THE AMERICAN ECONOMY

ISSN 1554-4400

THE AMERICAN ECONOMY

Kim Masters Evans

INFORMATION PLUS® REFERENCE SERIES
Formerly Published by Information Plus, Wylie, Texas

THOMSON
™
GALE

Detroit • New York • San Francisco • New Haven, Conn. • Waterville, Maine • London

The American Economy
Kim Masters Evans
Paula Kepos, Series Editor

Project Editor
John McCoy

Permissions
Lisa Kincade, Lista Person, Andrew Specht

Composition and Electronic Prepress
Evi Seoud

Manufacturing
Cynde Bishop

ISBN-13: 978-0-7876-5103-9 (set)
ISBN-10: 0-7876-5103-6 (set)
ISBN-13: 978-1-4144-0740-1
ISBN-10: 1-4144-0740-8
ISSN: 1554-4400

This title is also available as an e-book.
ISBN-13: 978-1-4144-2868-0 (set), ISBN-10: 1-4144-2868-5 (set)
Contact your Thomson Gale sales representative for ordering information.

Printed in the United States of America
10 9 8 7 6 5 4 3 2 1

TABLE OF CONTENTS

This chapter traces the development of the nation's capitalistic free-market economy and reviews the social and political events that have shaped the government's economic policy. It also introduces some basic terms of economics, such as supply and demand, inflation, gross national product, recession, and depression.

Economists use mathematical measures called economic indicators to gauge the overall health of the national economy. Although the most recent values present a relatively positive picture of economic health, public opinion polls show a strongly negative viewpoint among some segments of the population. Possible reasons for these differences are explored.

American consumers fuel economic growth by spending large sums of money. This chapter reviews the rise of the consumer culture in the United States and discusses the role of personal consumption expenditures in the nation's gross domestic product. Consumer expenses that have risen dramatically in recent years, particularly those for medical care, are examined in detail.

The assumption of personal debt is at an all-time high in the United States, which has both good and bad consequences for the economy. Historical viewpoints on debt, the role of interest rates, and different kinds of debt, such as mortgages and consumer credit loans, are discussed. Also covered are issues related to bankruptcy and predatory lending practices.

This chapter presents the latest data on employment and compensation in the United States and examines the economic performance and projections for various job sectors. Other topics include labor unions, government programs that protect worker rights, and the controversies over foreign workers in the United States and American jobs moving out of the country.

American businesses show great diversity in size and legal structure, ranging from self-employed individuals to multinational corporations. Businesses are discussed in terms of their economic performance, federal regulation, market power, and perceived social responsibilities. Recent corporate scandals and concerns over lack of competition in some markets are also addressed.

There are many opportunities available in the American economy for saving and investing. This chapter describes the major types of investments, with focus on home ownership and the stock and bond markets. Government regulation of these markets is also reviewed.

Wealth is defined not only by income but also by ownership of assets—real estate, stocks, bonds, and other securities. Unequal wealth distribution among Americans is a major cause of controversy, viewed by some as a natural consequence of capitalism and by others as a symptom of deep sociopolitical problems.

Government bodies at the local, state, and federal levels play a major role in the U.S. economy by redistributing money and providing employment. At the federal level the government has assumed an extremely large national debt that has consequences for present and future generations of Americans. Finally, the federal government manipulates the economy through spending and monetary policies.

The U.S. economy is preeminent in the world when it comes to national production. However, America buys far more from foreign lands than it sells to them. Economists disagree about whether this trade imbalance is good or bad for the United

States. Major trade agreements, the International Monetary Fund and the World Bank, economic sanctions, and the increasing trend toward global free trade, or globalization, are also discussed in this chapter.

PREFACE

The American Economy is part of the *Information Plus Reference Series*. The purpose of each volume of the series is to present the latest facts on a topic of pressing concern in modern American life. These topics include today's most controversial and most studied social issues: abortion, capital punishment, care for the elderly, crime, the environment, health care, immigration, minorities, national security, social welfare, women, youth, and many more. Although written especially for the high school and undergraduate student, this series is an excellent resource for anyone in need of factual information on current affairs.

By presenting the facts, it is Thomson Gale's intention to provide its readers with everything they need to reach an informed opinion on current issues. To that end, there is a particular emphasis in this series on the presentation of scientific studies, surveys, and statistics. These data are generally presented in the form of tables, charts, and other graphics placed within the text of each book. Every graphic is directly referred to and carefully explained in the text. The source of each graphic is presented within the graphic itself. The data used in these graphics are drawn from the most reputable and reliable sources, in particular from the various branches of the U.S. government and from major independent polling organizations. Every effort has been made to secure the most recent information available. The reader should bear in mind that many major studies take years to conduct and that additional years often pass before the data from these studies are made available to the public. Therefore, in many cases the most recent information available in 2007 dated from 2004 or 2005. Older statistics are sometimes presented as well, if they are of particular interest and no more-recent information exists.

Although statistics are a major focus of the *Information Plus Reference Series*, they are by no means its only content. Each book also presents the widely held positions and important ideas that shape how the book's subject is discussed in the United States. These positions are explained in detail and, where possible, in the words of their proponents. Some of the other material to be found in these books includes: historical background; descriptions of major events related to the subject; relevant laws and court cases; and examples of how these issues play out in American life. Some books also feature primary documents or have pro and con debate sections giving the words and opinions of prominent Americans on both sides of a controversial topic. All material is presented in an even-handed and unbiased manner; the reader will never be encouraged to accept one view of an issue over another.

HOW TO USE THIS BOOK

The American economy at the beginning of the twenty-first century is enormous, and enormously complicated. Workers, employers large and small, consumers, the equities markets, the U.S. government, and the world economy are constantly interacting with each other to affect the U.S. economy and, through it, each other. The American economy produces and consumes raw materials, services, manufactured goods, and intellectual property in vast amounts. This book describes the vast size and scope of the American economy, explains how it functions, and examines some of the challenges it faces, such as inflation, government regulation, off-shoring, and corporate scandals.

The American Economy consists of ten chapters and three appendixes. Each of the chapters is devoted to a particular aspect of the U.S economy. For a summary of the information covered in each chapter, please see the synopses provided in the Table of Contents at the front of the book. Chapters generally begin with an overview of the basic facts and background information on the chapter's topic, then proceed to examine subtopics of particular interest. For example, Chapter 10: International Trade and America's Place in the Global Economy begins by comparing the size and scope of the U.S. economy with that of the world as a whole, and with other countries. The factors that have contributed to the United States becoming the world's largest economy are discussed. Next, the chapter presents statistics on the import and export of goods and services between the United States and the rest of the world. The trade deficit that the United States has with the rest of the world is given particular attention, and contrasting opinions on its importance are explained. The chapter then moves on to a description of some of the international trade agreements and organizations that are most important to the United States, including discussion of criticisms of these trade structures. The chapter concludes with sections on a variety of controversial issues related to world trade, such as the globalization and anti-globalization movements, foreign ownership of U.S. assets, and the difficulty of enforcing intellectual property rights in a global market. Readers can find their way through a chapter by looking for the section and subsection headings, which are clearly set off from the text. Or, they can refer to the book's extensive Index, if they already know what they are looking for.

Statistical Information

The tables and figures featured throughout *The American Economy* will be of particular use to the reader in learning about this topic. These tables and figures represent an extensive collection of the most recent and valuable statistics on the U.S. economy—for example, graphics in the book cover the spending habits of the typical consumer; employment in manufacturing and service industries; the gross national product; the trade deficit; and consumer debt levels. Thomson Gale believes that making this information available to the reader is the most important way in which we fulfill the goal of this book: to help readers understand the issues and controversies surrounding the American economy and reach their own conclusions.

Each table or figure has a unique identifier appearing above it for ease of identification and reference. Titles for the tables and figures explain their purpose. At the end of each table or figure, the original source of the data is provided.

In order to help readers understand these often complicated statistics, all tables and figures are explained in the text. References in the text direct the reader to the relevant statistics. Furthermore, the contents of all tables and figures are fully indexed. Please see the opening section of the Index at the back of this volume for a description of how to find tables and figures within it.

Appendixes

In addition to the main body text and images, *The American Economy* has three appendixes. The first is the Important Names and Addresses directory. Here the reader will find contact information for a number of government and private organizations that can provide further information on aspects of the economy. The second appendix is the Resources section, which can also assist the reader in conducting his or her own research. In this section the author and editors of *The American Economy* describe some of the sources that were most useful during the compilation of this book. The final appendix is the Index.

ADVISORY BOARD CONTRIBUTIONS

The staff of Information Plus would like to extend its heartfelt appreciation to the Information Plus Advisory Board. This dedicated group of media professionals provides feedback on the series on an ongoing basis. Their comments allow the editorial staff who work on the project to continually make the series better and more user-friendly. Our top priorities are to produce the highest-quality and most useful books possible, and the Advisory Board's contributions to this process are invaluable.

The members of the Information Plus Advisory Board are:

- Kathleen R. Bonn, Librarian, Newbury Park High School, Newbury Park, California
- Madelyn Garner, Librarian, San Jacinto College—North Campus, Houston, Texas
- Anne Oxenrider, Media Specialist, Dundee High School, Dundee, Michigan
- Charles R. Rodgers, Director of Libraries, Pasco-Hernando Community College, Dade City, Florida
- James N. Zitzelsberger, Library Media Department Chairman, Oshkosh West High School, Oshkosh, Wisconsin

COMMENTS AND SUGGESTIONS

The editors of the *Information Plus Reference Series* welcome your feedback on *The American Economy*. Please direct all correspondence to:

Editors
Information Plus Reference Series
27500 Drake Rd.
Farmington Hills, MI 48331-3535

CHAPTER 1
THE AMERICAN ECONOMY—HISTORICAL OVERVIEW

*It is not what we have that will make us a great nation;
it is the way in which we use it.*

—Theodore Roosevelt, 1886

The workings of the American economy are complex and often mysterious, even to economists. At its simplest, the economy runs on three major sectors: consumers, businesses, and government. (See Figure 1.1.) Consumers earn money and exchange much of it for goods and services from businesses. These businesses use the money to produce more goods and services and to pay wages to their employees. Both consumers and businesses fund the government sector, which spends and transfers money back into the system. The banking system plays a crucial role in the economy by providing the means for all sectors to save and borrow money. Finally, there are the stock markets, which allow consumers to invest their money in the nation's businesses—an enterprise that further fuels economic growth for all sectors. Thus, the U.S. economy is a circular system based on interdependent relationships in which massive amounts of money change hands. The historical developments that produced this system are important to understand, because they provide key information about what has made the U.S. economy such a powerful force in the world.

DEFINING THE AMERICAN ECONOMY

The term "market economy" describes an economy in which the forces of supply and demand dictate the way in which goods and resources are allocated and what prices will be set. The opposite of a market economy is a "planned economy," in which the government determines what will be produced and what prices will be charged. In a market economy producers anticipate what products the market will be interested in, and at what price, and they make decisions about what products they will bring to market and how these products will be produced and priced.

Market economies foster competition among businesses, which typically leads to lower prices and is generally considered beneficial for both workers and consumers. A planned economy, on the other hand, is directed by a central government that has a far greater degree of influence over prices and production, as well as tighter regulation of industries and manufacturing procedures. The United States has a "mixed economy," which combines aspects of a market economy with some central planning and control to create a system with a high degree of market freedom along with regulatory agencies and social programs that promote the public welfare.

This mixed economy did not develop overnight. It has evolved over more than two centuries and has been shaped by American experiences at various times with hardship, war, peace, and prosperity.

HISTORICAL TRENDS

Colonial Times

When European colonists first came to the "New World," they found a vast expanse of land inhabited by Native Americans. Many of the first colonies were business ventures called "charter companies" that were financed by wealthy English businessmen and landowners. The colonies were granted limited economic and political rights by the king of England. After profits proved to be disappointing, many of the investors turned over the companies to the colonists themselves. These actions were to have far-reaching consequences on the shape of America. A report titled *The U.S. Economy: A Brief History* published by the U.S. Department of State (http://usinfo.state.gov/products/pubs/oecon/chap3.htm) notes: "The colonists were left to build their own lives, their own communities, and their own economy."

At first the colonists were preoccupied with merely surviving. Eventually they engaged in commerce with

FIGURE 1.1

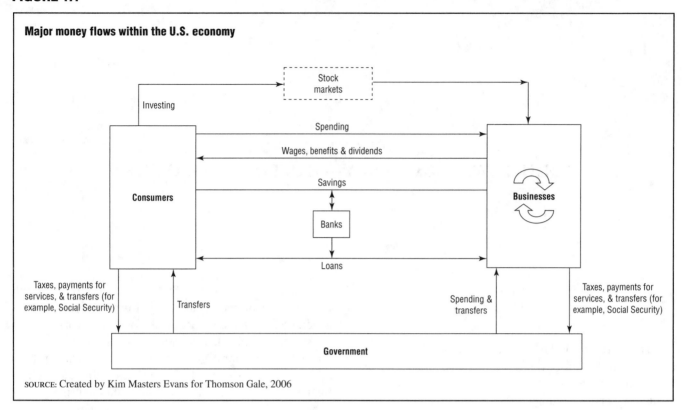

Major money flows within the U.S. economy

SOURCE: Created by Kim Masters Evans for Thomson Gale, 2006

Europe by exploiting the natural resources of their new homeland. The main agricultural products of the colonies were tobacco, wheat, rye, barley, rice, and indigo plant. Other important exports were animal furs, products from fish and whales, and timber. Shipbuilding became a major industry in New England.

Political and Industrial Revolution

Frustrated with the political and economic interference of England, the colonists banded together to forge a new nation—the United States of America. The push for independence from Britain, which culminated in the Revolutionary War (1775–83), was driven by economic and political motivations, including the desire for greater self-governance and tax relief.

In 1776 a book was published in England that would have long-reaching effects on the new United States. Scottish philosopher Adam Smith wrote *An Inquiry into the Nature and Causes of the Wealth of Nations*. The book was remarkable for many reasons. It discussed economic principles in a commonsense, nonmathematical manner and argued that the forces of supply and demand affect prices and wages. It criticized the restrictions and regulations common in European countries, and it advocated free and open trade within and between countries and abolishment of wage and price controls. Smith believed that an "invisible hand" was guiding workers seeking to better their private finances, which in turn helped nations achieve prosperity. In other words, people who work hard for their own gain unconsciously contribute to national wealth. The principles of a competitive marketplace with little government interference were adopted by the new United States and dominated the nation's economic policy for more than a century.

During the late 1700s Britain and the newly formed United States underwent a major social and economic change from agriculture to industry. The Industrial Revolution saw the introduction of the steam engine, cotton gin, and other machines capable of increasing production while decreasing human labor. Farming, in particular, became much less labor-intensive, freeing up people to pursue other forms of employment. Over the next century the United States would change from an agrarian-based nation to one in which the majority of income was generated by manufacturing, trade, and business providing services to consumers. (See Figure 1.2.)

The 1800s—Expansion and Civil War

The 1800s were a period of enormous growth for the United States in terms of territory, population, and economic might. Settlers spread from the East and South across the Midwest to the West Coast. A massive railroad system was built across the country. Gold was discovered in the western territories. More than two dozen states were added to the union. Expansionism was accompanied by violent conflicts with Britain (the War of 1812), Mexico (the Mexican-American War, 1846–48), and Spain (the Spanish-American War, 1896). In addition,

FIGURE 1.2

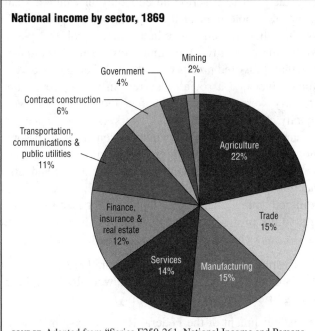

National income by sector, 1869

- Mining 2%
- Government 4%
- Contract construction 6%
- Transportation, communications & public utilities 11%
- Finance, insurance & real estate 12%
- Services 14%
- Manufacturing 15%
- Trade 15%
- Agriculture 22%

SOURCE: Adapted from "Series F250-261. National Income and Persons Engaged in Production, by Industry Divisions: 1869–1970," in *Historical Statistics of the United States, Colonial Times to 1970, Bicentennial Edition, Part 1, Chapter F: National Income and Wealth*, U.S. Department of Commerce, U.S. Census Bureau, September 1975, http://www2.census.gov/prod2/statcomp/documents/CT1970p1.zip (accessed June 16, 2006)

the so-called Indian Wars were waged for many years against Native American tribes.

The Northeast developed thriving industries, and cities swelled with hundreds of thousands of European immigrants. Although the South remained largely rural and agricultural, mechanical innovations, like the cotton gin, changed the region's focus. Cotton became a major crop and was exported to textile mills in the North and overseas. Unfortunately, much of the economic success of the South was based on the use of slave labor.

Deep divisions arose between factions in the North and South on the morality of slavery and associated political and economic issues, which led to the devastating American Civil War in 1861. By the time the war ended in 1865 the factories of the Northeast had become extremely important in fueling America's economy.

The Gilded Age

In 1873 American author Mark Twain cowrote with his neighbor Charles Dudley Warner a novel entitled *The Gilded Age*, which describes an American society in which unscrupulous businessmen and corrupt politicians pursue quick fortunes at the expense of the common people. Indeed, the decades following the Civil War were characterized by scandals involving high-level politicians making money from crooked business deals, as well as an

unprecedented boom in business. The resulting social atmosphere was one of decadence among the upper classes contrasted with poverty and labor unrest among the lower classes.

During the late 1800s the U.S. economy surged on a wave of industrialization and mechanized production. Industries boomed in iron, steel, lumber, precious metals, railroading, and petroleum. Some enterprising businessmen became extremely wealthy during the period, including John D. Rockefeller and Andrew Carnegie. Such men were called "captains of industry" by those who admired them and "robber barons" by those who despised them.

The U.S. government had a hands-off approach to business regulation, a tactic described by the French term *laissez-faire* (leave alone or "do as you please"). It was generally believed that the government should not interfere in economic affairs but should instead allow supply and demand and competition to operate unfettered, resulting in a "free market."

The gilded age is notable for a growth in corporations. A corporation is a legally defined entity that may receive financial support from numerous investors but is treated as an individual under the law. A corporation is granted a state charter including specific rights, privileges, and liabilities. This type of business organization became very popular in the late 1800s. It allowed people to invest in businesses without taking on all of the responsibilities and risks of being a business owner. State charters limited the liability of individual investors, who were paid dividends in proportion to their share of investment in the corporation.

Some corporations grew through mergers or by buying out the companies of their competitors. Then they developed a business structure called a trust, in which the component companies were managed by a small group of people called a board of trustees. These corporations controlled nearly all of the business in their respective industries, a condition known as monopolization. The public feared that trusts squelched competition that helped keep prices in check. In 1890 the U.S. Congress passed the Sherman Antitrust Act. Its stated purpose was "to protect trade and commerce against unlawful restraints and monopolies." But due to court challenges, the law was not successfully applied until the early 1900s.

Panics and Depressions

In economic terms a "panic" is a widespread occurrence of public anxiety about financial affairs. People lose confidence in banks and investments and want to hold onto their money instead of spending it. This can lead to a severe downturn, or depression, in the economic condition of a nation. The U.S. economy suffered from panics and depressions even during the booming growth of the 1800s and early 1900s. Although economists argue about the exact definitions of panics and depressions, in general it is agreed that economic downturns occurred in the United States in 1819, 1837, 1857, 1869, 1873, 1893, and 1907.

The crises were triggered by a variety of factors. Common problems included too much borrowing and speculation by investors and poor oversight of banks by the federal government. Speculation is the buying of assets on the hope that they will greatly increase in value in the future. During the 1800s many speculators borrowed money from banks to buy land. Huge demand caused land prices to increase dramatically, often above what the land was actually worth in the market. Poorly regulated banks extended too much credit to speculators and to each other. When a large bank failed, there was a domino effect through the industry, which caused other banks and businesses to fail.

A panic or depression results in a downward economic spiral in which individuals and businesses are afraid to make new investments. People rush to pull their money from banks. As panic spreads, banks demand that borrowers pay back money, but borrowers may lack the funds to do so. Consumers are reluctant to spend money, which negatively affects businesses. Demand for products goes down, and prices must be lowered to move merchandise off of shelves. This means less profit for business owners. Businesses lay off employees to cut costs and do not hire new employees. As more people become unemployed or fearful about their jobs, there is even less spending in the marketplace, which leads to more business cutbacks and so forth. The cycle continues until some compelling change takes place to nudge the economy back into a positive direction.

The Twentieth Century Begins

The early twentieth century was a time of social and political change in the United States. Public disgust at the corruption and greed of the gilded age encouraged a movement called progressivism. Progressives promoted civic responsibility, workers' rights, consumer protection, political and tax reform, "trust busting," and strong government action to achieve social improvements. The progressive era greatly affected the U.S. economy because of its focus on improving working conditions for average Americans. Successes for the progressives included child labor restrictions, improved working conditions in factories, compensation funds for injured workers, a growth surge in labor unions, federal regulation of food and drug industries, and the formation of the Federal Trade Commission to oversee business practices.

Some people viewed the progressive movement as an attack on capitalism and a prelude to socialism. The American economy was first described as "capitalist"

by the German economist Karl Marx (1818–83), who used the term to describe an economy in which a small group of people control the capital, or money available for investment, and, by extension, control the power within the economy. A common criticism of capitalism was that it favored profits over the well-being of workers. Marx advocated a socialist system in which wealth and property were not held by a few individuals but were equally distributed among all workers under a heavily planned economy. The socialist movement gained some momentum during the progressive era, thanks in large part to its ties to organized labor. In the presidential election of 1912 the socialist candidate Eugene V. Debs garnered more than nine hundred thousand votes— around 6% of the popular vote. But socialism soon faded as a serious challenge to American capitalism.

Despite its laissez-faire attitude, in 1913 the federal government took two actions that were to have long-lasting effects on the U.S. economy:

- Establishment of the Federal Reserve System to serve as the nation's central bank, furnish currency, and supervise banking
- Ratification of the Sixteenth Amendment to the U.S. Constitution authorizing the collection of income taxes

World War I and Inflation

In 1914 World War I began in Europe. The U.S. entered the conflict in April 1917 and was engaged until the war ended in November 1918. Although the nation spent only nineteen months at war, the U.S. economy underwent major changes during this period.

It is sometimes said that "war is good for the economy" because, during a major war, the federal government spends large amounts of money on weapons and machinery through contracts with private industries. These industries hire more employees, which reduces unemployment and puts more money into the hands of consumers to spend in the marketplace. This benefits other businesses not directly involved in the war effort. On the surface, these economic effects appear positive. However, major wars almost always result in high inflation rates.

Inflation is an economic condition in which the purchasing power of money goes down because of price increases in goods and services. For example, if a nation experiences an inflation rate of 3% in a year, an item that cost $1.00 at the beginning of the year will cost $1.03 at the end of the year. Inflation causes the "value" of a dollar to go down over the course of the year. In general, small increases in inflation occur over time in a healthy growing economy, because demand slightly outpaces supply. Economists consider an inflation rate of 3% or

FIGURE 1.3

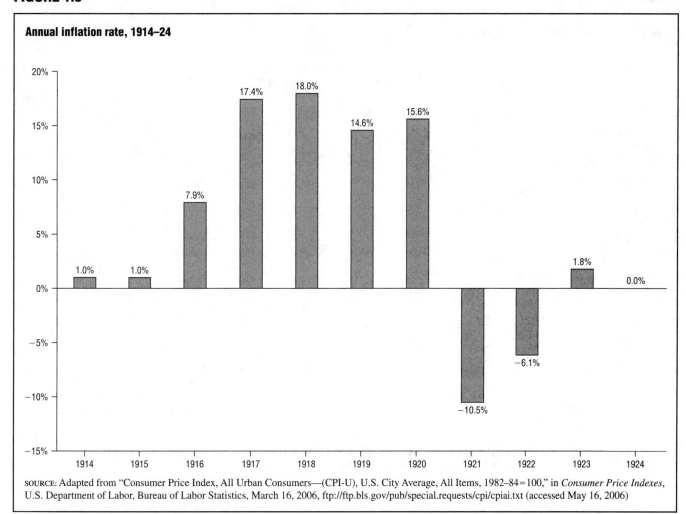

Annual inflation rate, 1914–24

SOURCE: Adapted from "Consumer Price Index, All Urban Consumers—(CPI-U), U.S. City Average, All Items, 1982–84=100," in *Consumer Price Indexes*, U.S. Department of Labor, Bureau of Labor Statistics, March 16, 2006, ftp://ftp.bls.gov/pub/special.requests/cpi/cpiai.txt (accessed May 16, 2006)

less a year to be tolerable. During a major war the supply and demand ratio becomes distorted. This occurs when the nation produces huge amounts of war goods and far fewer consumer goods, such as food, clothing, and cars. This lack of supply and anxiety about the future drive up the prices of consumer goods, making it difficult for people to afford things they need or want.

During World War I the federal government intervened in private industry to support war needs and exert some control over supply and demand dynamics. Agencies were created to oversee the production of war goods, food, fuel, and nonmilitary ships. Although the government tried to impose some level of price control in the food and fuel industries, inflation still occurred. According to the U.S. Census Bureau's *Historical Statistics of the United States* (1975), the prices for many consumer goods nearly doubled between 1915 and 1920. Figure 1.3 shows the average annual inflation rate from 1914 through 1924. The inflation rate was unusually high from 1916 through 1920, peaking at 18% in 1918. Wartime inflation was particularly hard on nonworking citizens, such as the elderly and sick, because there were no large

government programs in place at that time to assist needy people.

A lasting legacy of World War I was the assumption of large amounts of debt by the federal government to fund the war effort. Figure 1.4 shows the enormous differences that occurred between government revenues (receipts) and spending during the war years. In 1919 government spending peaked at nearly $18.5 billion; revenues for that year were just over $5 billion. The government made up the difference by borrowing money. One method used was the selling of Liberty bonds. Bonds are a type of financial asset—an IOU that promises to pay back at some future date the original purchase price plus interest.

The Roaring Twenties

The Roaring Twenties began with a whimper; there was a severe economic downturn in 1921. But this crisis was followed by several years of robust economic growth. Mass production and the availability of electricity led to huge consumer demand for household appliances. Installment plans became a popular means

FIGURE 1.4

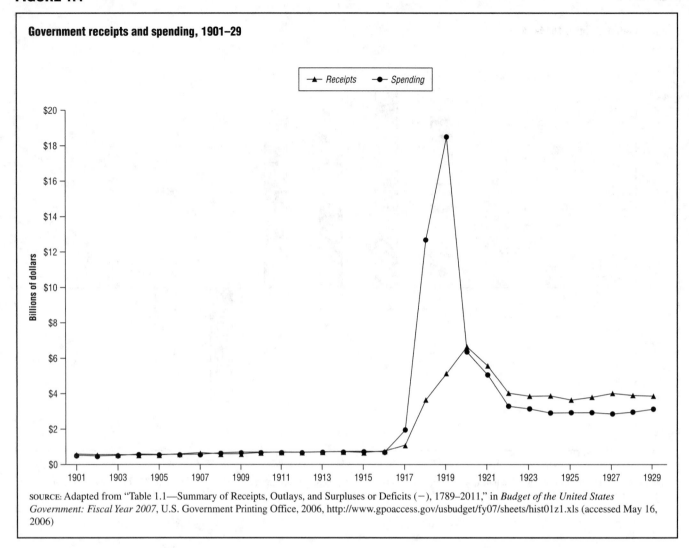

Government receipts and spending, 1901–29

SOURCE: Adapted from "Table 1.1—Summary of Receipts, Outlays, and Surpluses or Deficits (−), 1789–2011," in *Budget of the United States Government: Fiscal Year 2007*, U.S. Government Printing Office, 2006, http://www.gpoaccess.gov/usbudget/fy07/sheets/hist01z1.xls (accessed May 16, 2006)

for middle-class Americans to purchase expensive long-lasting (durable) goods like refrigerators, washing machines, and automobiles.

Americans also began spending more money on entertainment. They bought radios and went in large numbers to see motion pictures and baseball games. The automobile became a necessity, rather than a luxury, for many people. Booming car sales boosted the petroleum and housing markets and allowed city dwellers to move to the suburbs.

The prosperity of the 1920s was not shared by all Americans. During World War I demand for agricultural goods had skyrocketed, particularly in Europe. Overoptimistic farmers borrowed heavily to pay for tractors and other farm equipment, only to see food prices plummet during the 1920s when supply outpaced demand. Financial problems in the agricultural industry directly impacted a lot of Americans. In addition, banks in rural areas were stressed by farmers who were unable to pay back loans. The agricultural crisis was accompanied by

downturns in the coal mining and railroad industries that affected many workers.

In the late 1920s the stock market became a major factor in the U.S. economy. Investors were richly rewarded, as stocks increased dramatically in value. Many people took out loans from banks to pay for stock or purchased stock by "buying on margin." In this arrangement an investor would make a small down payment (as little as 10%) on a stock purchase. The remainder of the balance would be paid (in theory) by the future increase in the stock value. Buying on margin was widely practiced by optimistic investors of the time. University of Wisconsin history professor William Tishler notes: "By 1929, much of the money that was invested in the stock market did not actually exist" ("The Crash and the Great Depression," 2000, http://us.history.wisc.edu/hist102/lectures/textonly/lecture18.html).

Black Tuesday—October 29, 1929

On October 29, 1929, the stock market crashed. For months, President Herbert Hoover and other influential

FIGURE 1.5

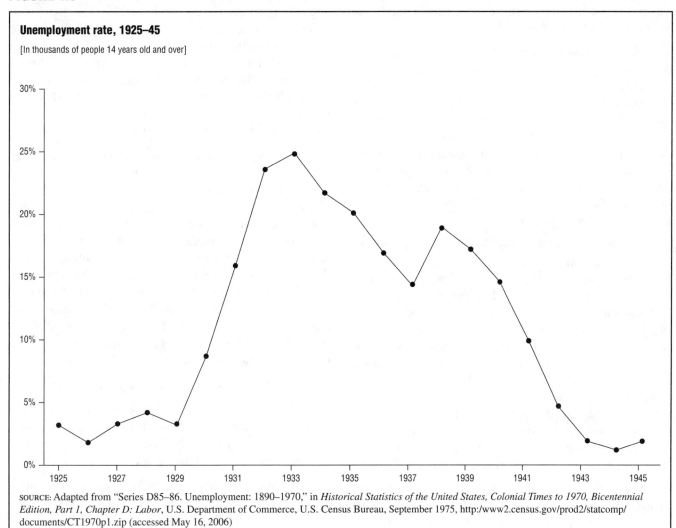

Unemployment rate, 1925–45

[In thousands of people 14 years old and over]

SOURCE: Adapted from "Series D85–86. Unemployment: 1890–1970," in *Historical Statistics of the United States, Colonial Times to 1970, Bicentennial Edition, Part 1, Chapter D: Labor*, U.S. Department of Commerce, U.S. Census Bureau, September 1975, http://www2.census.gov/prod2/statcomp/documents/CT1970p1.zip (accessed May 16, 2006)

people had warned that there was too much speculation in the stock market and that stock prices were higher than the actual worth of the companies. In the fall of 1929 investors began to get nervous. On October 24, 1929, there was a selling frenzy as people tried to get rid of stocks they thought might be overvalued. The day was dubbed "Black Thursday." The following day the market rebounded somewhat, and stock prices climbed back upward. But the recovery was short-lived.

On Tuesday, October 29, 1929, panic selling took place all day. Stock values dropped dramatically. The drawback to buying on margin was that if a stock value went down by a certain amount, the lender would make a "margin call" asking the buyer for more cash up front. If the margin buyer could not pay, the lender sold the stock to recoup the money. As "Black Tuesday" progressed, desperate margin buyers paid lenders all their cash in savings in hopes of saving their stock for the expected recovery, but no recovery came. As stock values fell further, lenders demanded more money. By the end of the day many margin buyers had lost their life savings and their stock.

Those who managed to hold on to their stock found it was worth only a fraction of its former value.

According to economist Harold Bierman, Jr., the American stock market lost almost 90% of its value between 1929 and 1932 ("The 1929 Stock Market Crash," August 11, 2004, http://eh.net/encyclopedia/article/Bierman.Crash).

The Great Depression

The United States economy suffered a devastating downturn following the stock market crash. The depression was so deep and lasted so long—more than a decade—that it is called the Great Depression.

Historically, economic depressions had been short downturns with limited consequences. They were temporary dips in an overall trend of American prosperity. The Great Depression was a completely different experience. It brought long-term unemployment and hardship to millions of people. The unemployment rate soared from 3.2% in 1929 to nearly 25% in 1933. (See Figure 1.5.) It remained more than 10% through the end of the 1930s. The public lost confidence in the stock market, the banking system, and big business.

Like all previous depressions, this one included a downward cycle in which businesses reduced spending and production and laid off employees. Unemployed workers and those fearful of losing their jobs cut back on spending, which forced businesses to lay off more people. The economy underwent "deflation"—a condition where a lack of money among consumers depresses demand and pushes prices downward. Lower prices for agricultural and industrial goods hurt farmers and businesses, particularly those with high debt. Consumers also had assumed high levels of debt during the 1920s.

The Great Depression was aggravated by a crisis in the banking industry. Some banks had invested heavily in the stock market using their depositors' money or loaned large amounts of money to stock market investors. These banks failed after the crash, and the depositors lost their savings. Fear of further failures caused "bank runs," in which large numbers of depositors rushed to withdraw their money at the same time. This caused more bank failures, which perpetuated the cycle. In addition, some economists believe that the banking market became over-saturated during the 1920s with underfunded and loosely regulated banks that loaned money too easily. These institutions were already financially troubled before the crash and could not survive the stress.

America's Great Depression was felt worldwide, particularly in other industrialized countries. By the 1920s the United States played a major role in world commerce by exporting and importing large amounts of goods and investing money in foreign businesses. A prolonged downturn in American production, spending, and investing combined with the banking crisis had international consequences. Europe, in particular, suffered financially as it struggled to recover from the devastation of World War I.

The New Deal

When the Great Depression first began, the laissez-faire attitude still dominated political opinion. Some economists, including Andrew Mellon (1855–1937), who served as Secretary of the Treasury from 1921 through 1932, advised President Hoover not to interfere. These economists took the traditional viewpoint that supply and demand factors would eventually equilibrate, and the economy would recover on its own. Hoover was not convinced. He tried a variety of tax adjustments, asked industry not to cut wages, and pushed for public works projects. But the depression only deepened.

By 1932 Americans were ready for a change in leadership. New York State Governor Franklin D. Roosevelt (FDR) promised "a new deal" for the nation. He was

elected in a landslide and developed a government that aggressively acted in economic affairs. The New Deal included a wide variety of programs intended to bring relief to suffering Americans, revive farming and business, and reform the stock market and banking industry. After more than seventy years, economists still argue about whether the New Deal was actually good for the nation. They all agree, however, that it was a turning point in American economic history.

Some New Deal programs did not survive court challenges. The National Industrial Recovery Act of 1933 encouraged companies within industries to form alliances and set prices and wages. The companies that participated were exempt from antitrust laws that ordinarily would have forbidden such collusion. In 1935 the U.S. Supreme Court ruled the law unconstitutional. The Agricultural Adjustment Act (AAA) of 1933 paid farmers to reduce production. It was thought that lower supply would raise prices and improve the living conditions of farmers. In 1936 the U.S. Supreme Court invalidated parts of the AAA. But the payment of farm subsidies became a permanent component of U.S. economic policy.

Other legacies of the New Deal include:

- Federal Securities Act (1933)—Regulated the selling of investment instruments (such as stock) to ensure that buyers are better educated about their purchases and to prevent fraudulent practices

- Securities Exchange Act (1934)—Regulated the stock exchanges and created the U.S. Securities and Exchange Commission

- Glass-Steagall Banking Act (1933)—Separated the commercial and investment banking industries and established the Federal Deposit Insurance Corporation (FDIC) to safeguard depositors' money

- National Labor Relations Act (1935)—Guaranteed the right of employees in most private industries to organize, form labor unions, and bargain collectively with their employers; established the National Labor Relations Board

- Social Security Act (1935)—Established a program to provide federal benefits to the elderly and assist the states in providing for "aged persons, blind persons, dependent and crippled children, maternal and child welfare, public health, and the administration of unemployment compensation laws"

Government employment programs under the Public Works Administration, Works Project Administration, and Civilian Conservation Corps put people to work building roads, dams, bridges, airfields, and post offices and developing national parks for tourism. According to economics writer Robert Samuelson, as many as ten to twelve million Americans were employed in these programs at various times during the 1930s ("Great Depression," http://www.econlib.org/library/Enc/Great Depression.html#biography).

Perhaps the greatest legacy of FDR's New Deal was the new role of the federal government as a manipulator of economic forces and a provider of benefits to the needy. This change in American policy was seen as a wise and compassionate move by some people and as a dangerous shift toward socialism by others. In American history the New Deal is considered the birth of "big government."

By 1940 the unemployment rate was 14.9%. (See Figure 1.5.) Although down from a peak of 25% in 1933, the rate was still very high by historical standards. Nearly a decade of New Deal programs had softened the hardship suffered by many Americans, but had not boosted the country out of the Great Depression. It was going to take a war to accomplish that task.

World War II

During the 1930s Germany, led by the dictator Adolf Hitler (1889–1945), began aggressive military campaigns against its neighboring countries, followed by similar moves by Japan and Italy. Many in the United States were determined to keep the nation out of these international conflicts, but in 1939 Britain, France, and Canada declared war on Germany after Germany invaded Poland. The Germans began a devastating bombing campaign of London called a *blitzkrieg* ("lightning war"). By 1941 Germany and its Italian and Japanese allies had occupied France and war had spread throughout Europe, North Africa, parts of China, and the North Atlantic and South Pacific seas.

In the United States, FDR publicly adhered to the isolationist sentiment of the American public; but as early as 1939 he began quietly expanding the nation's military capabilities. On December 29, 1940, he gave a radio address in which he reiterated his goal of keeping the United States out of the war, but he warned that the very survival of the United States would be jeopardized if Great Britain were to be defeated. He pledged to provide America's allies with "implements of war," saying "we must be the great arsenal of democracy." FDR believed that American industrial power would save Great Britain and its allies from defeat. In his address FDR noted:

> Manufacturers of watches, farm implements, linotypes, cash registers, automobiles, sewing machines, lawn mowers, and locomotives are now making fuses, bomb packing crates, telescope mounts, shells, pistols, and tanks. But all our present efforts are not enough. We must have more ships, more guns, more planes, more of everything. This can only be accomplished if we discard the notion of business as usual.

On December 7, 1941, Japanese forces attacked Pearl Harbor in Oahu, Hawaii, where members of the U.S. Navy, Army Air Corps, and Marines were stationed. The attack killed more than twenty-four hundred American service people and civilians. Within days, the United States was at war with Japan, Germany, and Italy. "Business as usual" was a thing of the past.

Although the U.S. officially entered World War II in 1941, it had been gearing up its industries for war for more than a year. This experience at mobilization (converting civilian industries to produce military goods) proved to be invaluable. The federal government established a host of agencies to oversee wartime production, labor relations, and prices. Efforts were made to avoid the huge inflation increase that had occurred during World War I. Rationing was instituted on some goods to prevent dramatic price increases. By and large, these efforts were successful. Figure 1.6 shows the annual rates of inflation experienced in the United States between 1940 and 1950. Inflation spiked during the early years of the war and immediately after but was not consistently high over the decade.

Businesses rushed to increase production and hire workers to produce the goods needed for the war effort. Unemployment dropped dramatically and wages went up, particularly for workers in low-skilled factory jobs. Laborers found themselves in high demand and joined labor unions in record numbers to consolidate their power and seek better working conditions.

World War II was an expensive endeavor for the United States. But it was believed that the stakes were so high that the war had to be won at any cost. As shown in Figure 1.7, government spending during the war far outpaced revenues. By 1945 the government was spending around $90 billion per year and taking in revenues around half that amount. Once again, the difference was made up by borrowing.

The flood of American goods and military might turned the tide of the war. By early 1945 Germany and Italy had been defeated. In August of that year Japan surrendered after suffering two devastating hits by U.S. atomic bombs. World War II was over, and a new world order had been established. The United States abandoned its isolationist stance and assumed an active role in international affairs.

Keynesian Economics

The Great Depression shook many peoples' beliefs in the laissez-faire approach to economics advocated by Adam Smith in the eighteenth century. During the 1930s and 1940s different approaches to capitalism began to receive serious attention. One of the most famous economists of the time was John Maynard Keynes (1883–1946). Keynes (pronounced "canes") was an

FIGURE 1.6

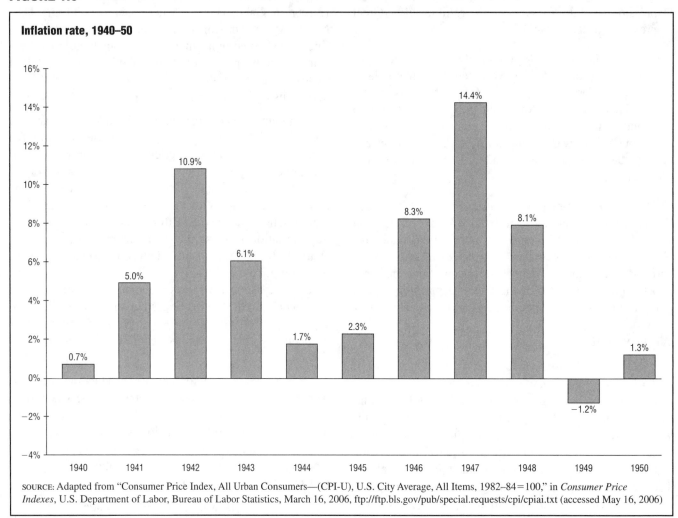

Inflation rate, 1940–50

SOURCE: Adapted from "Consumer Price Index, All Urban Consumers—(CPI-U), U.S. City Average, All Items, 1982–84=100," in *Consumer Price Indexes*, U.S. Department of Labor, Bureau of Labor Statistics, March 16, 2006, ftp://ftp.bls.gov/pub/special.requests/cpi/cpiai.txt (accessed May 16, 2006)

English expert in the application of economic theory to real-world problems. He published several influential books, including *The Economic Consequences of the Peace* (1919) and the *General Theory of Employment, Interest and Money* (1936). In the latter book Keynes advocated strong government intervention in the economy as a remedy for the ongoing economic depression.

Politicians of the 1930s were not completely convinced by Keynes's arguments, particularly in regards to government spending. Maintaining a balanced federal budget was considered so sacred that the governments of Hoover and Roosevelt were reluctant to veer far from that precedent. But following World War II it appeared obvious that huge government spending had helped fuel recovery from the Great Depression. Keynes's theories on capitalism, unemployment, and business cycles became highly regarded, and he is credited with inventing macroeconomics. This is a "big picture" approach that measures broad trends in an economy, such as employment and inflation, and the way these trends interact. In contrast, microeconomics analyzes the economy on a smaller scale—for example, by studying the supply

and demand factors at work in individual markets or industrial segments.

Keynesian economics became the operating principle of the U.S. government in the post–World War II era. Although Keynes had his critics, and his methods have been revised over time, he is considered by many to be the father of the mixed economy system used in the United States to this day.

The National Income and Product Accounts

One innovation of the 1940s was the National Income and Product Accounts (NIPAs), which are compilations of national economic data. Prior to that time there was a lack of comprehensive macroeconomic data on the nation's inputs and outputs, such as labor and production of goods and services. This problem became apparent during the Great Depression when the Hoover and FDR administrations were forced to make decisions based on fragmented and incomplete data on the nation's financial condition. As a result, the federal government asked researchers at the National Bureau of Economic Research (NBER) at the City University

FIGURE 1.7

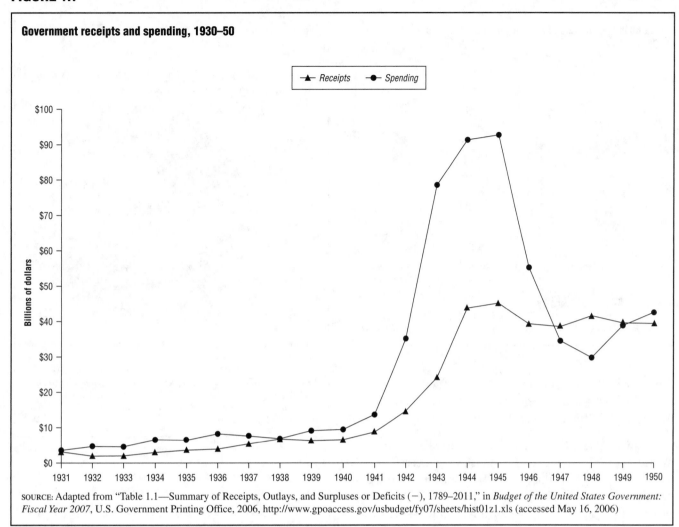

Government receipts and spending, 1930–50

SOURCE: Adapted from "Table 1.1—Summary of Receipts, Outlays, and Surpluses or Deficits (−), 1789–2011," in *Budget of the United States Government: Fiscal Year 2007*, U.S. Government Printing Office, 2006, http://www.gpoaccess.gov/usbudget/fy07/sheets/hist01z1.xls (accessed May 16, 2006)

of New York to begin estimating national income (wages, profits, rent, etc.). The NBER had been founded in 1920 as a private nonprofit organization dedicated to economic research.

During World War II the federal government began compiling another macroeconomic measure called the gross national product (GNP). The GNP is the amount in dollars of the value of final goods and services produced by Americans over a particular time period. For example, the GNP for 1945 was nearly $212 billion (*Historical Statistics of the United States*, September 1975). GNP is calculated by summing consumer and government spending, business and residential investments, and the net value of U.S. exports (exports minus imports).

At first GNP estimates were made annually; eventually they were calculated on a quarterly basis. The GNP provides a valuable tool for tracking national productivity over time. By the end of the 1940s an entire set of NIPAs had been developed to report macroeconomic data on the state of the U.S. economy.

A Postwar Spending Spree

Following World War II many U.S. industries demobilized from producing military goods and returned to producing consumer goods. Well-paid workers who had been frustrated by wartime shortages were ready to spend money. Returning soldiers received government incentives to buy houses and start businesses. Postwar euphoria drove a spending spree and a baby boom. The birth rate increased from an average of 19.2 births per one thousand population in the 1930s to 24.8 births per one thousand population in the 1950s. (See Figure 1.8.)

Growing families purchased bigger houses, many of which were built in the suburbs. The suburban population shift was accompanied by a growth in shopping centers, supermarkets, and car ownership. According to the U.S. State Department's *Outline of U.S. History*, annual production of automobiles quadrupled between 1946 and 1955. Television and air conditioning became widely available following World War II. Air conditioning spurred migration from the Northeast and Midwest to the Southeast and Southwest. By the end of the 1950s

FIGURE 1.8

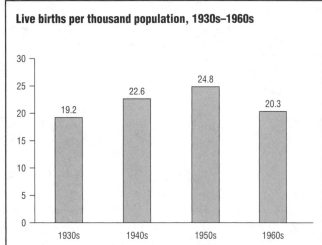

Live births per thousand population, 1930s–1960s

SOURCE: Adapted from "Series B1-4. Live Births, Deaths, Marriages, and Divorces: 1909–1970," in *Historical Statistics of the United States, Colonial Times to 1970, Bicentennial Edition, Part 1, Chapter B: Vital Statistics and Health and Medical Care*, U.S. Department of Commerce, U.S. Census Bureau, September 1975, http:/www2.census.gov/prod2/statcomp/documents/CT1970p1.zip (accessed May 18, 2006)

FIGURE 1.9

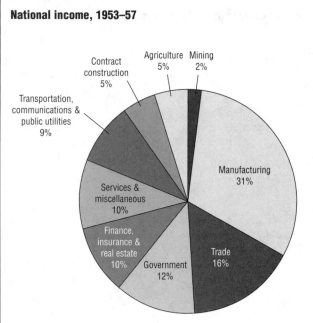

National income, 1953–57

SOURCE: Adapted from "Series F250-261. National Income and Persons Engaged in Production, by Industry Divisions: 1869–1970," in *Historical Statistics of the United States, Colonial Times to 1970, Bicentennial Edition, Part 1, Chapter F: National Income and Wealth*, U.S. Department of Commerce, U.S. Census Bureau, September 1975, http://www2.census.gov/prod2/statcomp/documents/CT1970p1.zip (accessed May 18, 2006)

three-fourths of all American families owned at least one television set. Television advertising reached a large audience and promoted more consumer spending.

New industries in aviation and electronics arose after World War II. Many existing industries underwent consolidation and growth as corporations merged into giant conglomerates. Figure 1.9 shows the national income produced by the business sector for 1953 to 1957. Manufacturing accounted for nearly a third of the national income during this period.

The 1950s also experienced a boom in business franchises. In this arrangement an individual could purchase permission from a company in one geographic area to sell the company's products or services in another area. Franchising proved to be a very effective means of spreading brand recognition and was widely practiced in the surging "fast food" industry. In 1955 Des Plaines, Illinois, became the site of the first McDonald's franchise after businessman Raymond Kroc became a franchisee for the McDonald brothers, who owned a small chain of restaurants in California. By 1959 there were more than one hundred McDonald's franchises around the country. Over the next decade franchising was practiced in a number of other businesses, many of which grew into major corporations.

Dwight D. Eisenhower was president from 1953 through 1961. His administration is associated with a growing economy that experienced low inflation rates and general prosperity. But the prosperity of the 1950s was not shared equally in American society. Once again, farmers found themselves in trouble due to overproduction.

Oversupply of agricultural goods meant lower prices (and lower profits). Agriculture became increasingly an industry in which large "factory farms" run by corporations were able to survive, while many smaller farmers could not compete.

Minority populations (largely African-American) also suffered financial hardship during this era. Figure 1.10 shows the dramatic difference between the unemployment rates for whites and minorities during the postwar decades. By the mid-1950s unemployment among minorities was twice as high as it was among white workers, a disparity that lingered well into the 1960s. It was in this atmosphere that the civil rights movement gained in strength and urgency. In 1954 segregation was ruled unconstitutional by the U.S. Supreme Court. A year later African-American seamstress and activist Rosa Parks was arrested in Alabama for refusing to move from the "white" section of a public bus. This incident spurred a bus boycott and ultimately brought Martin Luther King, Jr., and other leaders of the movement to national prominence.

The Cold War, Korea, and Vietnam

The United States left World War II in sound economic shape. All other industrialized nations had suffered great losses during the war in their infrastructure, financial stability, and populations. The United States invested heavily in the postwar economies of Western Europe and

FIGURE 1.10

Unemployment rate by race, 1948–70

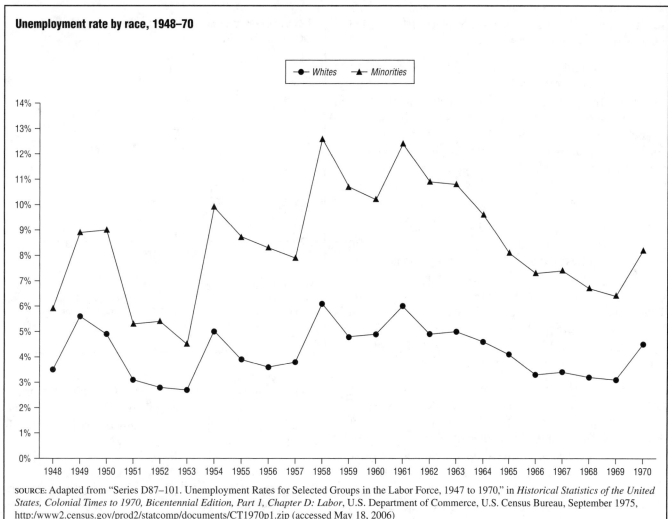

SOURCE: Adapted from "Series D87–101. Unemployment Rates for Selected Groups in the Labor Force, 1947 to 1970," in *Historical Statistics of the United States, Colonial Times to 1970, Bicentennial Edition, Part 1, Chapter D: Labor*, U.S. Department of Commerce, U.S. Census Bureau, September 1975, http:/www2.census.gov/prod2/statcomp/documents/CT1970p1.zip (accessed May 18, 2006)

Japan, hoping to instill an atmosphere conducive to peace and the spread of capitalism. U.S. barriers to foreign trade were relaxed to build new markets for American exports and to allow some war-ravaged nations to make money selling goods to American consumers.

The Soviet Union had been a wartime ally of the United States, but relations became strained after World War II ended. The Soviet Union had adopted communism following a period of revolution and civil war in the late 1910s and early 1920s. During World War II the Soviet Union "liberated" a large part of Eastern Europe from Nazi occupation. Through various means the Union of Soviet Socialist Republics (USSR) assumed political control over these nations. The USSR had been largely industrialized prior to World War II and quickly regained its industrial capabilities. It soon took a major role in international affairs, placing it in direct conflict with the only other "superpower" of the time—the United States. A "cold war" began between two rich and powerful nations that had completely different political, economic, and social goals for the world.

The cold war was fought mostly by politicians and diplomats. A direct and large-scale military conflict between U.S. and Soviet forces never occurred. But an expensive arms race began in which both sides produced and stockpiled large amounts of weapons as a show of force to deter a first strike by the enemy. In addition, both sides provided financial and military support to countries around the world in an attempt to influence the political leanings of those populations. Communist China joined the cold war during the 1950s and often partnered with the USSR against U.S. interests.

In 1950 North Korean forces backed by the Soviet military invaded South Korea, setting off the Korean War (1950–53). The United States was caught off guard by the invasion, but rushed to defend South Korea from a communist takeover. Over the next three years U.S. and allied forces under the United Nations fought against North Korean and Chinese troops supported by the Soviet Union. The war ended in a stalemate with both sides back where they had started—on either side of the thirty-eighth parallel (a line of latitude). In 1953 a cease-fire agreement ended the armed conflict in Korea. North Korea remained under communist control, while South Korea became a democracy protected by United Nations troops (primarily U.S. forces).

Also during the 1950s, the U.S. military became involved in a conflict between communist North Vietnam and noncommunist South Vietnam. The United States sent thousands of "military advisors" to South Vietnam during the late 1950s and early 1960s in an effort to bolster the defenses of the country. In 1964 the conflict escalated into full-scale civil war. Once again, the U.S. found itself in a remote Asian country trying to prevent the spread of communism.

The fight in Vietnam turned out to be a long and difficult one in which U.S. forces, assisted by a handful of other countries, were pitted against highly motivated forces equipped and backed by the USSR and China. The U.S. was engaged in the Vietnam War for more than a decade before withdrawing its last troops in 1975 and leaving South Vietnam to a communist takeover. According to *Outline of U.S. History*, the total cost of the Vietnam war exceeded $150 billion.

In both the Korean and Vietnam wars the U.S. chose to fight in a limited manner without using its arsenal of nuclear weapons or engaging Chinese or Soviet troops directly for fear of sparking another world war. Full-scale mobilization of U.S. industries was not required for these wars, as it had been during World War II. Instead, a defense industry developed during the cold war to supply the U.S. military on a continuous basis with the arms and goods it wanted. In a 1961 speech, outgoing President Dwight D. Eisenhower described this arrangement to the American public:

> We can no longer risk emergency improvisation of national defense; we have been compelled to create a permanent armaments industry of vast proportions. Added to this, three and a half million men and women are directly engaged in the defense establishment. We annually spend on military security more than the net income of all United States corporations.

Figure 1.11 shows the percentage of the national budget that was devoted to national defense between 1940 and 1970. Spending on national defense soared during World War II and then declined dramatically following the war's end. But military spending quickly climbed again as the cold war heated up, remaining above 40% for nearly two decades.

The Birth of the Modern Fed

The nation's central bank—the Federal Reserve System—was formed in 1913 to furnish currency and supervise financial institutions. Gradually it took on other roles that affected the amount of money circulating in the United States and the interest rates charged by banks to

FIGURE 1.11

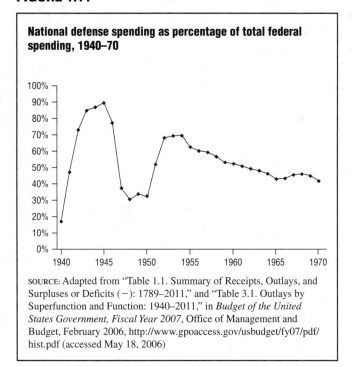

National defense spending as percentage of total federal spending, 1940–70

SOURCE: Adapted from "Table 1.1. Summary of Receipts, Outlays, and Surpluses or Deficits (−): 1789–2011," and "Table 3.1. Outlays by Superfunction and Function: 1940–2011," in *Budget of the United States Government, Fiscal Year 2007*, Office of Management and Budget, February 2006, http://www.gpoaccess.gov/usbudget/fy07/pdf/hist.pdf (accessed May 18, 2006)

their customers. The Federal Reserve System comprises twelve regional banks located around the country and overseen by a seven-member board of governors headquartered in Washington, D.C.

The Fed, as it came to be called, was designed to be as independent as possible from political pressures from the U.S. president and the Congress. This safeguard was included to prevent the Fed from having to bow to demands for short-term economic fixes requested by politicians seeking reelection. The Fed was charged with taking a big-picture, long-term approach to economic policy for the good of the nation as a whole.

From its inception until the early 1950s the Fed was influenced by the policies of the U.S. Department of the Treasury, a federal agency created in 1789. During the late 1940s Fed and Treasury officials disagreed about how best to handle the large debt accumulated by the United States during World War II. This conflict and other contentious issues led to a new agreement, or accord, between the two agencies about the roles of each in the U.S. economy. This accord is considered the birth of the modern Fed, an organization that has grown to exert great power in the U.S. economy (Robert L. Hetzel and Ralph F. Leach, "After the Accord: Reminiscences on the Birth of the Modern Fed," *Economic Quarterly*, volume 87/1, winter 2001, http://www.richmondfed.org/publications/economic_research/economic_quarterly/pdfs/winter2001/leach.pdf).

The chairman of the board of governors at the time of the accord was William McChesney Martin, Jr. (1906–98).

Martin was a dynamic leader who maintained his post for nearly two decades. Under his leadership the Fed assumed greater control over the nation's financial policies. This control was exercised primarily by influencing interest rates on loans. Lowering interest rates encouraged borrowing, which put more money into circulation for spending or investing. However, if demand outpaced supply, price inflation became a problem. Then, the Fed would raise interest rates to make borrowing less attractive and dampen demand. Martin reportedly summed this up as follows: "You have to take away the punch bowl when the party is warming up." His policy proved to be fruitful during the prosperous decades of the 1950s and 1960s.

The 1960s—Social Upheaval and Economic Growth

The 1960s were a time of social and economic change for the United States. The decade began with the election of President John F. Kennedy, who promised to ensure economic growth and address America's growing social problems. In 1963 Kennedy's efforts were cut short by his assassination. Lyndon B. Johnson took over as president and dramatically enlarged the federal government and its role in socioeconomic affairs. Johnson's administration initiated large-scale programs for the needy, including the health care programs Medicare (for the elderly) and Medicaid (for the poor), jobs programs, federal aid to schools, and food stamps for low-income Americans. The so-called "war on poverty" and the escalating war in Vietnam proved to be very expensive. At the same time, the United States was pursuing a costly (but ultimately successful) endeavor to land astronauts on the moon before the end of the decade.

Consumer and government spending drove the nation's GNP during the 1960s. It grew to $977 billion by 1970. But inflation became a problem (as it often does in a fast-growing economy) in the late 1960s. At the macroeconomic level there was too much money in the hands of consumers, which resulted in consumer demand that was higher than supply. By 1970 the inflation rate had reached 5.7%.

The nation was preoccupied with the explosive social problems of the time. During the mid- to late 1960s the country was plagued by protests against the Vietnam War and riots in blighted urban areas populated by poor African-Americans. By 1968 there were half a million American troops in Vietnam. Nightly television coverage provided a bleak picture of the war's progress and helped turn public opinion against the war and President Johnson. In 1968 Johnson announced he would not seek reelection. That same year Martin Luther King, Jr., and Robert Kennedy—John Kennedy's brother and an aspiring presidential candidate—were assassinated.

The United States left the 1960s having experienced the longest continuous stretch of positive GNP growth in history—the first quarter of 1961 through the last quarter of 1969 (National Bureau of Economic Research, http://www.nber.org/cycles.html/). But high inflation was about to become a major problem.

The 1970s: Stagflation and Energy Crises

Stagflation is a word coined during the 1970s to describe an economy suffering stagnation, high inflation, and high unemployment all at the same time. This combination of economic problems was unprecedented in U.S. history. Previously, high inflation had occurred when the economy was growing quickly, such as during World War II. But high production had meant high employment levels. By contrast, economic downturns were associated with higher unemployment but lower inflation (and even deflation). These relationships had been considered natural and certain.

The 1970s were unique, because both unemployment and inflation were high, by historical standards. Economist Robert Barro invented a new term called the Misery Index to describe this condition. The Misery Index is computed by summing the unemployment rate and inflation rate. Figure 1.12 shows the annual Misery Index calculated for 1968 through 1983. By the mid-1970s each rate exceeded 5%.

There were three presidents during the 1970s—Richard Nixon, Gerald Ford, and Jimmy Carter. Each tried a variety of measures to stem stagflation, but none was considered effective. Nixon implemented wage and price controls and increased government spending. In 1973 he resigned under threat of impeachment for his role in the Watergate scandal. Vice President Gerald Ford assumed the presidency. Economic problems continued, and in 1976 the country elected Jimmy Carter as the new president. Carter had emphasized the high Misery Index during his presidential campaign, but his administration was unable to turn the tide. By 1980 the Misery Index had climbed to 20%.

FOREIGN OIL AND COMPETITION. America's economic problems were aggravated by its dependence on foreign oil and competition from foreign industries. In 1973 Middle Eastern members of the Organization of Petroleum Exporting Countries (OPEC) halted oil exports to the United States in retaliation for U.S. support of Israel. The oil embargo lasted five months. When shipments resumed, the price of oil had dramatically increased. Americans faced high prices, long lines, and shortages at the gas pumps. Figure 1.13 shows that the average retail price of gasoline surged from around thirty-five cents per gallon in 1972 to $1.35 per gallon in 1981. A fifty-five mile per hour speed limit was imposed on the nation's interstates to save fuel. The federal government called on Americans to conserve energy and provided an example by not lighting the

FIGURE 1.12

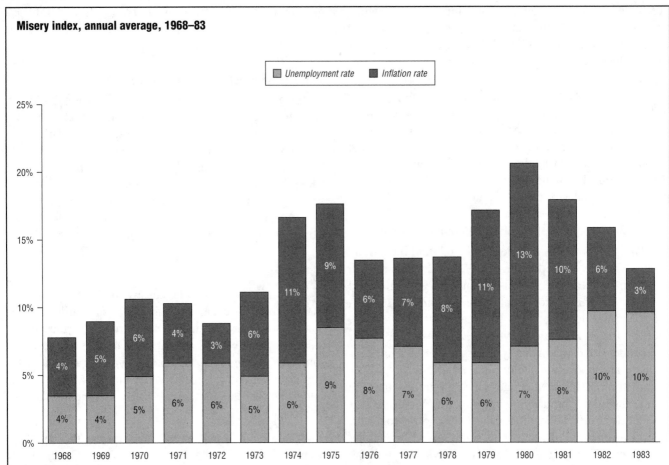

Misery index, annual average, 1968–83

SOURCE: Adapted from "Labor Force Statistics from the Current Population Survey: Unemployment Rate, Annual Average," in *Bureau of Labor Statistics Data*, U.S. Department of Labor, Bureau of Labor Statistics, 2006, http://data.bls.gov/PDQ/servlet/SurveyOutputServlet?data_tool=latest_numbers& series_id=LNU04000000&years_option=all_years&periods_option=specific_periods&periods=Annual+Data (accessed May 20, 2006) and from "Consumer Price Index, All Urban Consumers—(CPI-U), U.S. City Average, All Items, 1982–84=100," in *Consumer Price Indexes*, U.S. Department of Labor, Bureau of Labor Statistics, March 16, 2006, ftp://ftp.bls.gov/pub/special.requests/cpi/cpiai.txt (accessed June 12, 2006)

White House Christmas tree. During the late 1970s a revolution in oil-rich Iran brought a second wave of shortages to U.S. energy supplies.

The "energy crisis" of the 1970s had a ripple effect through the U.S. economy, causing the prices of other goods and services to increase. Lower profits and uncertainty about the future caused businesses to slow down and reduce their workforces. At the same time, American industries in steel, automobiles, and electronics endured stiff foreign competition, particularly from Japan. Small energy-efficient Japanese cars became very popular in the United States. By 1980 gasoline cost more than $1.00 per gallon, which was quadruple the price in 1970. American car makers struggled to compete, having always relied on consumer demand for large automobiles—now considered "gas-guzzlers."

DEREGULATION. One of the measures that President Carter took to combat stagflation was deregulation. For decades certain industries in the United States had been given government immunity from market supply and demand factors. The railroad, trucking, and airline industries were prime examples. Companies in these industries were guaranteed rates and routes and were allowed to operate contrary to antitrust laws. In 1978 the airline industry was deregulated; airlines began to compete with each other over fares and routes, and new companies entered the industry. Some of the large, well-established companies were unable to compete in the new environment and went out of business. But demand increased as prices came down and flying became available to many more Americans. By 1980 deregulation had been completed or was underway for the railroad, trucking, energy, financial services, and telecommunications industries.

The 1980s—Recession and Reaganomics

In November 1980 the American people elected Ronald Reagan as the new president. Inflation was at 13% that year—incredibly high for a peacetime economy. Unemployment was at 7%, meaning that millions of people were unemployed and faced with rapidly increasing prices in the marketplace. The economic

FIGURE 1.13

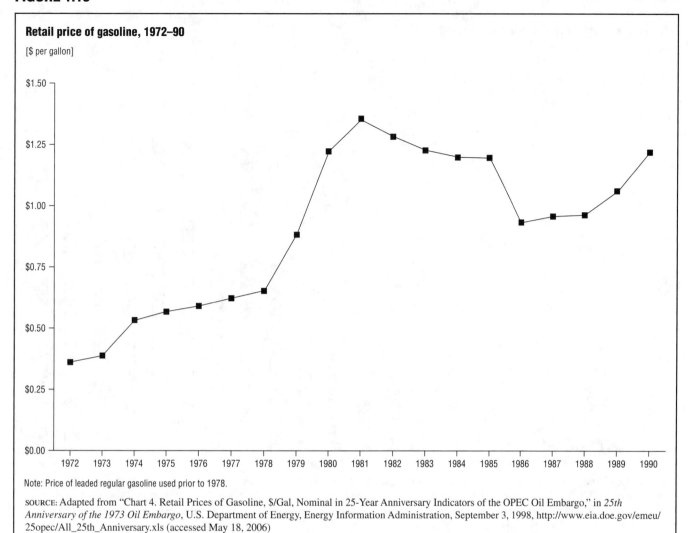

Retail price of gasoline, 1972–90

[$ per gallon]

Note: Price of leaded regular gasoline used prior to 1978.

SOURCE: Adapted from "Chart 4. Retail Prices of Gasoline, $/Gal, Nominal in 25-Year Anniversary Indicators of the OPEC Oil Embargo," in *25th Anniversary of the 1973 Oil Embargo*, U.S. Department of Energy, Energy Information Administration, September 3, 1998, http://www.eia.doe.gov/emeu/25opec/All_25th_Anniversary.xls (accessed May 18, 2006)

situation was dire, and drastic measures would be required to turn the economy around.

SLAYING THE INFLATIONARY DRAGON. In late 1979 President Carter had appointed a new governor of the Federal Reserve, Paul Volcker, who promised to "slay the inflationary dragon." Volcker began by tightening the nation's money supply. This had the effect of making credit more difficult to obtain, which drove up interest rates. The government knew that rising interest rates would probably trigger a production slowdown (a recession) that would push unemployment even higher. It was a trade-off that policymakers during the previous decade had been unwilling to accept.

Volcker forged ahead with his policies, and by the early 1980s interest rates had reached historical highs. Figure 1.14 shows that the prime loan rate—the interest rate that banks charge their best customers—peaked at 21.5% in December 1980. In 1981 the average interest rate for a conventional thirty-year mortgage soared to 18.45%, the highest rate ever recorded by the Federal

FIGURE 1.14

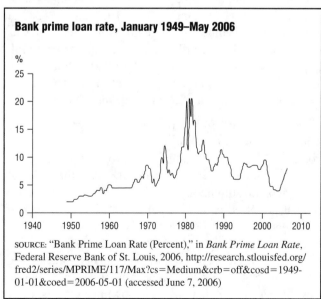

Bank prime loan rate, January 1949–May 2006

SOURCE: "Bank Prime Loan Rate (Percent)," in *Bank Prime Loan Rate*, Federal Reserve Bank of St. Louis, 2006, http://research.stlouisfed.org/fred2/series/MPRIME/117/Max?cs=Medium&crb=off&cosd=1949-01-01&coed=2006-05-01 (accessed June 7, 2006)

FIGURE 1.15

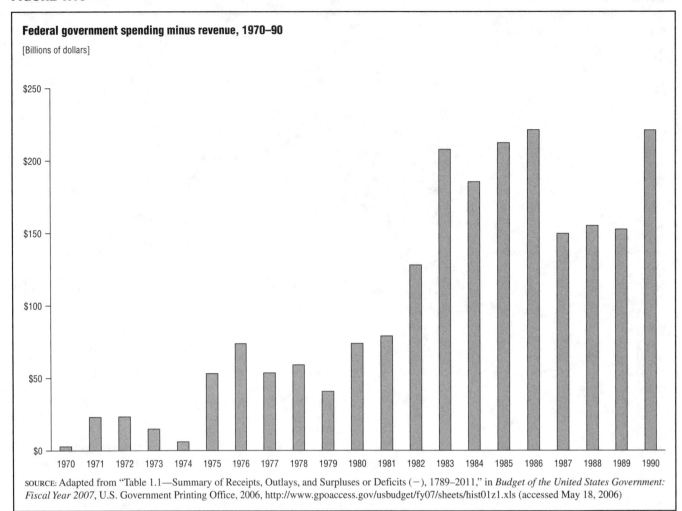

Federal government spending minus revenue, 1970–90

[Billions of dollars]

SOURCE: Adapted from "Table 1.1—Summary of Receipts, Outlays, and Surpluses or Deficits (−), 1789–2011," in *Budget of the United States Government: Fiscal Year 2007*, U.S. Government Printing Office, 2006, http://www.gpoaccess.gov/usbudget/fy07/sheets/hist01z1.xls (accessed May 18, 2006)

Home Loan Mortgage Corporation (http://research.stlouisfed.org/fred2/data/MORTG.txt).

Lack of credit caused a business slowdown—a reduction in GNP growth (or recession). As expected, the recession put more people out of work. Unemployment climbed at first, averaging 10% in 1982 and 1983, but then began to decline. By the end of the decade it was down around 5%. The inflation rate dropped from a high of 13% in 1980 to less than 5% by 1989. Although the spike in unemployment had been painful for Americans, the inflationary dragon was finally dead.

REAGANOMICS. When Reagan took office in 1981 he brought a new approach to curing the nation's financial woes: supply-side economics. Traditionally, the government had focused on the demand side—the role of consumers in stimulating businesses to produce more. Reagan preferred economic policies that directly helped producers. Professor Paul Johnson of Auburn University describes the philosophy this way: "Supply-side policy analysts focus on barriers to higher productivity—identifying ways in which the government can promote faster economic growth over the long haul by removing impediments to the supply of, and efficient use of, the factors of production" (http://www.auburn.edu/~johnspm/gloss/supply_side).

One of the cornerstones of supply-side economics is reducing taxes so that people and businesses have more money to invest in private enterprise. Reagan enacted tax cuts through two pieces of legislation: the Economic Recovery Tax Act of 1981 and the Tax Reform Act of 1986. The result was a much lower number of tax brackets (the various rates at which individuals are taxed based on their income), a broader tax base (wealth within a jurisdiction that is liable to taxation), and reduced tax rates on income and capital gains (the profit made from selling an investment, such as land).

At the same time, Reagan pushed for greater national defense spending as part of his "peace through strength" approach to the Soviet Union and selective cuts in social services spending. But no cuts were made to the largest and most expensive programs within the social services budget. The combination of all these factors resulted in high federal deficits during the 1980s. In other words, the federal government was spending more than it was making each year. As shown in Figure 1.15, the federal

FIGURE 1.16

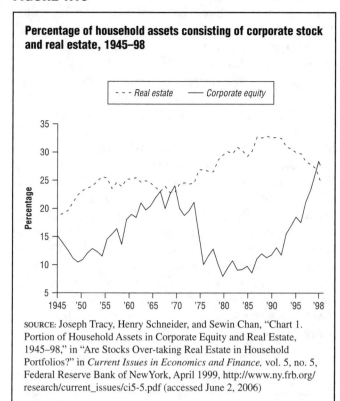

Percentage of household assets consisting of corporate stock and real estate, 1945–98

- - - Real estate   —— Corporate equity

SOURCE: Joseph Tracy, Henry Schneider, and Sewin Chan, "Chart 1. Portion of Household Assets in Corporate Equity and Real Estate, 1945–98," in "Are Stocks Over-taking Real Estate in Household Portfolios?" in *Current Issues in Economics and Finance,* vol. 5, no. 5, Federal Reserve Bank of New York, April 1999, http://www.ny.frb.org/research/current_issues/ci5-5.pdf (accessed June 2, 2006)

deficits of the mid-1980s were more than twice what they had been during the mid-1970s. In 1981 the national debt (the sum of all accumulated federal deficits since the nation began) reached $1 trillion.

The 1990s—Sparkling Economic Performance

The 1990s were a time of phenomenal economic growth for the United States, even amid the shadows of war and an ever-increasing federal deficit. In August 1990 the military forces of Iraq under President Saddam Hussein invaded the small neighboring country of Kuwait. President George H. W. Bush had taken office in 1989 and quickly acted to put together a coalition of international forces that successfully forced Iraq out of Kuwait. The Gulf War, as it came to be known, was short-lived and would be seen as a triumphant, if incomplete, victory by allied forces. Although his military strength was weakened, Hussein was not removed from power in Iraq and continued to pose foreign relations problems for the United States for many years.

President Bush had been elected in large part because of his promise not to raise taxes. During the campaign he famously said, "Read my lips: No new taxes." But the promise was not one he could keep given the economic realities of the time. During the late 1980s there had been a severe financial crisis in the savings and loan industry, which had been recently deregulated. A series of unwise loans and poor business decisions left most of the indus-

try in shambles and necessitated a government bailout. According to the U.S. Department of State, by 1993 the cost of the bailout had exceeded $500 billion ("Outline of U.S. History," November 2005, http://usinfo.state.gov/products/pubs/histryotln/order.htm). At the same time, the government faced rapidly rising expenditures on health care programs for the elderly (Medicare) and the needy (Medicaid). Bush reluctantly agreed to a tax increase, a move that was politically damaging. In 1992 he lost his reelection bid to Arkansas Governor Bill Clinton, who was reelected in 1996.

By and large the 1990s were a period of peace and prosperity for America. The cold war ended when the Soviet Union disintegrated into individual republics. Technological innovations, particularly in the computer industry, helped push the economy to new heights. Sterling business success led to robust investor confidence in the stock markets. Figure 1.16 shows the portion of household assets invested in real estate and corporate equity (stocks) between 1945 and 1998. Although real estate was the preferred investment through nearly all of this period, the 1990s witnessed tremendous increases in the holdings of corporate equity by the average American. In the mid-1980s the average household had only 10% of its assets in corporate equity. By 1998 this percentage had reached nearly 30%, roughly equal to the percent held in real estate. The Dow Jones Industrial Average is a stock market index—a measure used by economists to gauge the value (and performance) of the stock of thirty large companies. Between the late 1970s and the late 1990s the index soared from around one thousand points to eleven thousand points—reflecting the tremendous value gained by these companies over that time period.

The combination of low interest rates, low unemployment, and high investment rates and business growth combined to greatly expand the U.S. economy. In a 1999 speech, Chairman of the Federal Reserve Board Alan Greenspan described the expansion as "America's sparkling economic performance."

The 2000s—Hardship, War, Peace, and Prosperity

In January 2001 George W. Bush was inaugurated as the nation's new president. He entered office with plans to overhaul many federal programs and enacted a tax cut within the first few months of his administration. On September 11, 2001, four commercial airliners were commandeered by hijackers. Two of the planes were flown into the twin towers of the World Trade Center in New York City. A third plane was flown into the Pentagon in Washington, D.C. The fourth plane crashed in a field in Pennsylvania after passengers likely struggled with their hijackers. The attacks killed more than twenty-nine hundred people and stunned the world.

Intelligence revealed that the hijackers were Middle Eastern terrorists associated with the group al-Qaida, led by Osama bin Laden. The U.S. believed that bin Laden was being harbored by the Taliban government of Afghanistan and demanded that he be turned over to authorities. After the Taliban refused to do so, the United States military invaded Afghanistan. Although the military operations were technically a success, the U.S. was not able to capture bin Laden and found itself in a lingering guerilla-type conflict with Taliban and al-Qaida fighters.

The so-called 9/11 attacks dramatically altered the priorities of the U.S. government. The president called for a worldwide war against terrorism and created a new Department of Homeland Security to strengthen national security. In 2003 an allied military force comprised mostly of American and British troops invaded Iraq. The allied forces met little resistance from Iraqi forces, and the war was declared over in less than a month. But, as in Afghanistan, the United States found itself trying to establish order in a country in which pockets of insurgents (well-armed and determined guerillas and terrorists) managed to wreak havoc and kill American soldiers and innocent civilians. As of the fall of 2006 the U.S. military continued its presence in Afghanistan and Iraq. Both nations were trying to rebuild with U.S. assistance. Fox News reported in September 2005 that the Afghanistan and Iraq campaigns had cost the United States more than $300 billion at that time (September 10, 2005, http://www.foxnews.com/story/0,2933,169035,00.html).

The 9/11 attacks had numerous direct effects on the U.S. economy. Investor nervousness brought a short-lived dip in the stock markets. The tourism industry suffered a major setback, and insurance companies had to make massive payouts to settle claims. There were also costs to the government for rescue and recovery operations. Longer-term effects include the financial repercussions of new national security and antiterrorism measures implemented at home and abroad.

THE INTERNET BUBBLE BURSTS. During the late 1990s the stock market witnessed tremendous growth, driven in large part by investor enthusiasm for Internet-related businesses. Access to the Internet became widespread in America and much of the developed world, creating many new market opportunities for entrepreneurs. Investors enthusiastically poured money into the stock of these new businesses. NASDAQ is U.S.-based stock market on which the stock of many technology companies is traded. The NASDAQ composite index is a measure of the performance of many of the stocks on NASDAQ. In 1990 the index was less than five hundred. In early 2000 it peaked above four thousand during the height of the Internet stock craze. Many of the stocks had become overvalued; their high prices could not be sustained based on the actual financial results that the companies were producing. What followed was a sharp market correction, as investors sold off many Internet-based stocks and the prices plummeted. By late 2002 the NASDAQ composite index was around twelve hundred, from which it slowly began to climb again.

In economics a "bubble" is a phenomenon in which investors overzealously invest (speculate) in a particular commodity or market sector that becomes overvalued. Excitement about possible gains overrules frank analysis of the underlying financial factors. Unfortunately, the very existence of a bubble is not evident until after the fact, when the bubble has burst and much value has been lost in the investments and the businesses involved.

THE DECADE SO FAR. The early 2000s have proved to be expensive years for the U.S. economy, with the 9/11 attacks, the wars and rebuilding efforts in Iraq and Afghanistan, the bursting of the Internet bubble, corporate scandals, devastating hurricanes that hit the U.S. Gulf Coast in 2005, and rising energy costs. But relatively prosperous conditions have continued for the U.S. economy, as witnessed by continuing growth in the gross domestic product (GDP), relatively low unemployment rates, and moderate rates of inflation.

CHAPTER 2
ECONOMIC INDICATORS AND PUBLIC PERCEPTIONS

Because the U.S. economy is so large and complex, it is difficult to assess its overall health at any given time. Economists use a variety of numerical measures to analyze and track macroeconomic factors, such as employment and production. These economic indicators are widely broadcast in the media and are the subject of much analysis by leaders in government, industry, and the financial markets. The American public tends to gauge the health of the economy based on other factors, including their own personal and community-wide experiences and expectations. As such, the public's perception of the economy is sometimes at odds with the numerical measures so valued by economists. Analysts refer to this discrepancy as "Main Street versus Wall Street," and it has been quite in evidence during the 2000s.

ECONOMIC INDICATORS

Economists gauge the strength of the economy using data on wages, spending, saving, unemployment, and the production and consumption of goods and services. Some of these data are called economic indicators, because they provide key information about the macroeconomic condition of the country. One example is the National Income and Product Accounts (NIPAs) compiled by the Bureau of Economic Affairs under the U.S. Department of Commerce. The U.S. Census Bureau, U.S. Department of Labor, and some private organizations also publish key economic indicators, as shown in Table 2.1.

Three of the most important and telling economic indicators are the gross domestic product (GDP), consumer price index, and the unemployment rate.

Gross Domestic Product

The GDP measures in dollars the total value of U.S. goods and services newly produced or newly provided in a given time period. It is calculated and published by the U.S. Bureau of Economic Affairs and is one of the most important and accurate ways the government tracks the health of the economy. The GDP can be calculated in different ways. One method is called the expenditure approach. It sums all of the spending that takes place during a specified time period on final goods and services that are newly produced or newly provided. The components of this calculation are:

- Consumption—the amount spent by consumers on final goods and services. This includes food, clothing, household appliances, etc., and payments for medical care, haircuts, dry cleaning, and other types of services. One major item not included in this category is the purchase of residential housing, which is considered an investment, rather than a consumption expense.

- Investment—this category has three components. One is the amount spent by businesses on assets they will use to provide goods and services (for example, new machines and equipment, warehouses, software, and company vehicles). Also included are changes in the value of business inventories. This amount can be positive or negative. Residential housing is the third component of the investment category.

- Government expenditures—the amount spent by the government (local, state, and federal) on final goods and services. This category does not include transfer payments to the public (such as Social Security and unemployment compensation) because those expenditures do not represent goods or services purchased.

- Net exports—the difference between the value of U.S. exports and imports. In other words, net exports equal the amount that foreigners paid for American goods minus the amount that Americans spent on foreign goods. If the United States exports more than it imports, this value will be positive. If the country imports more than it exports, the value will be negative.

TABLE 2.1

Key economic indicators for U.S. economy

Economic indicator	Description	Source	Website
Gross domestic product	Value of goods and services produced in a given time period.	U.S. Department of Commerce, Bureau of Economic Affairs http://www.bea.gov/bea	http://www.bea.gov/bea/dn/home/gdp.htm
Personal income and outlays	Personal income, disposable personal income, and personal consumption expenditures.		http://www.bea.gov/bea/dn/home/personalincome.htm
Corporate profits	Corporate profits based on current production.		http://www.bea.gov/bea/dn/home/corporateprof.htm
Fixed assets	Net stocks, depreciation, and investment for private residential and nonresidential fixed assets.		http://www.bea.gov/bea/dn/home/fixedassets.htm
Balance of payments (International transactions)	Quarterly trade in goods, services, income, unilateral transfers, and financial assets.		http://www.bea.gov/bea/di/home/bop.htm
Consumer price index	Monthly changes in the prices paid by urban consumers for a representative basket of goods and services.	U.S. Department of Labor, Bureau of Labor Statistics http://www.bls.gov	http://www.bls.gov/cpi/
Producer price index	Group of indexes that measure the average change over time in the prices received by U.S. producers of goods and services.		
Unemployment rate	Number of unemployed people divided by total labor force. Based on monthly survey.		http://www.bls.gov/cps/home.htm
Monthly retail trade	Survey of companies that sell merchandise and related services to final consumers.	U.S. Department of Commerce, U.S. Census Bureau http://www.census.gov/econ/www/	
Monthly wholesale trade	Survey of companies that are primarily engaged in merchant wholesale trade in the U.S.		
Consumer confidence index	Consumers' assessment of economic conditions based on monthly surveys of a representative sample of 5,000 U.S. households.	The Conference Board http://www.conference-board .org/economics	http://www.conference-board.org/economics/ consumerConfidence.cfm
Leading indicators	Index based on vendor performance, stock prices, consumer expectations, manufacturers' new orders, manufacturing hours, interest rate spread, building permits, claims for unemployment insurance, and real money supply.		http://www.conference-board.org/economics/
ISM report on business®	Economic activity in many manufacturing and nonmanufacturing industries based on orders, production, employment, supplier deliveries, imports, prices, and inventories.	Institute for Supply Management http://www.ism.ws/ISMReport/	http://www.ism.ws/ISMReport/

SOURCE: Created by Kim Masters Evans for Thomson Gale, 2006

It should be noted that GDP counts only the final value paid for goods and services, not the value of intermediate transactions. For example, the value of steel sold by a steel company to an automaker is not counted. The value of the car made from the steel is counted when the car is sold in the marketplace. To be counted in GDP a product must be new. The sales of used items are not included.

COMPARISON WITH GROSS NATIONAL PRODUCT (GNP). Prior to 1991 the U.S. government used an economic indicator called the gross national product (GNP) to measure U.S. productivity. The GNP was calculated the same way that the GDP is calculated today, except that the GNP included the contribution of U.S. production in foreign countries (for example, an American-owned factory in Mexico). GDP includes only production occurring within the boundaries of the United States.

NOMINAL VERSUS REAL GDP. Economists refer to GDP values as being nominal (based on current dollar values) or real (based on inflation-adjusted dollar values). Consider a simple example in which a nation's only production is one thousand identical new cars produced and sold each year. Assume this nation suffers from inflation, meaning that the price charged and paid for each car increases each year. A graph of this nation's GDP would go upward, indicating that production increases each year, while actually it is just the price of the cars that is increasing.

To remedy this problem, economists adjust the actual GDP values (nominal values) to account for inflation. The adjusted values are called "real" GDP values. They are useful for comparing GDP changes over time. Figure 2.1 shows real GDP values for the U.S. economy from 1929 through 2005. These values were calculated assuming that

FIGURE 2.1

Real gross domestic product, 1929–2005

[Billions of year 2000 dollars]

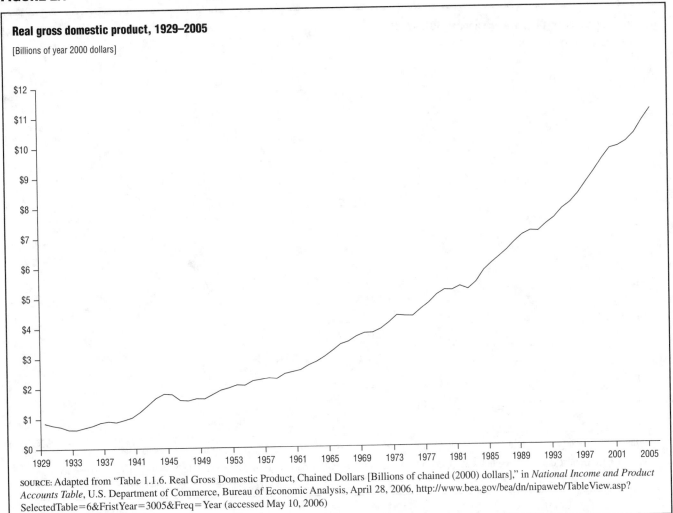

SOURCE: Adapted from "Table 1.1.6. Real Gross Domestic Product, Chained Dollars [Billions of chained (2000) dollars]," in *National Income and Product Accounts Table*, U.S. Department of Commerce, Bureau of Economic Analysis, April 28, 2006, http://www.bea.gov/bea/dn/nipaweb/TableView.asp? SelectedTable=6&FristYear=3005&Freq=Year (accessed May 10, 2006)

a dollar had the exact same value over time—the value it had in the year 2000.

Consumer Price Index

The consumer price index (CPI) provides a measure of price changes in consumer goods and services over a specific period of time. Each month the U.S. Bureau of Labor Statistics (BLS), a division of the U.S. Department of Labor, calculates the purchase price of a fixed "basket" of thousands of goods and services commonly purchased for consumption by American households. These purchases are divided into eight major categories:

- Food and beverages—at-home and away-from-home consumption

- Housing—includes rent of primary residence or owners' equivalent rent

- Apparel

- Transportation—includes insurance payments

- Medical care

- Recreation—includes pet expenses

- Education and communication—includes computer software

- Other goods and services—haircuts, cigarettes, funeral expenses, etc.

The basket price includes sales and excise taxes paid on goods purchased. Payments for income taxes and investments, such as stocks and bonds, are not included.

An index is a tool useful for comparing changes over time. The index for the basket price for a selected time period is arbitrarily set to one hundred. This is the reference index. All other basket prices are compared with the reference index using this equation: index = (basket price/ reference basket price) × 100. Therefore, a graph of CPI data over time does not show the actual prices paid for the baskets but rather a series of index numbers useful for determining price changes. Figure 2.2 shows the average annual CPI for 1913 through 2005. It uses the time period of 1982 through 1984 as the reference time period for which the CPI value is arbitrarily set to one hundred.

FIGURE 2.2

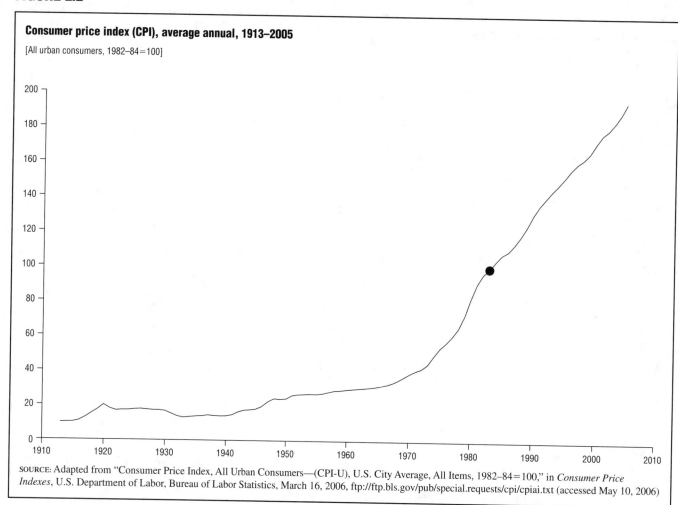

Consumer price index (CPI), average annual, 1913–2005

[All urban consumers, 1982–84=100]

SOURCE: Adapted from "Consumer Price Index, All Urban Consumers—(CPI-U), U.S. City Average, All Items, 1982–84=100," in *Consumer Price Indexes*, U.S. Department of Labor, Bureau of Labor Statistics, March 16, 2006, ftp://ftp.bls.gov/pub/special.requests/cpi/cpiai.txt (accessed May 10, 2006)

Percent changes in price between two years can be determined based on the difference in index values. For example, in 1985 the CPI was 108. By 2005 it had risen to 195—a difference of 87 index points. Dividing 87 by 108 and multiplying by 100 provides a percentage difference of 81%. On average, prices increased by 81% over this twenty-year period.

The data presented in Figure 2.2 are for urban households. According to the BLS, the urban CPI (CPI-U) represents the buying habits of approximately 87% of the U.S. population (http://www.bls.gov/cpi/cpifaq.htm). The BLS also calculates a CPI for urban dwellers employed in clerical or wage occupations. This CPI-W covers a subset of people included in the CPI-U. This subset represents approximately 32% of the U.S. population. In addition to the national average, the BLS publishes CPI data for specific regions of the United States and for dozens of metropolitan areas.

CALCULATING INFLATION RATES FROM THE CPI. Price inflation can be defined as the increase in price over time of a fixed basket of goods and services. Thus, the CPI provides economists with a tool for quantifying inflation rates. The percent change in CPI from year to year is the inflation rate for that year. Figure 2.3 shows the annual inflation rate for the U.S. economy for each year between 1915 and 2005 based on CPI-U data. The CPI-U for 2004 was 189; for 2005 it was 195. The inflation rate was ([195-189]/189) × 100 = 3%. This means that, on average, the price of consumer goods and services increased by 3% between 2004 and 2005. It also means that the purchasing power of a dollar went down over that time. For example, a candy bar that cost $1.00 in 2004 cost $1.03 in 2005.

In general, annual inflation rates of 2–3% are considered signs of a healthy growing economy where demand slightly outpaces supply. Larger inflation rates can be worrisome. The U.S. economy has suffered from double-digit inflation rates due to the effects of both world wars and during the 1970s and very early 1980s. Deflation (lowering of average prices) occurred during the 1920s and 1930s.

Unemployment Rate

The U.S. government calculates the nation's unemployment rate for a given time period by dividing the number of unemployed people by the total labor force

FIGURE 2.3

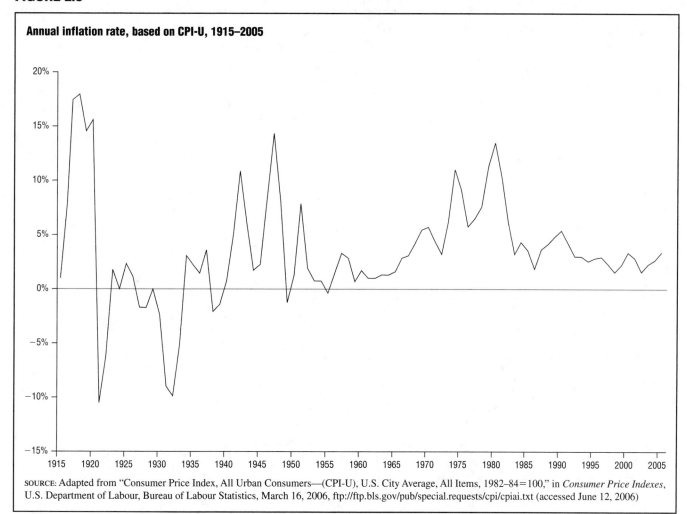

Annual inflation rate, based on CPI-U, 1915–2005

SOURCE: Adapted from "Consumer Price Index, All Urban Consumers—(CPI-U), U.S. City Average, All Items, 1982–84=100," in *Consumer Price Indexes*, U.S. Department of Labour, Bureau of Labour Statistics, March 16, 2006, ftp://ftp.bls.gov/pub/special.requests/cpi/cpiai.txt (accessed June 12, 2006)

(unemployed plus employed people). The employment status of people is determined based on responses by the public to a monthly government survey called the Current Population Survey (CPS). The CPS is administered by the U.S. Census Bureau for the BLS. According to the BLS, the survey is administered to more than sixty thousand households per month (http://www.bls.gov/cps/uiclaims.htm).

The BLS counts people as being unemployed if they meet all of the following criteria:

- Do not have a job

- Have actively looked for work in the prior four weeks

- Are currently available for work

The BLS does not consider active-duty military personnel or institutionalized workers (such as prison inmates) to be in the labor force. In addition, some Americans are neither employed nor unemployed under the BLS definitions and thus are not in the labor force. The most obvious examples are patients in long-term care facilities and retirees. Many students and stay-at-home parents would also fall into this category.

Figure 2.4 shows the U.S. unemployment rate for 1925 through 2005. For years through 1945 the rate is calculated based on people age fourteen and older. Due to the passage of child labor laws, the unemployment rate for years following 1945 includes only people age sixteen and older. The unemployment rate soared during the Great Depression, reaching nearly 25% in 1933. More typically, it has ranged between 3% and 8%. During the early 1980s the unemployment rate was nearly 10%, its highest rate since the 1930s. Since 1995 is has hovered between 4% and 6%, generally considered to be a reasonable range for a healthy economy.

Critics believe that the BLS data are not representative of the nation's actual unemployment rate, because the data do not include people who become discouraged and quit actively looking for work.

THE NUMERICAL STATE OF THE U.S. ECONOMY

Government and industry statistics on the state of the U.S. economy are released with varying frequency. Some economic indicators are published monthly, while others are published quarterly. Three government agencies—the

FIGURE 2.4

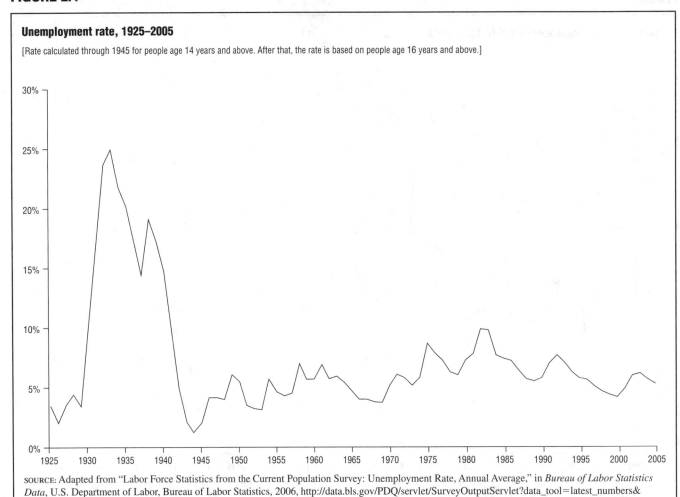

Unemployment rate, 1925–2005

[Rate calculated through 1945 for people age 14 years and above. After that, the rate is based on people age 16 years and above.]

SOURCE: Adapted from "Labor Force Statistics from the Current Population Survey: Unemployment Rate, Annual Average," in *Bureau of Labor Statistics Data*, U.S. Department of Labor, Bureau of Labor Statistics, 2006, http://data.bls.gov/PDQ/servlet/SurveyOutputServlet?data_tool=latest_numbers& series_id=LNU04000000&years_option=all_years&periods_option=specific_periods&periods=Annual+Data (accessed May 20, 2006)

BLS, the Bureau of Economic Affairs (BEA), and the U.S. Census Bureau—publish updated economic indicators on a regular basis.

BLS: Unemployment, Wages, and Prices

The U.S. Department of Labor's BLS publishes an online source called "U.S. Economy at a Glance" that includes the latest statistics gathered by the agency on unemployment, wages, prices, and other economic factors. Table 2.2 shows the latest data available up to May 2006.

The unemployment rate in May 2006 was 4.6%. The rate had dropped slightly from December 2005, when it was 4.9%. Comparison with the historical unemployment chart in Figure 2.4 shows that this rate is a moderate rate for post–depression America.

The BLS also tracks changes in nonfarm payroll employment and average hourly earnings. These data are based on monthly surveys conducted of 160,000 businesses and government agencies as part of the agency's Current Employment Statistics program (http://www.bls.gov/ces/). As shown in Table 2.2, approximately

seventy-five thousand new jobs were added in May 2006, and the average hourly wage for production and nonsupervisory workers was $16.62. Both numbers were based on preliminary estimates. Figure 2.5 shows the monthly change in the number of nonfarm payroll employees from January 2004 through May 2006. The seventy-five thousand new jobs added during May 2006 represent the lowest monthly increase recorded since October 2005.

The consumer price index (CPI) increased by 0.6% from March 2006 to April 2006. This value was relatively high compared with the changes reported for the four preceding months.

There are three other indexes reported by the BLS:

- Producer price index (PPI)—a family of indexes that measure changes over time in the selling prices received by the makers and providers of goods and services. As shown in Figure 2.6, the PPI has risen dramatically over the past two decades from its reference value of one hundred in 1982. Table 2.2 indicates the PPI increased by 0.9% from March 2006 to April

TABLE 2.2

U.S. Department of Labor economic indicators, December 2005–May 2006

Data series	Dec 2005	Jan 2006	Feb 2006	Mar 2006	Apr 2006	May 2006
Unemployment rate[a]	4.9	4.7	4.8	4.7	4.7	4.6
Change in payroll employment[b]	145	154	200	175	126*	75*
Average hourly earnings[c]	16.35	16.40	16.47	16.51	16.61*	16.62*
Consumer price index[d]	−0.1	0.7	0.1	0.4	0.6	0.4
Producer price index[e]	0.7	0.3	−1.3*	0.5*	0.9*	0.2*
U.S. import price index[f]	0.0	1.2	−0.8	−0.1	2.1	1.6
Employment cost index[g,i,j]	0.8		0.6			
Productivity[h]	−0.3		3.7			

*Preliminary

[a]In percent, seasonally adjusted. Annual averages are available for Not Seasonally Adjusted data.
[b]Number of jobs, in thousands, seasonally adjusted
[c]For production and nonsupervisory workers on private nonfarm payrolls, seasonally adjusted
[d]All items, U.S. city average, all urban consumers, 1982-84=100, 1-month percent change, seasonally adjusted
[e]Finished goods, 1982=100, 1-month percent change, seasonally adjusted
[f]All imports, 1-month percent change, not seasonally adjusted
[g]Compensation, all civilian workers, quarterly data, 3-month percent change, seasonally adjusted
[h]Output per hour, nonfarm business, quarterly data, percent change from previous quarter at annual rate, seasonally adjusted
[i]Includes wages, salaries, and employer costs for employee benefits.
[j]See www.bls.gov/ncs/ect/cimapnote#

SOURCE: Adapted from *U.S. Economy at a Glance*, U.S. Department of Labor, Bureau of Labor Statistics, June 29, 2006, http://www.bls.gov/eag/eag.us.htm (accessed July 4, 2006)

2006. PPI values can differ from CPI values due to factors such as taxes and distribution costs.

- U.S. import price index (MPI)—indicates monthly changes in the prices of nonmilitary goods and services imported to the U.S. from the rest of the world. The MPI increased by 1.6% between April and May 2006. The BLS also tracks an export price index as part of its International Price Program.

- Employment cost index (ECI)—tracks quarterly changes in nonfarm civilian business labor costs based on a national compensation survey. It includes wages, salaries, and employer costs for employee benefits. The ECI increased by 0.6% from fourth quarter 2005 to first quarter 2006.

Finally, the *U.S. Economy at a Glance* includes a measure of national productivity (or efficiency). This number is a quarterly estimate of the change in output per hour of nonfarm businesses. It is calculated by comparing the amount of goods and services produced with the inputs that were used to produce them. According to the BLS, productivity was up 3.7% in first quarter 2006 compared with fourth quarter 2005.

BEA: GDP, Income, Savings, and Profits

The BEA's Web site publishes an "Overview of the Economy" that includes the latest agency statistics for GDP, corporate profits, personal income and savings, and other economic factors. It should be noted that until they are dubbed "final," these statistics are estimates and are frequently revised by the BEA as new data become available.

REAL GDP. Figure 2.7 shows the quarterly changes in real GDP for second quarter 2002 through first quarter 2006. Real GDP grew by 5.3% during first quarter 2006, based on preliminary estimates. This value represents a substantial improvement from the previous quarter and strong growth compared with the rest of the range. According to a BEA news release dated May 26, 2006, the first quarter 2006 real GDP growth was primarily due to increases in consumer spending on durable (long-lasting) goods; U.S. exports; federal government spending; and business investment in equipment and software. Overall, real GDP grew by 3.5% during 2005, from $10.76 trillion in 2004 to $11.13 trillion in 2005 (note that real GDP values are based on year 2000 dollars; http://www.bea.gov/bea/newsrelarchive/2006/gdp106p.pdf).

NOMINAL GDP. The BEA reports that nominal GDP (GDP in current dollars) was $12.5 trillion in 2005. A breakdown by component is detailed in Table 2.3 and shown graphically in Figure 2.8.

Personal consumption expenditures (PCE) accounted for two-thirds of positive GDP during 2005. This is consumer spending on goods and services. Services accounted for more than half of PCE, totaling $5.2 trillion. Medical care was the largest single service component, accounting for $1.5 trillion of the total. Housing costs were the second-largest component, at $1.3 trillion. Spending on nondurable goods, such as food, clothing, etc., amounted to $2.6 trillion, or 19%, of positive GDP. Durable goods expenditures totaled just over $1 trillion, or 8%, of positive GDP.

Private investments totaled $2.1 trillion in 2005 and accounted for 16% of positive GDP. More than half of this total was devoted to nonresidential (business) investments in structures, equipment, and software. Residential fixed investment totaled $756.3 billion. The contribution from the change in private inventories was $18.9 billion.

Government spending and investment amounted to $2.4 trillion, or 18%, of positive GDP. State and local governments accounted for more than half of this total. Net exports were a negative contributor to GDP during 2005, because the value of imports ($2 trillion) was greater than the value of exports ($1.3 trillion).

PERSONAL INCOME AND SAVINGS. The BEA also tracks changes in personal income and its disposition. Personal income includes wages and salaries (the largest component), wage and salary supplements (for example, employer contributions to private pension funds on behalf of employees), rental income, proprietors' income (earned

FIGURE 2.5

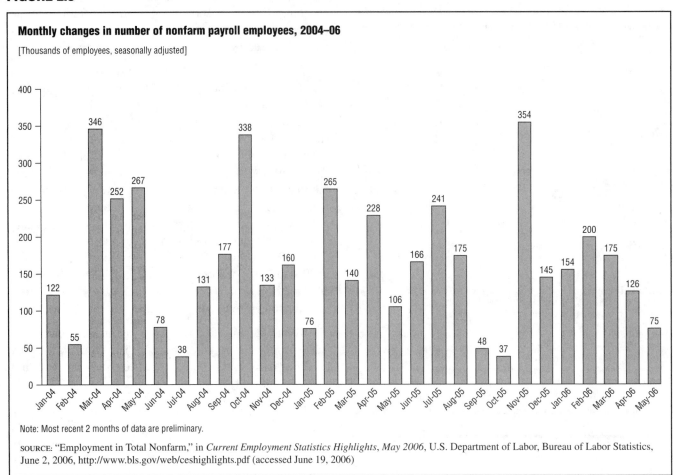

Monthly changes in number of nonfarm payroll employees, 2004–06

[Thousands of employees, seasonally adjusted]

Note: Most recent 2 months of data are preliminary.

SOURCE: "Employment in Total Nonfarm," in *Current Employment Statistics Highlights*, *May 2006*, U.S. Department of Labor, Bureau of Labor Statistics, June 2, 2006, http://www.bls.gov/web/ceshighlights.pdf (accessed June 19, 2006)

by entrepreneurs, small businesses, and farmers), and interest and dividend income. Most of the data are based on private and government payrolls. In a May 26, 2006, news release (http://www.bea.gov/bea/newsrelarchive/2006/pi0406.pdf), the BEA reported that personal income increased by 0.4% in April 2006. This was very similar to changes recorded in the previous four months.

Disposable personal income (DPI) is the amount of income received by people after taxes are subtracted. In other words, DPI is the income available to people for spending or saving. According to the BEA, DPI increased by 0.4% in April 2006 compared with March 2006. Personal savings (DPI minus personal outlays) was negative $147 billion in April 2006. Negative personal savings from current income occurs in three situations:

- People spend more than their DPI and borrow money to pay for the difference—for example, from credit cards or home equity loans.

- People sell investments or other assets to finance their excess outlays.

- People spend savings left over from previous periods.

CORPORATE PROFITS. The BEA reports that corporate profits from current product increased $116.5 billion

during first quarter 2006 after a $185.8 billion increase during fourth quarter 2005. The amount of internal funds available to corporations for investment increased by nearly $85 billion in first quarter 2006.

The Census Bureau: Housing Starts and Home Sales

A high rate of home ownership is considered a positive sign of financial health by the U.S. government. As such, the U.S. Census Bureau tracks two important indicators in this area: housing starts and home sales. Housing starts is the number of new housing units (or homes) that have been started over a particular period. According to the U.S. Census Bureau, nearly 1.6 million single-family homes were started in May 2006. This value is up from around 1.2 million homes started in mid-2000. In general, monthly housing start numbers increased steadily during the early 2000s. (See Figure 2.9.) In April 2006 nearly six million existing homes were sold, up from around four million sold per month in mid-1997. In September 2006, however, the National Association of Realtors reported that during the previous month, for the first time in eleven years, the median price of a single family home was lower than it had been a year before. Economists speculated that this could be the beginning of a significant downturn in the real estate market.

FIGURE 2.6

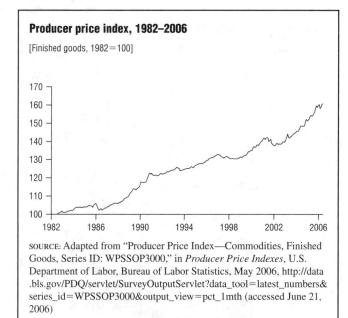

Producer price index, 1982–2006

[Finished goods, 1982=100]

SOURCE: Adapted from "Producer Price Index—Commodities, Finished Goods, Series ID: WPSSOP3000," in *Producer Price Indexes*, U.S. Department of Labor, Bureau of Labor Statistics, May 2006, http://data .bls.gov/PDQ/servlet/SurveyOutputServlet?data_tool=latest_numbers& series_id=WPSSOP3000&output_view=pct_1mth (accessed June 21, 2006)

FIGURE 2.7

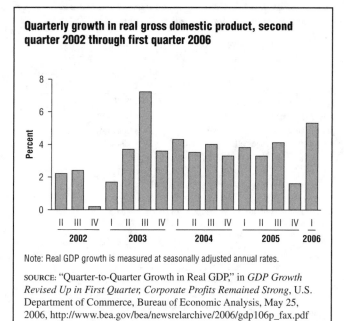

Quarterly growth in real gross domestic product, second quarter 2002 through first quarter 2006

Note: Real GDP growth is measured at seasonally adjusted annual rates.

SOURCE: "Quarter-to-Quarter Growth in Real GDP," in *GDP Growth Revised Up in First Quarter, Corporate Profits Remained Strong*, U.S. Department of Commerce, Bureau of Economic Analysis, May 25, 2006, http://www.bea.gov/bea/newsrelarchive/2006/gdp106p_fax.pdf (accessed June 7, 2006)

PUBLIC PERCEPTION OF THE ECONOMY

According to the government's various economic indicators, the condition of the U.S. economy is good overall. In reality, the state of the nation's economy is a reflection of the financial condition of the hundreds of millions of individuals and businesses that contribute to it. Thus, economic conditions at the national level can be quite different from those experienced by people at the regional and local levels. In addition, the public's perception of the nation's financial condition often proves to be quite different from that indicated by numerical measures.

Regional and Local Economies

Part of microeconomics study involves the economic health of various geographical regions and communities. A regional economy can be an area as small as a neighborhood or as large as a group of states with climate, geography, industry, or culture in common. The relative strength of a regional economy reflects broader national trends. For example, in the late nineteenth and early twentieth centuries—with the economy of the American South in shambles after the Civil War—northern cities attracted millions of workers to their rapidly growing industrial centers, such as the steel mills of Pittsburgh and the car factories of Detroit. Later, as the population migrated elsewhere, this region became known as the Rust Belt. Similarly, in the late twentieth century, western states experienced substantial growth with the rise of the computer industry, thanks in large part to Microsoft, which is headquartered in Seattle, Washington, and the "dotcom" companies centered in California's Silicon Valley. Other major economic regions of the United

States include the Farm Belt of the Great Plains and the Sun Belt states of the South and southwestern United States, with warm climates that make them popular tourist destinations and strong agricultural regions.

When a region or community experiences a serious economic downturn—such as that which happened in the upper Midwest, when the auto and steel manufacturers starting losing ground to foreign competitors, and in the Farm Belt, with the rise of agribusiness and the subsequent demise of the small family farm—its citizens often fall into a cycle of unemployment and poverty, leading federal and local governments and private nonprofit organizations to step in and offer assistance.

The Role of the Individual in the Economy

Almost every aspect of American life is influenced by, and further influences, the economy. Whether individuals drive or fly on their next vacation, how a person will pay for college and save for his or her retirement, what advertisements a person sees, what movies an individual watches, and what magazines a person reads all involve making economic decisions, which then impact the way the economy functions. If a person works or plans to work, that person is a small but important part of the economy. Likewise, every time an individual buys goods or saves money, he or she is participating in economic activity.

Economists maintain that the better off the economy is, the better its participants will be. In a healthy economy people tend to have more job security, earn more money, and are able to increase opportunities for themselves and

TABLE 2.3

Composition of gross domestic product, 2005

[Billions of current dollars, seasonally adjusted at annual rates]

	Component	Percent of positive GDP
Gross domestic product:	**$12,487.10**	
Personal consumption expenditures	**$8,745.70**	66%
Durable goods	$1,026.50	8%
Motor vehicles and parts	$446.8	3%
Furniture and household equipment	$373.2	3%
Other	$206.4	2%
Nondurable goods	$2,564.40	19%
Food	$1,218.6	9%
Clothing and shoes	$345.4	3%
Gasoline, fuel oil, and other energy goods	$310.6	2%
Other	$689.8	5%
Services	$5,154.90	39%
Housing	$1,281.5	10%
Household operation	$481.8	4%
Electricity and gas	$201.7	2%
Other household operation	$280.1	2%
Transportation	$321.2	2%
Medical care	$1,510.0	11%
Recreation	$355.2	3%
Other	1,205.3	$0.09
Gross private domestic investment	**$2,105.00**	16%
Nonresidential fixed investment	$1,329.8	10%
Structures	$335.1	3%
Equipment and software	$994.7	8%
Residential fixed investment	$756.3	6%
Change in private inventories	$18.9	0.1%
Government consumption		
Expenditures and gross investment	**$2,362.90**	18%
Federal	$877.7	6.6%
State and local	$1,485.2	11.2%
Net exports of goods and services	**−$726.50**	
Exports	$1,301.20	
Goods	$905.6	
Services	$395.6	
Imports	$2,027.70	
Goods	$1,700.7	
Services	$327.0	

SOURCE: Adapted from "Table 3. Gross Domestic Product and Related Measures: Level and Change from Preceding Period," in *Gross Domestic Product: Fourth Quarter 2005 (Final); Corporate Profits: Fourth Quarter 2005*, U.S. Department of Commerce, Bureau of Economic Analysis, March 30, 2006, http://www.bea.gov/bea/newsrelarchive/2006/gdp405f.pdf (accessed June 12, 2006)

FIGURE 2.8

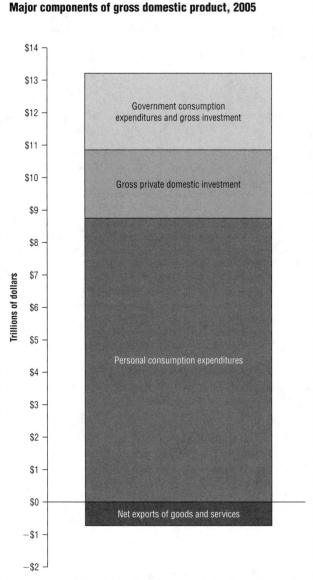

Major components of gross domestic product, 2005

SOURCE: Adapted from "Table 3. Gross Domestic Product and Related Measures: Level and Change from Preceding Period," in *Gross Domestic Product: Fourth Quarter 2005 (Final); Corporate Profits: Fourth Quarter 2005*, U.S. Department of Commerce, Bureau of Economic Analysis, March 30, 2006, http://www.bea.gov/bea/newsrelarchive/2006/gdp405f.pdf (accessed June 12, 2006)

their families—thus lifting their overall quality of life. But in an unstable, bad economy—such as in the United States during the Great Depression and during recessions—people are less certain of the future, face increasing pressures at work and may lose their jobs, and have less flexibility in being able to pay for goods and services, which in turn impacts trends in employment, interest rates, the cost of living, the money supply, and all other aspects of the economy, on both the macro and micro levels.

Public Opinion Polls

RATING THE ECONOMY. The Gallup Organization is a U.S.-based firm that conducts frequent public opinion polls to gauge the mood and attitudes of the American people on a variety of subjects. Economic issues are a frequent topic covered by Gallup polls. Since 1992 Gallup has asked poll participants to provide their assessment of the overall economic condition of the country by rating it as excellent, good, only fair, or poor. In a poll conducted in July 2006 Gallup found that only 5% of respondents rated the economy as excellent. Another 33% felt it was good, while 42% thought the economy was only fair. Another 19% gave the economy a poor rating, and 1% had no opinion. These results were published by Gallup in "Americans Still Dour on U.S. Economy" (http://www.galluppoll.com/content/default.aspx?ci=23782).

FIGURE 2.9

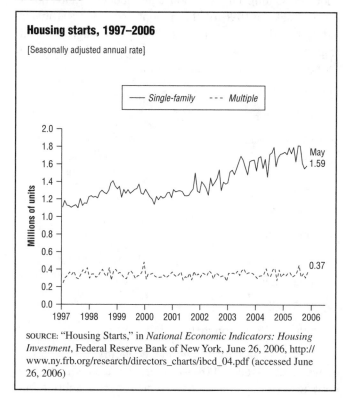

Housing starts, 1997–2006

[Seasonally adjusted annual rate]

SOURCE: "Housing Starts," in *National Economic Indicators: Housing Investment*, Federal Reserve Bank of New York, June 26, 2006, http://www.ny.frb.org/research/directors_charts/ibcd_04.pdf (accessed June 26, 2006)

In the same poll the participants were asked to give their opinion on whether economic conditions in the country as a whole are getting better or getting worse. The results indicate that 28% of those asked believed that the nation's economy is getting better. A much higher number, 64%, felt the economy was getting worse. A small percentage (7%) thought the economy was remaining basically the same, and 2% had no opinion.

ECONOMIC ATTITUDES. Gallup uses poll response data to calculate a value it calls the economic attitudes index. People describing the economy as excellent or good and either staying the same or getting better are considered to have a "positive" attitude. Those who believe the economy is fair or poor and either staying the same or getting worse are considered to have a "negative" attitude. Other viewpoints outside of these two categories are considered "mixed." In July 2006 just over half (52%) of those asked had a negative outlook on the economy, compared with only 22% with a positive outlook.

Gallup notes that economic attitudes vary based on the family income and political persuasion of the poll respondents. Thirty percent of respondents making $75,000 or more per year had a positive outlook, and 43% had a negative outlook. By contrast, only 11% of those making less than $20,000 per year had a positive outlook, while a much higher number (65%) had a negative outlook. There were also large differences based on political party affiliation. Nearly two-thirds of Democrats

(65%) and Independents (60%) had a negative outlook, compared with only 32% of Republicans. Similarly, while 43% of Republicans had a positive outlook, only 18% of Independents and 9% of Democrats did so ("Politics Dominate Consumers' Views of Economy," June 9, 2006, http://www.galluppoll.com/content/default.aspx?ci=23260). Obviously personal financial conditions and political philosophies shape American views about the economy.

REASONS FOR GOOD AND BAD GRADES. In May 2006 Gallup conducted a poll with the specific aim of exploring the reasoning behind Americans' attitudes about the economy. Participants were asked to rate the economy as "mostly good" or "mostly bad." Then they were asked to name the reasons for their opinion of the nation's economic condition. The top five reasons given by people rating the economy as "mostly good" were as follows:

- Employment situation—47%
- Consumer spending—12%
- Improving economy—11%
- Stock market—11%
- Real estate boom—7%

Nearly half (47%) of those who described the economic condition as "mostly good" pointed to the employment situation as their reason for giving the economy a positive grade.

The people who rated the economy as "mostly bad" were more divided in their responses:

- High energy prices—26%
- Employment situation—21%
- Inflation/rising costs—14%
- Job outsourcing—10%
- Lack of money—9%

Interestingly, the employment situation was a key motivator for both good and bad attitudes about the economy.

The results are analyzed by Frank Newport in "Exploring What's behind Americans' Attitudes about the Economy." Newport notes that some economists and politicians believe that the public is "not aware enough" of the data-based indicators published on the state of the economy. This could explain some of the negativity that Newport says economists believe is out of synch with the "economic reality." Newport describes the Main Street versus Wall Street differences: "It may simply be a case of differential or selective exposure to information. Some Americans may pay attention to reports that the national jobless rate is falling, while others pay attention to reports of corporate downsizing, layoffs, and outsourcing. It is also possible that some

Americans may be looking at employment from a personal or local perspective, reflecting the differences in employment from family to family and region to region."

Some analysts believe that the pessimistic viewpoint is a result of negative economic trends that are not reflected in the economic indicators published by the government. In January 2006 this issue was examined by the Economic Policy Institute (EPI) in "Why People Are So Dissatisfied with Today's Economy" (Lee Price, http://www.epi.org/content.cfm/ib219). The EPI is a nonprofit nonpartisan think tank that stresses "concern for the living standards of working people." The EPI report notes that two million new jobs were created during 2005, a number much heralded by the Bush administration as a sign of a healthy economy. However, the EPI says the rate of job growth (1.5%) is low based on historical data. For example, job growth from 1994 to 1995 was 3.1%, and it was 5.3% from 1977 to 1978.

During 2006 the EPI and other analysts have also maintained that low unemployment and inflation rates reported in recent years do not accurately reflect economic conditions in the nation. In its definition of the unemployed, the government includes only unemployed people who are actively looking for work. Some analysts believe that many people have become discouraged by poor job prospects and have quit looking for work. Thus, these people are not counted by the government. In addition, analysts claim that wage increases are not keeping pace with inflation, and that inflation-adjusted pay rates are actually declining for many low-income and middle-income Americans. For example, the EPI report cited above notes that real (inflation-adjusted) wages for people in the lowest twentieth percentile of the income scale declined by 0.8% between 2003 and 2005 and by 0.6% for people in the middle of the income scale.

There is no doubt that overall public attitudes about the economy have worsened during the 2000s, even as economic indicators seem to have brightened. In June 2006 the Gallup Organization compiled yearly averages dating back to 1996 of the nation's economic attitudes index based on poll results. The percentage of poll respondents expressing a "negative" attitude about the economy each year was as follows:

- 1996—39%
- 1997—34%
- 1998—22%
- 1999—19%
- 2000—20%
- 2001—46%
- 2002—46%
- 2003—50%
- 2004—42%
- 2005—52%
- 2006—53% (through June only)

Public negativity about the economy rose sharply between 2000 and 2001—a year characterized by the horrific terrorist attacks on the nation and a brief but sharp economic recession. The subsequent years have included American involvement in wars in Afghanistan and Iraq, a difficult struggle against terrorism, devastating hurricanes, and ballooning energy costs. Thus, public angst about the economy could be due to a combination of financial, political, and social factors, none of which are accurately reflected by the economic indicators. One eloquent explanation for this discrepancy was coined more than three decades ago by Robert F. Kennedy, the younger brother of U.S. President John F. Kennedy. In 1968, only months before he was assassinated, Robert F. Kennedy said: "The gross national product measures neither our wit nor our courage, neither our wisdom nor our learning, neither our compassion nor our devotion to country. It measures everything, in short, except that which makes life worthwhile."

CHAPTER 3
THE AMERICAN CONSUMER

The use of money is all the advantage there is in having money.

—Benjamin Franklin, 1736

Americans love to spend money, and their aggressive spending helps fuel both the American and the global economies, as imported goods are widely available and popular in the American market. In fact, consumer spending is the single largest contributing factor to the nation's growth in gross domestic production. High consumer spending rates produce a ripple effect that spreads across many other macroeconomic sectors, including employment, wages, corporate profits, and interest rates.

THE RISE OF THE CONSUMER CULTURE
World War II

World War II (1939–45) is generally credited with lifting the United States out of the Great Depression—the period of economic disaster that lasted from 1929 through the early 1940s. The urgent need for weapons, tanks, planes, and other war goods led the government to invest heavily in getting the nation's factories running again, especially after the United States joined the fighting in late 1941. At the war's end, many factories were converted into facilities to manufacture civilian products such as appliances and automobiles, for which demand was especially high after the war.

RATIONING AND THE WAR PRODUCTION BOARD. During the war, citizens were encouraged to exercise restraint in spending in order to conserve materials for the war effort. Some items were temporarily banned from public use; for example, platinum was declared a "strategic metal" to be used only in the manufacture of military goods, so its use in jewelry making was halted. The government also established rationing—tight controls over how much of an item a person could use or consume in a certain amount of time. All citizens were issued coupon books for rationed items every six months; once they used up their coupons for the month, they had to wait until the next month to buy more rationed goods. Coffee, sugar, meat, butter, and canned vegetables were rationed, as were gasoline, rubber, silk (which was used to make parachutes), fuel oil, and other goods put to military purposes. "Victory gardens" became common as the government encouraged Americans to plant their own vegetables rather than buying them.

In 1942 the War Production Board (WPB) was created to oversee production programs for war-related commodities. The agency's first move was to halt all American automobile production and order car factories to produce only planes, tanks, machine guns, diesel engines, and military trucks. Producers of other consumer goods were also ordered to join the war effort; for example, a domestic housewares company called International Silver converted its manufacturing facilities to the production of military goods such as surgical instruments, machine-gun clips, and gasoline bombs. To conserve materials needed to clothe soldiers and make other fabric items for the war effort, the WPB regulated every aspect of U.S. clothing design. Silk stockings were banned, so women drew seams on the backs of their legs to simulate them. The WPB mandated that dresses and skirts be made shorter, and men's suits—marketed as "victory suits"—had narrower lapels and pants with no cuffs, to conserve fabric. Women's two-piece bathing suits became popular because they used less fabric than one-piece suits.

The Postwar Boom

When the war came to an end in 1945, Americans were divided about becoming consumers again. While some had felt deprived for so long that they could not wait to start spending, others were reluctant. To help create jobs for the tens of thousands of soldiers returning to the workforce from the war and build on the country's newfound economic prosperity, the government, along with businesses and marketing firms, began a campaign to stir up consumer activity. Spending was promoted as a civic duty and an expression of patriotism rather than a personal indulgence.

THE COLD WAR: BEATING COMMUNISM BY SHOPPING. By the late 1940s the cold war—a decades-long period of political tension between the United States and the former Soviet Union that began just after World War II and ended in the early 1990s—was well underway. To contrast the U.S. open market system with Soviet socialism—under which private ownership was generally disallowed—U.S. politicians argued that widespread ownership of more possessions would create greater social equality, thereby proving the superiority of the market system. Consumer spending, therefore, acted as a function of the drive to defeat communism.

HOME OWNERSHIP. Foremost on the list of items that many American citizens wanted was new housing, and the ideal housing, according to the standards of the time, was a mass-produced single-family home in the suburbs. According to Lizabeth Cohen ("The Landscape of Mass Consumption," February 2003, http://www.nthposition.com/landscapeofmass.php), residential housing construction after the war occurred at rates never before seen in the United States, with the federal government helping veterans buy homes with guaranteed loans and connecting the new suburbs to cities with an immense system of federally built highways. Between 1947 and 1953, the number of people living in the suburbs increased by 43%, and by 1960 62% of Americans owned their own homes.

AUTOMOBILES. Home ownership generated the need for many items, but few had more far-reaching effects than automobiles. With such a large proportion of Americans living in the suburbs, the ability to commute to work and shopping centers became essential, so a family car went from being a luxury to being a necessity in the 1950s. This was the birth of the American car culture. Then, as now, a new car represented a substantial investment. The average income in the 1950s was $3,216 per year, and the cost of a Ford automobile was between $1,399 and $2,262—at least half of a family's annual income.

Car ownership led to more travel, which spawned more business opportunities. Fast food restaurants allowed people to eat in their cars. Motels ("motor hotels") provided inexpensive places to stay (and park cars) overnight. Convenience stores sprang up along the new highways, encouraging drivers to stop and shop while they were on the road. Even the camping and outdoor industry saw a rush to its products, as Americans purchased campers and other outdoor equipment and took to the road for family vacations. By 1950, 60% of American households had a car, and transportation-related expenses accounted for one out of every seven dollars spent by the typical American household (Jerome Segal, Cynthia Pansing, and Brian Parkinson, "What We Work for Now: Changing Household Consumption Patterns in the Twentieth Century," Common Assets Program, December 2001, http://www.rprogress.org/newpubs/2001/whatwework.pdf).

TELEVISION. Along with the widespread ownership of automobiles, the introduction of television into daily U.S. life represented one of the most important social, economic, and technological changes of the twentieth century. Television was promoted as a social equalizer that would, again, prove the superiority of American capitalism over Soviet communism. With such unprecedented access to information, U.S. citizens were predicted to achieve equality across all classes and social groups. In 1945 there were about seven thousand working television sets and nine television stations in the country; in 1950, when the total U.S. population was about 151 million, 3.8 million homes, or 9% of all households, had television sets. By the end of 1952, the number of households with TVs had grown to twenty million, and there were more than ninety-eight television stations ("The History of Film and Television," http://www.high-techproductions.com/historyoftelevision.htm). In 1993, 98% of American households had at least one television, and 64% had two or more.

Like automobiles, televisions were substantial financial investments for families in the middle of the century. A typical Philco Model 1403 TV cost $199, while the higher-end Admiral Home Entertainment TV System cost $549. Television commercials provided a new way to advertise consumer products in American homes, and advertisers were quick to recognize their effectiveness. In 1952 advertisers spent $288 million to purchase commercial airtime, an increase of more than 38% over the previous year.

CONTEMPORARY CONSUMER SPENDING

The U.S. Department of Labor's Bureau of Labor Statistics (BLS) tracks consumer spending and publishes the results in two different formats. Personal Consumer Expenditure (PCE) data are used on a quarterly basis to calculate the nation's GDP. PCE is based on aggregate data (data summed to represent the entire population). The BLS also publishes an annual Consumer Expenditure Survey that estimates the consumer spending of an average American household during a year.

One economic indicator extremely relevant to consumer spending is the inflation rate based on the Consumer Price Index (CPI). Table 3.1 shows the annual percent change in the CPI for all urban consumers (CPI-U) for all items and specific categories of items from 2001 through 2005. These numbers represent annual inflation rates. The overall inflation rate for 2005 was

TABLE 3.1

Annual percent change in the urban Consumer Price Index (CPI-U) for selected expenditure categories, 2001–05

Expenditure category	December 2005 relative importance	Percent change for 12 months ended December—				
		2001	2002	2003	2004	2005
All Items	100.000	1.6	2.4	1.9	3.3	3.4
Food	13.942	2.8	1.5	3.6	2.7	2.3
Energy	8.685	−13.0	10.7	6.9	16.6	17.1
Household fuels	4.494	−3.4	1.0	7.1	8.4	18.0
Motor fuel	4.191	−24.8	24.6	6.8	26.1	16.2
All items less food and energy	77.373	2.7	1.9	1.1	2.2	2.2
Commodities less food and energy	22.319	−.3	−1.5	−2.5	.6	.2
All items less energy	91.315	2.8	1.8	1.5	2.2	2.2
Services less energy services	55.055	4.0	3.4	2.6	2.8	2.9
Commodities	40.790	−1.4	1.2	.5	3.6	2.7
Durables	11.576	−1.3	−3.3	−4.3	.4	−.5
Furniture and bedding	1.013	−3.1	−1.1	−1.6	−.2	.6
Televisions	.164	−10.8	−10.6	−14.3	−12.3	−14.4
New vehicles	5.155	2.1	−2.0	−1.8	.6	−.4
Used cars and trucks	1.799	−1.9	−5.5	−11.8	4.8	1.4
Personal computers and peripheral equipment	.236	−30.7	−22.1	−17.8	−14.2	−15.8
Nondurables	29.214	−1.4	3.1	2.4	4.8	3.9
Energy commodities	4.530	−24.5	23.7	6.9	26.7	16.7
Gasoline	4.148	−24.9	24.8	6.8	26.1	16.1
Fuel oil	.232	−26.7	14.7	7.8	39.5	27.2
Apparel	3.786	−3.2	−1.8	−2.1	−.2	−1.1
Medical care commodities	1.457	4.4	3.1	2.1	2.2	3.7
Prescription drugs and medical supplies	1.025	6.0	4.5	2.5	3.5	4.4
Services	59.210	3.7	3.2	2.8	3.1	3.8
Shelter	32.260	4.2	3.1	2.2	2.7	2.6
Owners' equivalent rent of primary residence	23.442	4.5	3.3	2.0	2.3	2.5
Rent of primary residence	5.832	4.7	3.1	2.7	2.9	3.1
Hotels and motels	2.460	−.8	.0	3.1	5.0	3.3
Utility natural gas service	1.530	−15.1	6.7	17.4	16.4	30.2
Electricity	2.625	6.1	−1.9	2.6	2.1	10.7
Medical care services	4.764	4.8	5.6	4.2	4.9	4.5
Airline fares	.673	−3.9	−2.4	−.1	−1.5	6.4
Telephone services	2.245	1.3	.2	−2.7	−2.5	.4
Motor vehicle insurance	2.301	7.3	9.0	4.5	3.4	1.0
Medical care	6.220	4.7	5.0	3.7	4.2	4.3

SOURCE: Adapted from Todd Wilson, "Table 2. Annual Percent Change in the Consumer Price Index for All Urban Consumers (CPI-U), Selected Expenditure Categories, 1996–2005," in "Consumer Prices Rose 3.4 Percent in 2005, About the Same as Last Year," *Monthly Labor Review*, Vol. 129, No. 5, May 2006, http://www.bls.gov/opub/mlr/2006/05/art1full.pdf (accessed June 30, 2006)

3.4%. Table 3.1 lists the inflation rates for many other goods and services purchased by American consumers.

Personal Consumer Expenditures

Table 3.2 shows that the nation's PCE totaled $8.7 trillion in 2005. Major PCE categories include durable goods (items expected to last at least one year, such as cars and refrigerators), nondurable goods (items expected to last less than one year, such as food and gasoline), and services. Note that housing is listed under services. This category includes rent paid by renters and the estimated equivalent of rent for owner-occupied houses (in other words, the amount of money the owner occupants would have paid if they had been renting the space from someone else).

Services accounted for the largest portion (59%) of PCE in 2005, totaling nearly $5.2 trillion. Medical care ($1.5 trillion) and housing ($1.3 trillion) were the two largest components of service spending. Americans spent nearly $2.6 trillion on nondurable goods in 2005. Nearly half of this amount ($1.28 trillion) was devoted to food. Another $1 trillion was spent on durable goods, such as motor vehicles and furniture.

PCE data are based on industry information. In other words, the BLS estimates consumer spending by calculating the final value of goods and services sold by businesses.

Consumer Expenditure Survey

Figure 3.1 shows results of the 2004 Consumer Expenditure (CE) Survey, which was published in November 2005. The average American household spent $43,395 during 2004. Nearly two-thirds of this amount was devoted to three expenses: housing ($13,918; 33%), transportation ($7,801; 18%), and food ($5,781; 13%). But the CE housing component does not include mortgage principal payments, because they are considered repayment of a loan, rather than a consumer expense. Thus, CE data underreport the true cost of housing for Americans with mortgages.

TABLE 3.2

Personal consumption expenditures (PCE), 2005

[Billions of current dollars, seasonally adjusted at annual rates]

	Component	Percent of PCE
Personal consumption expenditures	**$8,745.70**	
Durable goods	$1,026.50	12%
Motor vehicles and parts	$446.8	5%
Furniture and household equipment	$373.2	4%
Other	$206.4	2%
Nondurable goods	$2,564.40	29%
Food	$1,218.6	14%
Clothing and shoes	$345.4	4%
Gasoline, fuel oil, and other energy goods	$310.6	4%
Other	$689.8	8%
Services	$5,154.90	59%
Housing	$1,281.5	15%
Household operation	$481.8	6%
Electricity and gas	$201.7	2%
Other household operation	$280.1	3%
Transportation	$321.2	4%
Medical care	$1,510.0	17%
Recreation	$355.2	4%
Other	1,205.3	14%

SOURCE: Adapted from "Table 3. Gross Domestic Product and Related Measures: Level and Change from Preceding Period," in *Gross Domestic Product: Fourth Quarter 2005 (Final); Corporate Profits: Fourth Quarter 2005*, U.S. Department of Commerce, Bureau of Economic Analysis, March 30, 2006, www.bea.gov/bea/newsrelarchive/2006/gdp405f.pdf (accessed June 12, 2006)

FIGURE 3.1

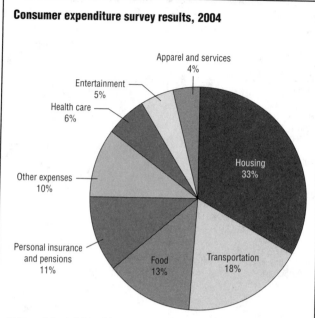

Consumer expenditure survey results, 2004

SOURCE: Adapted from "Average Annual Expenditures and Characteristics of All Consumer Units, Consumer Expenditure Survey, 2000–2004," in *Consumer Expenditure Survey*, U.S. Department of Labor, Bureau of Labor Statistics, April 2006, http://www.bls.gov/cex/2004/standard/multiyr.pdf (accessed June 12, 2006)

CE data are compiled based on consumer-supplied information. Purchase diaries are sent to sample households around the country. Participants record their everyday purchases and expenses in the diaries. Periodic interviews are conducted to collect diary information and quiz participants about their finances and spending habits. CE data are collected from households (called "consumer units") that are representative of the civilian noninstitutional population of the United States (that is, people not in the military and not in institutions, such as prisons or long-term care facilities).

According to the BLS, the average consumer unit in 2004 included 2.5 persons and had pretax annual income of $54,453. Most of the consumer units owned their homes (68%), and a large majority (88%) owned or leased at least one motor vehicle (http://www.bls.gov/cex/2004/standard/multiyr.pdf).

The CE survey results provide detailed data on American spending habits. For example, participants break down food purchases as to meal location (at home or away from home). The 2004 survey indicates that the average household spent $2,434 eating out, representing 42% of total food expenses. Each household averaged $130 per year for reading materials and $905 per year for educational expenses. Another $459 per year was spent on alcohol and $288 per year on tobacco products. The average American household reported donating $1,408 in cash to charitable causes.

HISTORICAL TRENDS IN CONSUMER SPENDING

Expenditures for some components making up PCE have changed dramatically over time. Figure 3.2 shows spending on medical care, housing, durable goods, nondurable goods, and "other" services as a percentage of total PCE for 1970, 1980, 1990, 2000, and 2005. These categories have historically been the five largest components of PCE.

The data show that the percentage of PCE dedicated to housing and durable goods remained steady between 1970 and 2005. Housing hovered between 14% and 16%, while durable goods stayed between 11.5% and 13.5%. A very slight downward trend is evident in the percent spent on durable goods over time. A much more dramatic decrease is seen in the percentage of PCE devoted to nondurable goods—from 42% in 1970 to 29% in 2000 and 2005. A percentage decrease in one component making up PCE means a percentage increase in one or more of the other components.

The percentage of PCE devoted to "other" services has increased slightly, from around 10.5% in 1970 and 1980 to around 14% in 2000 and 2005. Medical care increased from only 8% of PCE in 1970 to 17.3% in 2005. In other words, the percentage of PCE devoted to medical care more than doubled between 1970 and 2005.

FIGURE 3.2

Personal consumption expenditure components, selected years 1970–2005

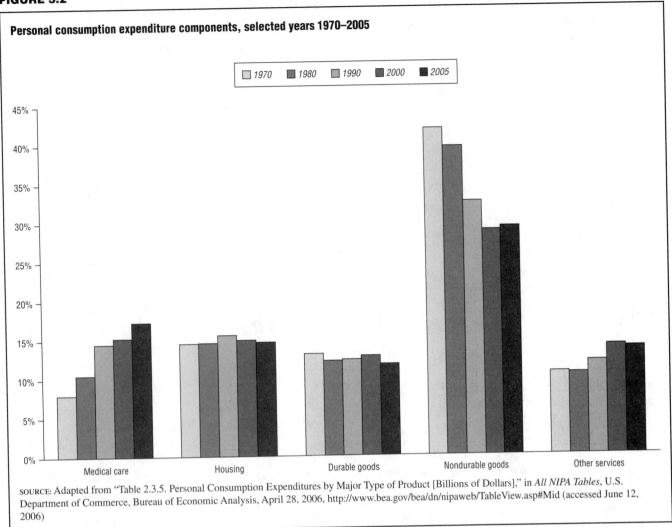

SOURCE: Adapted from "Table 2.3.5. Personal Consumption Expenditures by Major Type of Product [Billions of Dollars]," in *All NIPA Tables*, U.S. Department of Commerce, Bureau of Economic Analysis, April 28, 2006, http://www.bea.gov/bea/dn/nipaweb/TableView.asp#Mid (accessed June 12, 2006)

Nondurable Goods

Historically, food expenditures have accounted for roughly one-half of spending on PCE nondurable goods. For example, in 2005 food expenses totaled $1.2 trillion, a little less than half of the $2.6 billion spent on all nondurable goods. Other components of this category include clothes and shoes, energy goods (gasoline, fuel oil, coal, etc.), and miscellaneous nondurable goods.

Over the short term, food and energy prices can vary tremendously. Food prices are dependent on a variety of factors, including weather conditions (which affect growing costs), transportation and processing costs, and subsidies paid to farmers by the government that influence supply and demand ratios. Energy prices, particularly for oil, are affected by political and economic factors in the Middle East. Interestingly, energy prices in the United States can also be impacted by weather, as evidenced by the rise in gasoline prices following Hurricane Katrina and Hurricane Rita in 2005. Due to the volatile nature of food and energy prices, these costs are not included in the economic indicator called core inflation.

FOOD PRICES. One component of PCE that has become increasingly affordable over time is food. Figure 3.3 shows data from the U.S. Department of Agriculture (USDA) on food prices as a percentage of personal disposable income between 1929 and 2004. Personal disposable income is also known as after-tax income or "take-home pay." During the early 1930s the average American household spent nearly a quarter of its disposable income on food. By the 1960s the percentage had fallen to around 15% and continued to decrease. In 2004 American consumers spent just under 10% of their disposable income on food. Enormous gains in agricultural productivity and crop yields have kept food prices relatively low.

According to the USDA Economic Research Service, prices for food away from home increased by 3.1% in 2005, the highest annual increase since 1991. Strong consumer demand for restaurant meals is driving these price increases. But the 3.1% increase is less than the increase in the overall U.S. inflation rate in 2005 of 3.4% based on the CPI-U. Thus, the away-from-home food inflation rate was slightly less than the overall inflation rate.

FIGURE 3.3

Food expenditures as a percentage of disposable personal income, 1929–2004

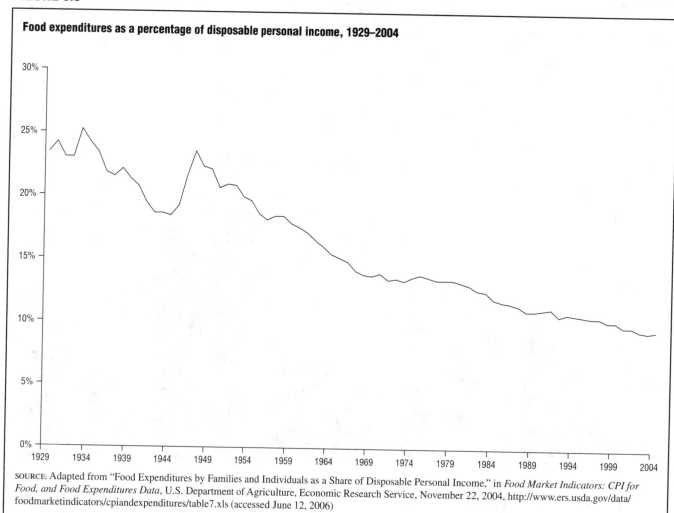

SOURCE: Adapted from "Food Expenditures by Families and Individuals as a Share of Disposable Personal Income," in *Food Market Indicators: CPI for Food, and Food Expenditures Data*, U.S. Department of Agriculture, Economic Research Service, November 22, 2004, http://www.ers.usda.gov/data/foodmarketindicators/cpiandexpenditures/table7.xls (accessed June 12, 2006)

In 2005 food-at-home prices increased by only 1.9%, below the ten-year-average increase of 2.6% for food-at-home and well below the overall U.S. inflation rate of 3.4%. Prices for fats, oils, and eggs actually declined during 2005. However, these declines were offset by increases in the price of fruits, vegetables, fish, and seafood. The USDA notes that robust competition between retail stores is contributing to low price increases in the food-at-home sector (http://www.ers.usda.gov/Briefing/CPIFoodAndExpenditures/outlook.htm).

ENERGY PRICES—GASOLINE. As shown in Table 3.2, nondurable energy goods accounted for only a small amount (4%) of PCE during 2005. This category does not include electricity and gas for household operation, which fall under services. Nondurable energy goods include products, such as gasoline, other motor fuels, and lubricants. In 2005 U.S. consumers spent nearly $311 billion on nondurable energy goods; gasoline accounted for the vast majority (93%) of this total.

According to the U.S. Department of Energy (DOE), the average retail price for a gallon of regular grade gasoline was $2.91 per gallon in May 2006. This value was up from $2.21 per gallon in May 2005. By August 2006 the price per gallon averaged just over $3.00. The price of gasoline increased dramatically over the year due to a variety of factors. The DOE's *Primer on Gasoline Prices* reports that the main causes were high worldwide demand, capacity shortages throughout the oil market system, and supply disruptions due to Hurricane Katrina (http://www.eia.doe.gov/bookshelf/brochures/gasolinepricesprimer/eia1_2005primerM.html).

As shown in Figure 3.4, the DOE notes that in May 2006 the retail price for a gallon of gasoline in the United States had four contributing components:

- Crude oil price—53%

- Refining costs and profits—22%

- Federal and state taxes—16%

- Distribution and marketing costs—9%

Thus, the cost of crude oil accounts for just over half of the retail price of gasoline. Crude oil is sold by the

FIGURE 3.4

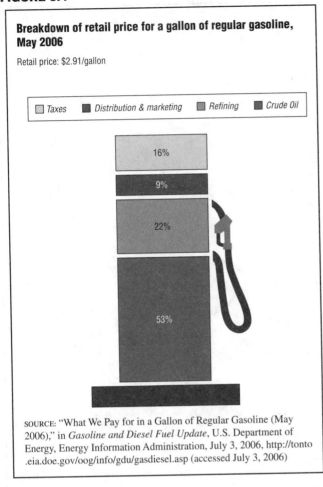

Breakdown of retail price for a gallon of regular gasoline, May 2006

Retail price: $2.91/gallon

☐ Taxes   ■ Distribution & marketing   ▨ Refining   ■ Crude Oil

16%

9%

22%

53%

SOURCE: "What We Pay for in a Gallon of Regular Gasoline (May 2006)," in *Gasoline and Diesel Fuel Update*, U.S. Department of Energy, Energy Information Administration, July 3, 2006, http://tonto .eia.doe.gov/oog/info/gdu/gasdiesel.asp (accessed July 3, 2006)

barrel, with each barrel containing forty-two U.S. gallons. At the beginning of 2005 the average worldwide price for crude oil was around $40 per barrel. By the beginning of 2006 the price was close to $55 per barrel and climbing. In July 2006 the price of crude oil rose to an all-time high of $78.40 per barrel before dropping slightly to $76.37 in early August ("Oil Prices Fall as Alaskan Oil Replaced," CBC News, August 8, 2006, http://www.cbc.ca/story/ business/national/2006/08/08/oil-prices.html?ref=rss).

As indicated in Figure 3.5 gasoline prices have been very volatile in the 2000s compared with the 1990s. The average retail price of a gallon of regular gasoline hovered just over one dollar throughout most of the 1990s and then began to rise dramatically. Figure 3.6 compares the nominal and real prices of gasoline from 1919 through 2005 and projects them through 2007. The nominal price is the price paid by consumers at the time. The real price is based on year 2005 dollars. In other words, the real price is adjusted to show what the price of gasoline would have been in previous years assuming that the value of a dollar was the same in that year as it was in 2005. Viewed in this context, the relatively high price of gasoline during the early 2000s appears to be in line with inflation-adjusted prices paid in previous years.

THE COST OF HOUSING AND HOUSEHOLD OPERATION

As shown in Table 2.3 in Chapter 2, the cost of housing was nearly $1.3 trillion during 2005 and accounted for 10% of positive GDP. Another $482 billion was spent on household operations—nearly half of this amount was devoted to electricity and natural gas expenses. It should be noted that the BLS calculates housing prices based on rent prices and owner-equivalent rents (the amounts that would be paid in rent if the owners were renting their dwellings to themselves).

The status of many consumer costs, including those for housing and household operation, is discussed by the BLS in "Consumer Prices Rose 3.4 Percent in 2005, About the Same as Last Year" published in the May 2006 issue of *Monthly Labor Review* (http:// www.bls.gov/opub/mlr/2006/05/art1full.pdf). According to the BLS, shelter costs increased by 2.6% during 2005, down slightly from a 2.7% increase in 2004. These rates are below the overall inflation rates for 2004 and 2005 of 3.3% and 3.4%, respectively.

The article in *Monthly Labor Review* notes that prices for household energy increased by nearly 18% in 2005, compared with a 7% increase in 2004. Natural gas accounted for most of the price escalation. Natural gas prices increased by more than 30% in 2005 due to production and supply problems after Hurricane Katrina and Hurricane Rita struck the Gulf Coast. Natural gas shortages led to increased demand and higher prices for coal, which pushed up electricity generation costs. Many power-generating facilities can burn either natural gas or coal and choose a fuel based on market factors. As a result, electricity prices were up by nearly 11% during 2005 after increasing by only 2% in 2004.

The annual inflation rates for shelter and household fuel prices for the years 2001 through 2005 are listed in Table 3.1.

THE COST OF MEDICAL CARE

In 2005 medical care expenditures topped $1.5 trillion and accounted for 11% of positive GDP. (See Table 2.3 in Chapter 2.) This made medical care a more expensive component than housing, food, or durable goods. Figure 3.7 shows that the U.S. Department of Health and Human Services (HHS) projects national health care expenditures to comprise an ever-increasing percentage of GDP through the year 2025.

Figure 3.8 compares the CPI-U between all items and medical care only on an annual basis between 1996 and 2005 using the time period of 1982–84 as the reference period (CPI=100). Medical inflation has outpaced overall inflation in each of these years. In other words, medical care prices are increasing at a faster pace than overall

FIGURE 3.5

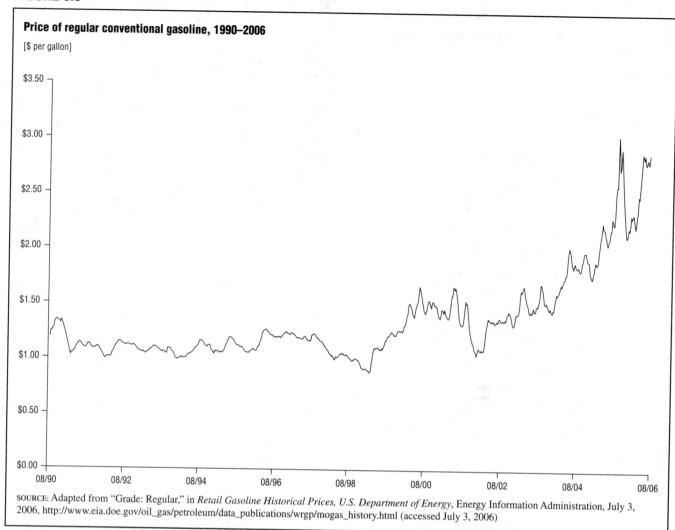

Price of regular conventional gasoline, 1990–2006

[$ per gallon]

SOURCE: Adapted from "Grade: Regular," in *Retail Gasoline Historical Prices, U.S. Department of Energy*, Energy Information Administration, July 3, 2006, http://www.eia.doe.gov/oil_gas/petroleum/data_publications/wrgp/mogas_history.html (accessed July 3, 2006)

prices in the economy. Medical inflation is blamed, in part, on technological advances in medicine that have increased expenses associated with the diagnosis and treatment of patients.

Recipients and Services

The Agency for Healthcare Research and Quality (AHRQ) is a division of the HHS. AHRQ conducts large-scale surveys of medical care recipients and providers as part of its Medical Expenditure Panel Survey (MEPS). The MEPS Web site (http://www.meps.ahrq.gov/) provides access to detailed data and reports on medical utilization and expenditures. As of June 2006, comprehensive MEPS data were available for calendar year 2003.

According to the AHRQ, just over 85% of the U.S. civilian noninstitutional population had some kind of medical expense during 2003. The rate was much higher among the elderly (people aged sixty-five and older); 96% of them reported having a medical expense during the year.

Overall, expenses for medical services (excluding insurance premiums) totaled $896 billion. A breakdown by type of service is shown in Figure 3.9. Hospital inpatient services accounted for more than one-third of the expenditures. Services from an office-based medical provider made up another 20% of the total, as did expenses for prescription medicines. The average expense during the year for each treated person was $3,601. According to the AHRQ, the average was slightly lower ($2,837 per treated person) for people under age sixty-four and much higher ($8,209 per treated person) for people age sixty-five and older.

Who Pays the Bill?

During 2003 private health insurance paid the largest portion (42%) of medical service expenditures. Another 20% was paid out of pocket, that is, directly by consumers. Medicare and Medicaid are government-operated health care programs. Medicare covers the elderly and includes some younger people with certain disabilities

FIGURE 3.6

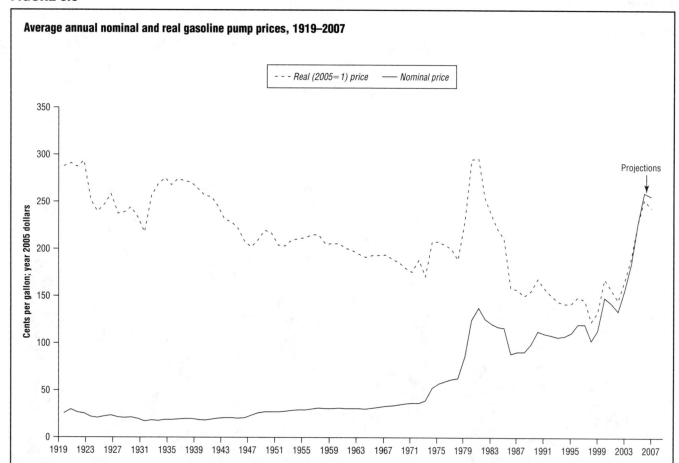

Average annual nominal and real gasoline pump prices, 1919–2007

- - - *Real (2005=1) price* —— *Nominal price*

Projections

History: Gasoline prices: Bureau of Labor Statistics (BLS) survey prices: 1919–1979: leaded regular; 1980–1981: unleaded regular; 1982–1994: Energy Information Administration (EIA) data extrapolated using BLS survey data; 1995–current: EIA survey. Real (inflation adjusted prices) price data is deflated by the consumer price index, source BLS, where year 2005=1. Forecast 2006–2007: gasoline prices, current short-term energy outlook (STEO). Forecasted consumer price index, global insight.

SOURCE: Adapted from "Real Gasoline Pump Price: Annual Average 1919–2007," in *Short Term Energy Outlook*, U.S. Department of Energy, Energy Information Administration, June 2006, http://www.eia.doe.gov/emeu/steo/pub/fsheets/PetroleumPrices_files/frame.htm (accessed June 12, 2006)

FIGURE 3.7

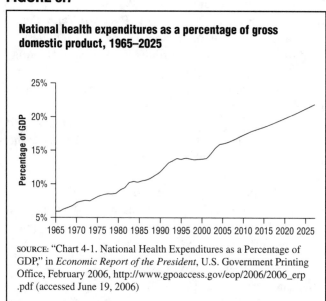

National health expenditures as a percentage of gross domestic product, 1965–2025

SOURCE: "Chart 4-1. National Health Expenditures as a Percentage of GDP," in *Economic Report of the President*, U.S. Government Printing Office, February 2006, http://www.gpoaccess.gov/eop/2006/2006_erp .pdf (accessed June 19, 2006)

and illnesses. Medicaid provides insurance coverage for needy people. During 2003 Medicare and Medicaid paid 20% and 9%, respectively, of the nation's health care expenditures. The additional 9% was paid by other sources, such as workers' compensation programs or automobile insurance companies.

OUT-OF-POCKET EXPENSES. Out-of-pocket expenses (those paid for by patients) for medical care amounted to $176 billion during 2003. The AHRQ notes that out-of-pocket expenses per consumer varied widely. The average was $707 per patient. But people younger than age eighteen had a much lower average of $261 per patient, while people age sixty-five and older had a much higher average of $1,547 per patient. Insurance coverage also played a major factor in out-of-pocket expenses. Those patients younger than age sixty-four without insurance had slightly higher out-of-pocket averages than those with insurance. Among the elderly, patients covered by only Medicare had a higher average ($1,754 per patient) than those covered by Medicare supplemented with

FIGURE 3.8

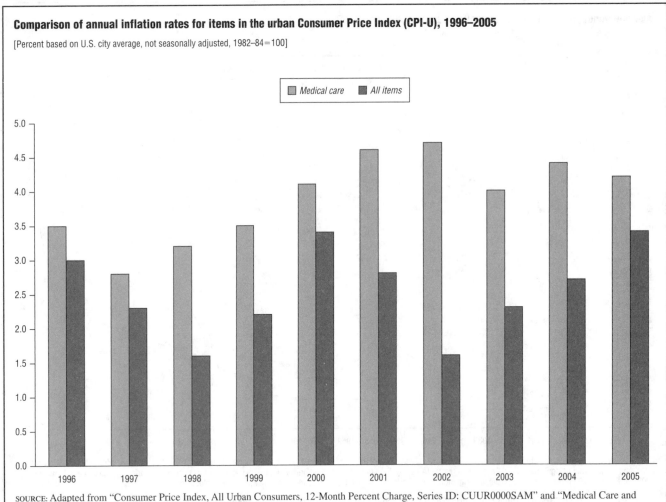

Comparison of annual inflation rates for items in the urban Consumer Price Index (CPI-U), 1996–2005

[Percent based on U.S. city average, not seasonally adjusted, 1982–84=100]

SOURCE: Adapted from "Consumer Price Index, All Urban Consumers, 12-Month Percent Charge, Series ID: CUUR0000SAM" and "Medical Care and Consumer Price Index, All Urban Consumers, 12-Month Percent Change, Series ID: CUUR0000SA0, All Items," in *Consumer Price Indexes*, U.S. Department of Labor, Bureau of Labor Statistics, June 16, 2006, http://www.bls.gov/cpi/home.htm#tables (accessed June 16, 2006)

private insurance ($1,552 per patient) or Medicare supplemented with other public insurance ($1,083 per patient).

The AHRQ reports that nearly half of all out-of-pocket expenses were devoted to prescription drug purchases.

Prescription Drug Expenses

As Figure 3.9 shows, expenses for prescription drugs accounted for almost 20% of all medical care expenses (excluding health insurance premiums) during 2003. According to the AHRQ, nearly $178 billion was spent on outpatient prescription drugs. A total of 2.8 billion prescriptions were purchased—an average of almost ten prescriptions per American. But prescription expenses were not spread evenly among the U.S. population. Around two-thirds of Americans (64%) actually had a prescription drug expense. Nearly half of these people were Medicare recipients. The average price paid for outpatient prescription drugs during 2003 was $950 per treated person.

The AARP (formerly the American Association of Retired Persons) is a nonprofit membership organization for people age fifty and older. According to its Web site, the organization has more than thirty-five million members. According to the April 2006 issue of the group's quarterly consumer newsletter *AARP Rx Watchdog Report* ("Brand-Name Drug Prices Keep Going Up," http://assets. aarp.org/www.aarp.org_/articles/legislative/watchdog_ april_04-web.pdf), the U.S. prices of 193 brand-name prescription drugs commonly used by the elderly increased by 6% during 2005 due to price hikes by manufacturers. The overall U.S. inflation rate for 2005 was 3.4% based on the CPI-U. The AARP says that price hikes on prescription drugs have been larger than the overall U.S. inflation rates every year between 2000 and 2005, sometimes by more than twice as much. For example, in 2003 and 2004 drug prices increased by more than 7% each year, while the overall inflation rates were less than 3% per year.

MEDICARE DRUG COVERAGE. Beginning in 2006, the Medicare health care program for elderly Americans began offering voluntary prescription drug coverage. For

FIGURE 3.9

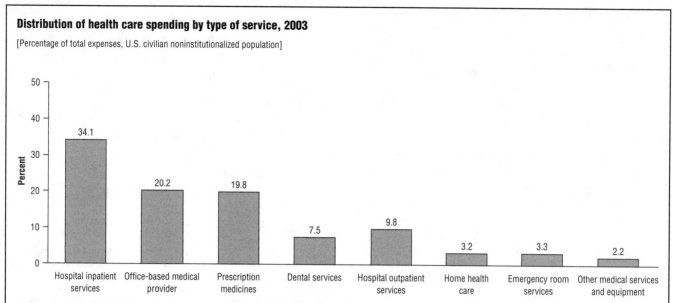

Distribution of health care spending by type of service, 2003

[Percentage of total expenses, U.S. civilian noninstitutionalized population]

Note: Categories do not add to 100.0 due to rounding, and hospital inpatient services include zero night hospital stays.

SOURCE: David Kashihara and Kelly Carper, "Figure 2. Distribution of Health Care Spending in the U.S. Civilian Noninstitutionalized Population, by Type of Service, Percentage of Total Expenses, 2003," in *National Health Care Expenses in the U.S. Civilian Noninstitutionalized Population, 2003*, U.S. Department of Health and Human Services, Agency for Healthcare Research and Quality, November 2005, http://www.meps.ahrq.gov/papers/st103/stat103 .pdf (accessed June 2, 2006)

a monthly premium, Medicare recipients can join one of many insurance plans designed to reduce their out-of-pocket expenses for prescription drugs. The "Medicare Part D" plan was authorized by the Medicare Prescription Drug, Improvement, and Modernization Act of 2003.

In June 2006 the HHS reported that thirty-eight million Medicare recipients were receiving comprehensive prescription drug coverage—thirty-three million from Medicare and five million from other plans. The total represents approximately 90% of all Medicare recipients. According to the HHS, more than 3.5 million prescriptions per day were being filled under the Part D program (http://hhs.gov/news/press/2006pres/20060614.html).

The federal government has touted the plan as a means for seniors to protect themselves from "unexpected drug costs." Critics say that the program was tailored to benefit the insurance suppliers and drug companies, rather than seniors. They point out that the participation of dozens of insurance companies as "middlemen" in the system increases the administrative costs of the plan and prevents the federal government from purchasing drugs in bulk at lower prices. In August 2006 the *San Francisco Chronicle* reported that profits were "higher than expected" during the second quarter of 2006 for the drug companies that produce medications commonly purchased under the plan and for the largest health insurers that participate in the plan (Victoria Colliver, "Medicare Drug Plan Is Prescribing Profits," August 4, 2006, http://sfgate.com/cgi-bin/article.cgi?file =c/a/2006/08/04/BUG2PKAJGH39.DTL).

IMPORTED PRESCRIPTION DRUGS. During the early 2000s the purchase of prescription drugs from other countries, particularly Canada, became popular with U.S. consumers due to cost concerns. Drugs manufactured in the United States are typically cheaper when purchased in other industrialized countries due to supply and demand factors, the strength of the U.S. dollar compared with foreign currencies, and price controls imposed on drugs by foreign governments. Potential cost savings prompted American consumers, especially the elderly, to fill their prescriptions with Canadian pharmacies—either in person or via the Internet. This practice was condemned by the pharmaceutical industry and the U.S. government, both of which warned against the dangers of buying drugs of unknown quality.

Technically, the purchase of foreign-sold prescription drugs is against U.S. law, even if the drugs originated in the United States. But the law was rarely enforced during the early 2000s. In March 2006 the *Boston Globe* reported that federal officials had begun confiscating foreign-sold prescription drugs mailed to U.S. consumers (Christopher Rowland, "U.S. Steps Up Seizures of Imported Drugs," March 26, 2006, http:// www.boston.com/yourlife/health/diseases/articles/2006/ 03/26/us_steps_up_seizures_of_imported_drugs/). The article states that the crackdown began in November 2005 and that more than thirteen thousand packages of drugs had been intercepted and seized at mail inspection facilities around the United States. The intended recipients received letters from the Department of Homeland

Security, U.S. Customs and Border Protection, notifying them that their medications had been confiscated.

According to the *Boston Globe*, a government spokesperson defended the seizures as a way of protecting the public from potentially unsafe medications. The Food and Drug Administration claims it has confiscated shipments of prescription drugs that were sold to U.S. consumers from Web sites claiming to be based in Canada that actually were based in developing countries. Critics of the seizures note that the enforcement policy took effect soon after the enrollment period began for the Medicare Part D program. They hint that the seizures were intended to discourage the elderly from buying imported drugs in favor of enrolling in the new drug coverage plan. U.S. Senator Bill Nelson of Florida pointed out that the federal government is unable to control the flow of illegal drugs into this country but noted, "By God, they can stop Grandma from saving $50 on her prescription drugs."

THE COST OF LIVING

The "cost of living" is a nontechnical term that refers to the cost of basic necessities to American households, such as food, clothing, and shelter. Although many factors affect the prices of these commodities, one economic factor has played a major role in recent decades: inflation. Because of inflation, the cost of living increases each year as the prices of necessities become more expensive. The consumer price index (CPI) is the economic indicator commonly used to gauge changes in inflation and the cost of living.

A cost of living adjustment (COLA) is an adjustment made to wages or benefits to compensate consumers for the effects of inflation. The government applies annual COLAs to increase the amounts paid out to recipients of certain benefits, such as Social Security and food stamps. This is designed to help people keep up with the rising cost of living due to inflation.

The COLA for Social Security recipients is calculated on the CPI for urban wage earners and clerical workers (CPI-W) from the third quarter of one year to the third quarter of the next year. For example, in December 2005 the government calculated a 4.1% increase in the CPI-W between third-quarter 2004 and third-quarter 2005. As a result, monthly Social Security benefits payable during 2006 were increased by 4.1%.

PUBLIC OPINION ON CONSUMER ISSUES

The Gallup Organization conducts numerous polls questioning Americans about their consumer habits and financial condition. In July 2005 pollsters asked Americans to rate various economic factors in terms of their threat level to the respondents' standard of living. As shown in Figure 3.10, medical costs and energy costs

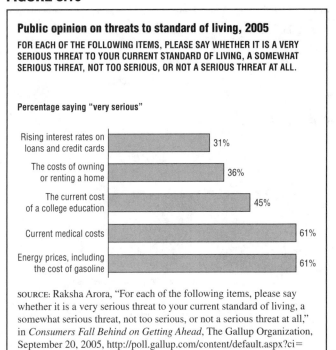

FIGURE 3.10

Public opinion on threats to standard of living, 2005

FOR EACH OF THE FOLLOWING ITEMS, PLEASE SAY WHETHER IT IS A VERY SERIOUS THREAT TO YOUR CURRENT STANDARD OF LIVING, A SOMEWHAT SERIOUS THREAT, NOT TOO SERIOUS, OR NOT A SERIOUS THREAT AT ALL.

Percentage saying "very serious"

Rising interest rates on loans and credit cards	31%
The costs of owning or renting a home	36%
The current cost of a college education	45%
Current medical costs	61%
Energy prices, including the cost of gasoline	61%

SOURCE: Raksha Arora, "For each of the following items, please say whether it is a very serious threat to your current standard of living, a somewhat serious threat, not too serious, or not a serious threat at all," in *Consumers Fall Behind on Getting Ahead*, The Gallup Organization, September 20, 2005, http://poll.gallup.com/content/default.aspx?ci= 18679 (accessed June 2, 2006). Copyright © 2005 by The Gallup Organization. Reproduced by permission of The Gallup Organization.

were each named by 61% of the poll participants as "very serious" threats. These two issues outranked consumer concerns about the cost of college education and housing and rising interest rates on debt.

In June 2006 Gallup asked poll participants to name the most important financial problem facing their family at that time. As Table 3.3 indicates, health care costs received the highest mention, being named by 16% of those asked. Energy costs were also an issue of concern, garnering mention by 13% of the respondents. Health care and energy costs have continuously been the two top-rated financial concerns named by Americans in similar polls conducted by Gallup since November 2005.

Gallup polling performed in May 2006 assessed consumers' views on the cost of various goods and services commonly purchased during the previous year. Table 3.4 lists the items that respondents were asked about. Nearly all participants (99%) answered that the price of gasoline had increased over the previous year. Majorities also said that costs for home energy, groceries, local property taxes, and health care had increased. Exactly half reported that state taxes had increased, while lower numbers said that federal income taxes and rent had gone up during the previous year.

CONSUMER SPENDING, JOB CREATION, AND INTEREST RATES

Consumer spending is essential to economic growth in America and is greatly affected by two things: employment and interest rates, which are interdependent factors

TABLE 3.3

Public opinion on the most important financial problem facing families, 2005–06

WHAT IS THE MOST IMPORTANT FINANCIAL PROBLEM FACING YOUR FAMILY TODAY?

Recent trend:	Jun 1–4, 2006	May 8–11, 2006	Apr 10–13, 2006	Feb 6–9, 2006	Dec 19–22, 2005	Nov 17–20, 2005
	%	%	%	%	%	%
Healthcare costs	16	17	18	17	15	16
Energy costs/oil and gas prices	13	20	12	8	14	11
Lack of money/low wages	12	14	12	11	12	11
High cost of living/Inflation	8	6	5	6	4	5
Too much debt/not enough money to pay debts	8	8	9	9	7	7
College expenses	8	9	8	8	7	8
Retirement savings	7	7	6	7	5	5
Cost of owning/renting a home	6	7	7	7	5	5
Taxes	5	5	4	5	4	4
Lack of savings	2	2	5	2	2	2
Unemployment/loss of job	2	3	3	6	6	8
Social security	2	2	1	1	1	*
Interest rates	1	1	2	1	1	1
Stock market/investments	1	1	1	*	*	1
Transportation/commuting costs	1	1	*	*	1	1
State of the economy	1	1	1	*	1	1
Controlling spending	*	*	1	1	1	1
Other	1	2	4	3	3	5
None	15	15	14	13	16	14
No opinion	5	2	4	4	2	4

Notes: Percentages add to more than 100% due to multiple responses.
*Less than 0.5%

SOURCE: Frank Newport, "What is the most important financial problem facing your family today?" in *Americans Paying More for Gas, Utilities, Food, and Healthcare*, The Gallup Organization, June 19, 2006, http://poll.gallup.com/content/default.aspx?ci=23371 (accessed June 19, 2006). Copyright © 2006 by The Gallup Organization. Reproduced by permission of The Gallup Organization.

TABLE 3.4

Public opinion on changes over the past year in income and spending, May 2006

THINKING BACK OVER THE PAST YEAR, WOULD YOU SAY THAT EACH OF THE FOLLOWING HAS GONE UP, REMAINED ABOUT THE SAME, (OR) GONE DOWN?

2006 May 22–24 (sorted by "gone up")	Gone up	Remained the same	Gone down
	%	%	%
The price you pay for a gallon of gasoline	99	1	*
The amount you pay for home utilities such as heating/electricity/water	82	16	2
The value of your home (*asked of homeowners*)	76	17	6
The price you pay for food and other groceries	73	26	1
Your local property taxes	70	28	2
The amount you pay for health insurance coverage	64	31	4
The amount of money you pay out-of-pocket for healthcare/prescription drugs	62	32	5
Your state taxes	50	48	2
Your federal income taxes	42	49	9
Your rent (*asked of renters*)	40	56	4
Your take-home pay after taxes and deductions	38	40	22
The amount of money you are able to put away in savings each month	19	35	46

Notes: Percentages were recalculated to add to 100%, based on those who had opinions.
*Less than 0.5%

SOURCE: Frank Newport, "Thinking back over the past year, would you say that each of the following has gone up, remained about the same, (or) gone down?" in *Americans Paying More for Gas, Utilities, Food, and Healthcare*, The Gallup Organization, June 19, 2006, http://poll.gallup.com/content/default.aspx?ci=23371 (accessed June 19, 2006). Copyright © 2006 by The Gallup Organization. Reproduced by permission of The Gallup Organization.

in the economy. Historically, when interest rates have been lower, people have spent more money, which has in turn stimulated the job market. And when people have steady and dependable work, they are more likely to spend money, which also adds jobs to the economy.

Consumer buying choices can also stimulate—and even shift—job growth among industries. The higher the demand is for certain products and services, the more growth those industries will experience. The goods and services that are purchased by the consumer are called final goods; those that are used in the production of final goods are called intermediate goods. Demand for both final and intermediate goods leads to expansion in their respective industries, which in turn adds jobs to the economy.

Interest Rates and Spending

Interest rates are determined by the Federal Reserve Board (commonly known as the Fed), which is the central bank of the United States. The Federal Reserve sets the federal funds rate (the interest rate banks charge for overnight loans to each other), which then influences the prime rate (the rate that banks charge their best custo-

mers; the prime rate usually is set at about three percentage points above the federal funds rate). From there, creditors set competitive rates for lending money to consumers. When interest rates are high, consumer spending, particularly for high-priced items such as cars and houses, tends to slow down because the cost of borrowing money is higher. Lower interest rates stimulate the economy because consumers can afford to borrow more at lower rates.

For example, the historically low interest rates of the early 2000s led to a high number of mortgage refinancings, which gave homeowners more money to spend monthly as their mortgage payments were lowered. Because of lower interest rates, many homeowners also had access to a source of disposable income unrelated to their wages: their homes. In 2003 American homeowners took advantage of rising property values and low interest rates by withdrawing $200 billion in equity from their homes. (Equity is the proportion of a house's mortgage value that a homeowner has paid off and actually owns; when people get a home equity loan, they have access to that part of their home's value in the form of credit, which they must then pay back.) In this sense, low interest rates are not always good for individual finances or the economy, because they lead to more debt in the form of home equity loans, car loans, and more credit cards.

CONSUMERISM

Some critics say that America's consumer habits are a sign of chronic overspending. In *The Overspent American: Why We Want What We Don't Need* (1998), Juliet B. Schor examines the tendency of Americans to overspend. Noting that "competitive acquisition" has been a hallmark of American life since the beginning, Schor writes that people used to compare themselves and their belongings with those who lived near them in circumstances similar to their own. More recently, however, as exposure to different economic classes has become commonplace—especially via television, movies, magazines, and the Internet, but also with coworkers and acquaintances—Americans began to compare themselves with people outside of their own economic group, usually looking to the upper classes for direction on what and how much to buy. This seemingly unrealistic comparison eventually became the norm, causing average Americans to expect their material status to equal that of those outside of what Schor calls their "reference groups"—the group of people each of us chooses to identify with most closely. The material possessions of one's reference group quickly come to be considered necessities rather than indulgences; Schor writes of the trend of overspending to keep up with others:

> Oddly, it doesn't seem as if we're spending wastefully, or even lavishly. Rather, many of us feel we're just making it, barely able to stay even. But what's remarkable is that this feeling is not restricted to families of limited income. It's a generalized feeling, one that exists at all levels. Twenty-seven percent of all households making more than $100,000 a year say they cannot afford to buy everything they really need. Nearly twenty percent say they "spend nearly all their income on the basic necessities of life." In the $50,000–100,000 range, 39 percent and one-third feel this way, respectively. Overall, half the population in the richest country in the world say they cannot afford everything they really need. And it's not just the poorest half.

Elizabeth Warren and Amelia Warren Tyagi find in *The Two-Income Trap: Why Middle-Class Mothers and Fathers Are Going Broke* (2003) that many Americans overspend for practical reasons, citing education as an example. While public schools were once considered more or less reliably similar in different communities, the perception in the 1990s and 2000s has been that families who plan to send their children to public schools must buy houses in more affluent neighborhoods whether or not they can afford them because those areas have better school districts. Many parents consider this to be a fair trade-off, but it often strains a family's finances. Additionally, Warren and Tyagi note that, unlike earlier generations that typically had one parent working full time and the other at home and available to take on a job to supplement the family's income if necessary, families in the late twentieth and early twenty-first centuries already tended to have both parents working full-time and putting about 75% of their pay toward household essentials.

CHAPTER 4
PERSONAL DEBT

Beautiful credit! The foundation of modern society.

—Mark Twain, *The Gilded Age*, 1873

He who goes a borrowing, goes a sorrowing.

—Benjamin Franklin, *Poor Richard's Almanack*, 1732–57

Personal debt has both good and bad effects on the U.S. economy. Americans borrow money to buy houses, cars, and other consumer goods. They also take out loans to pay for vacations, investments, and educational expenses. All of this spending helps businesses and boosts the nation's gross domestic product (GDP). As long as debt is handled prudently it can be a positive economic force. But some Americans take on too much debt and get into financial difficulties. Debt becomes a problem on a macroeconomic scale when people must devote large amounts of their disposable income to repaying loans instead of spending or investing their money.

In response to consumer demand, a credit industry has developed in the United States that encompasses a wide variety of businesses. Consumers and regulators complain that some creditors engage in practices that victimize debtors, particularly those that are poor and uneducated. In addition, identity theft has become a major problem in the industry. This is a crime in which personal and financial data are stolen so that criminals can use the good credit histories of others for illegal purposes.

HISTORICAL DEVELOPMENTS

For centuries religious teachings about making and taking loans affected societal attitudes about the appropriateness of personal debt. The promise to repay a loan was considered a sacred pledge; thus, violating such an agreement was morally reprehensible. The Bible and the Koran (the sacred text of Islam) include scriptures that were interpreted as prohibiting the charging of excessive interest (or even any interest) on loans made to certain groups of people. Granting or assuming debt were actions that aroused disapproval in many circumstances. In William Shakespeare's play *Hamlet*, first performed around 1600, one of the characters advises: "Neither a borrower, nor a lender be."

English common law allowed for imprisonment of debtors who could not repay their debts. This practice carried over to the fledgling United States. In fact, one of the signers of the Declaration of Independence, Robert Morris, was later imprisoned in Philadelphia for failing to repay personal debt. The use of debtor's prisons (or gaols) in America was gradually phased out during the 1800s due to changing societal attitudes and the enactment of bankruptcy laws.

Federal bankruptcy laws were passed in the United States in 1800, 1841, and 1867, as noted in *Debt's Dominion: A History of Bankruptcy Law in America* by David Skeel (2001). But each was in force for only several years before being repealed. Legislators had a difficult time drafting bills considered fair to both creditors and debtors. In 1898 a more workable law was passed that became the foundation for modern bankruptcy law.

As the twentieth century progressed, social taboos about personal debt diminished in the face of growing consumer demand for immediate access to goods. In 1919 the General Motors Acceptance Corporation (GMAC; the financial arm of the automobile company General Motors) formed to allow Americans to borrow money to acquire new automobiles. The venture proved to be wildly successful and inspired other companies to enter the credit business. During the prosperous 1920s middle-class Americans seized on the opportunity to use credit to buy newly available durable goods, such as appliances. Installment loans became a popular financing method. In the 1950s the first all-purpose credit cards were introduced. Over the next few decades their use became commonplace, representing a major shift in American buying habits and attitudes about the acceptability of debt.

CATEGORIES OF DEBT

Economists divide personal debt into two broad categories: investment debt and consumer debt. Money borrowed to buy houses and real estate is considered investment debt. Because most property appreciates (increases in value) over time, the debt assumed to finance its purchase will likely be a wise investment. Likewise, money borrowed to start a business or pay for a college education can bring financial benefits. All of this assumes that the investment was a wise one, and that the short-term costs of the debt can be borne. By contrast, consumer debt is assumed purely for consumption purposes. The money is spent to gain immediate access to goods and services that will not appreciate in value (and may well lose value) over time to help offset the costs of the debt.

Credit falls into two other categories: nonrevolving credit and revolving credit. Nonrevolving loans require regular payments of amounts that will ensure that the original debt (the principal) plus interest will be paid off in a particular amount of time. They are also known as closed-end loans and are commonly used to finance the purchase of real estate, cars, and boats or to pay for educational expenses. Nonrevolving loans feature predictable payment amounts and schedules that are laid out in amortization tables. The word "amortize" is derived from the Latin term *mort*, which means to kill or deaden. An amortization schedule details how a loan will be gradually eliminated (killed off) over a set period of time. Revolving debt is a different kind of arrangement in which the debtor is allowed to borrow against a predetermined total amount of credit and is billed for the outstanding principal plus interest. The loans typically require regularly scheduled minimum payments, but not a set time period for repaying the entire amount due. Credit card loans are the primary example of revolving debt.

Loans can also be secured or unsecured. A secured loan is one in which the borrower puts up an asset called collateral to lessen the financial risk of the loaner. If the borrower defaults (fails to pay back the loan) the loaner can seize the collateral and sell it to recoup some or all of the money that was loaned. Mortgages on homes and property and loans on cars, boats, motor homes, and other goods of high value are typically secured loans. In all of these cases the collateral can be legally repossessed by the loaners. Unsecured loans are not backed by collateral. They are granted solely on the good financial reputation of the borrower. Credit card debts and debts owed to medical practitioners and hospitals are the major types of unsecured debts.

HOUSEHOLD DEBT SERVICE

The Federal Reserve Board compiles an economic indicator called the household debt service ratio (DSR). The DSR is the ratio of household debt payments to disposable personal income (which is also known as after-tax income). It indicates the estimated fraction of disposable income that is devoted to payments on outstanding mortgage and consumer debt.

As shown in Figure 4.1, the DSR has gradually increased since the 1980s. In 1980 the debt service ratio was just over 11%. After climbing above 12% in the late 1980s, the DSR decreased in the early 1990s, dropping to less than 11%. It then began a gradual sustained climb. By the end of 2005, Americans as a whole were spending 13.86% of their disposable income on their debts.

INTEREST RATES

One of the chief factors affecting the amount of debt that people assume is the amount of interest charged on loans. Banks and other financial institutions charge interest to make money on loaning money. The interest rate charged must be low enough to tempt potential borrowers, but high enough to make a profit for lenders. In general, commercial lenders base their interest rates on the rates charged by the Federal Reserve (the Fed), the national bank of the United States. Lower interest rates encourage consumers to borrow money.

The Fed makes short-term loans to banks at an interest rate called the discount rate. If the Fed raises or lowers the discount rate, then banks adjust the federal funds rate, the rate they charge each other for loans. This affects the prime rate, the interest rate banks charge their best customers (typically large corporations), which in turn impacts the rates on other loans. Figure 1.14 in Chapter 1 shows the bank prime loan rate between 1949 and 2006. The rate has varied widely over time from around 2% in 1949 to more than 20% in the early to mid-1980s. Since 1990 the prime rate has consistently remained below 10% and even dipped below 5% in the early 2000s.

When a loan is granted the creditor sets terms that specify whether the interest rate to be paid will be fixed or variable. A fixed interest rate remains constant throughout the life of the loan. A variable rate changes and is typically tied to a publicly published interest rate, such as the prime rate. For example, a loan can be made with the stipulation that the interest rate charged each month will be one percentage point higher than the prime rate. As the prime rate changes, so will the interest rate on the loan and the borrower's monthly payments.

Table 4.1 shows the tremendous difference between loans with differing interest rates and repayment periods. A $100,000 mortgage with a thirty-year fixed interest rate

FIGURE 4.1

Household debt service ratio, 1980–2006

[Percent of disposable personal income, seasonally adjusted]

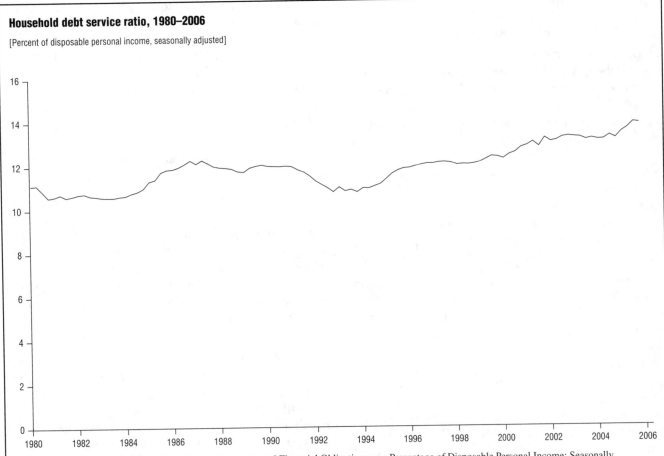

SOURCE: Adapted from "Household Debt Service Payments and Financial Obligations as a Percentage of Disposable Personal Income; Seasonally Adjusted," in *Household Debt Service and Financial Obligations Ratios*, The Federal Reserve, March 9, 2006, http://www.federalreserve.gov/releases/housedebt/default.htm (accessed June 17, 2006)

TABLE 4.1

Interest payments for particular loans

Interest rate	Years of loan	Amount borrowed	Total interest paid	Total principal + interest paid
5%	30	$100,000	$93,256	$193,256
10%	30	$100,000	$215,926	$315,926
15%	30	$100,000	$355,200	$455,200
5%	15	$100,000	$42,343	$142,343
10%	15	$100,000	$93,429	$193,429
15%	15	$100,000	$151,926	$251,926
12%	4	$20,000	$5,280	$25,280
12%	5	$20,000	$6,693	$26,693

SOURCE: Created by Kim Masters Evans for Thomson Gale, 2006

will be higher monthly payments. Borrowers must consider the financial consequences of monthly payments and interest rates to get a loan they can afford in the short and long term.

MORTGAGES

For most Americans a mortgage is the largest personal debt they will ever incur. Mortgage debt is a form of investment debt, because real estate usually increases in value. Thus, assuming mortgage debt is generally considered a sensible economic move, as long as the payments are well matched to the borrower's income and ability to pay.

Mortgage loans have been in use in Europe for centuries, developing along with private ownership of land. In modern times a mortgage represents a lien, or binding charge, against a piece of property for the payment of a debt. In other words, the loan is granted on the condition that the property can be claimed by the loaner (creditor) in the event the borrower defaults. If the loan is

of 5% will result in $193,256 being paid over the lifetime of the loan. The same loan at 10% interest will cost $315,926. Loans for new cars typically have a repayment period of four to five years. As shown in Table 4.1, a 12% fixed interest car loan for $20,000 paid over four years results in a total payment of $25,280. The same loan spread over five years will end up costing $26,693. But the trade-off to the borrower for a shorter loan period satisfactorily paid, full ownership of the property is granted to the borrower.

The Government's Role in Mortgages

Because high rates of home ownership are considered good for the U.S. economy, the government has taken an active role in the mortgage markets. Mortgage terms have changed dramatically since the early 1930s. At that time home buyers could borrow only up to half of a property's market value. A typical repayment plan included three to five years of regular payments and then one large "balloon" payment of the remaining balance. These terms discouraged many potential homeowners. As a result, the home ownership rate stood at around 40%, according to the Federal Housing Administration (FHA; http://www.hud.gov/offices/hsg/fhahistory.cfm). Most people preferred to rent.

During the 1930s the federal government introduced a variety of initiatives to boost a housing industry devastated by the Great Depression and increase home ownership. These efforts were focused on encouraging the supply side of the mortgage industry. They benefited consumers by enhancing the availability and flexibility of home mortgages. For example, amortization schedules covering fifteen years or more became common, eliminating balloon payments and making it much easier for consumers to afford houses. Following World War II the Veteran's Administration offered mortgages on favorable terms to returning veterans. Postwar economic prosperity and relatively low interest rates led to a housing boom. The FHA reports that by 2001 the nation's home ownership rate was in excess of 68%.

There are several agencies and organizations that operate under government control or mandate to increase home ownership among Americans.

FEDERAL HOUSING ADMINISTRATION. The FHA was created in 1934 and later placed under the oversight of the U.S. Department of Housing and Urban Development (HUD). The FHA provides mortgage insurance on loans made by FHA-approved lenders to buyers of single- and multifamily homes. FHA-insured loans require less cash down payment from the home buyer than most conventional loans. The insurance provides assurances to lenders that the government will cover losses resulting from homeowners defaulting on their loans. According to its Web site, updated in June 2005, the FHA has insured nearly thirty-three million home mortgages since 1934 and is the largest insurer of mortgages in the world.

FEDERAL NATIONAL MORTGAGE ASSOCIATION (FANNIE MAE). The Federal National Mortgage Association (FNMA or Fannie Mae) was created in 1938. Fannie Mae began buying FHA-insured mortgages from banks and other lenders, bundling the mortgages together and selling the mortgage packages as investments on the stock markets. In essence, Fannie Mae created a secondary market for home mortgages. Lenders benefited because they received immediate money that could be loaned to new customers. Home buyers benefited from the increased availability of mortgage loans. The mortgage packages were attractive to investors because the mortgages were backed by FHA insurance. In 1968 Fannie Mae was converted to a private organization and expanded its portfolio beyond FHA-insured mortgages. But as of 2006 it remained under congressional charter to enhance the availability and affordability of home mortgages for low- to middle-income Americans.

FEDERAL HOME LOAN MORTGAGE CORPORATION (FREDDIE MAC). The Federal Home Loan Mortgage Corporation (Freddie Mac) was created by the government in 1970 as a competitor for Fannie Mae, to prevent Fannie Mae's monopolization of the mortgage market. Like Fannie Mae, Freddie Mac sells home mortgages on the secondary market and is a private organization operating under a government charter.

Mortgage Interest Rates

Figure 4.2 shows the average interest rate on a thirty-year fixed mortgage between 1972 and 2005. Comparison with Figure 1.14 in Chapter 1 shows that mortgage rates mirror the ups and downs of the prime rate. Interest rates have been highly variable since the 1970s. Since the early 1980s, interest rates have decreased significantly, encouraging consumers to borrow money at unprecedented levels.

Creative financing terms introduced by creditors since the late 1990s have led to many alternatives to the conventional thirty-year fixed rate mortgage. Homebuyers can choose adjustable rate mortgages with variable interest rates or fixed-rate mortgages with shorter loan periods (for example, fifteen years instead of thirty years). Some creditors offer mortgages that allow homeowners to make interest-only payments for a short portion of the loan period. This is followed by a longer period of much higher monthly payments. Short-term payment schedules requiring one large balloon payment are also offered. Economists worry that mortgage arrangements with changeable monthly payments and balloon payments may pose a financial problem for homeowners who overestimate their ability to meet the costs of the mortgage.

Refinancing Mortgages

Most home mortgages cover long periods—up to thirty years. But interest rates can change dramatically in the short term, rising and falling in response to macroeconomic factors. Homebuyers who assume fixed-rate mortgages during times of high interest rates can ask creditors to refinance (adjust the mortgage terms) when

FIGURE 4.2

Interest rate on 30-year fixed mortgage, 1972–2005

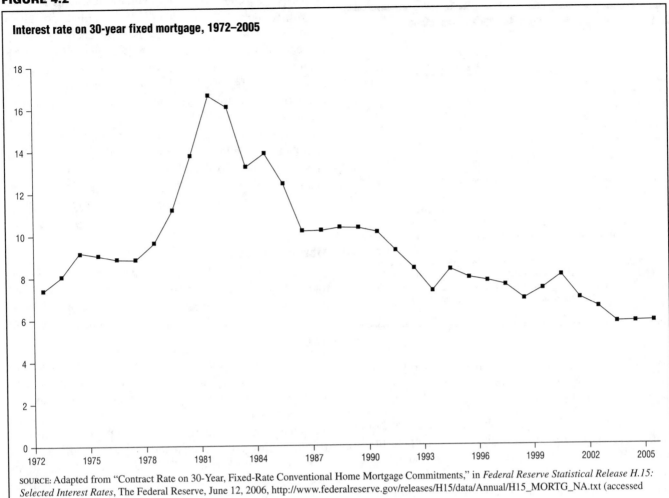

SOURCE: Adapted from "Contract Rate on 30-Year, Fixed-Rate Conventional Home Mortgage Commitments," in *Federal Reserve Statistical Release H.15: Selected Interest Rates*, The Federal Reserve, June 12, 2006, http://www.federalreserve.gov/releases/H15/data/Annual/H15_MORTG_NA.txt (accessed June 17, 2006)

interest rates go down. Basically, refinancing entails drawing up a new mortgage contract on a property. Because mortgage contracts are complicated legal documents, creditors usually charge fees to refinance mortgages. Thus, homeowners must weigh the long-term benefits of a reduced interest rate against the expense of refinancing fees.

During the 1990s and early 2000s interest rates trended downward, making mortgage refinancing very popular. This was particularly true for consumers who had purchased homes during the 1980s when interest rates were very high by historical standards.

Refinancing frequently results in lower monthly payments for the homeowner, due to the lower interest rate, and because refinancing is commonly performed after at least several years of payments have been made on the original loan. This frees up borrowers' money for consumer spending, investing, or saving. But refinances conducted with a long payment period will keep the homeowner in mortgage debt for a longer period of time than originally anticipated. Some homeowners opt for a

shorter loan payback period when they refinance. For example, consider a homeowner who has been paying for five years on a fixed-rate thirty-year mortgage. There are twenty-five years left in the repayment period. Refinancing at a much lower interest rate with a new fifteen-year payback period may not decrease the monthly payment, but it will reduce by ten years the amount of time the homeowner will be in mortgage debt.

Home Equity Loans

Real estate tends to appreciate in value. Thus, a property can increase in value above the amount originally paid for it (that is, the amount that was borrowed to pay for it). For example, imagine a homeowner who bought a house in 1990 for $100,000 under a thirty-year fixed-rate mortgage. After making mortgage payments for several years the homeowner discovers that the principal due on the loan has dropped to $90,000, but the property has increased in value to $140,000. The difference between the amount of principal owed (the outstanding loan balance) and the value of the property is $50,000 and is called home equity. Home equity is an

TABLE 4.2

Uses of funds liquefied in 2001 and 2002 refinancings

	Share of loans[a] (percent)	Share of dollars (percent)
Repayment of other debts	51	26
Home improvements	43	35
Consumer expenditures[b]	25	16
Stock market or other financial investment	13	11
Real estate or business investment	7	10
Taxes	2	2

[a]The percentages sum to more than 100 because multiple uses could be cited for a single loan.
[b]Includes vehicle purchases; vacation, education, or medical expenses; living expenses; and other consumer purchases.

SOURCE: Margaret M. McConnell, Richard W. Peach, and Alex Al-Haschimi, "Table 2. Uses of Funds Liquefied in 2001 and 2002 Refinancings," in "After the Refinancing Boom: Will Consumers Scale Back Their Spending?" *Current Issues in Economics and Finance*, Vol. 9, No. 12, Federal Reserve Bank of New York, December 2003, http://www.newyorkfed.org/research/current_issues/ci9-12.pdf (accessed June 22, 2006). Data from Glenn Canner, Karen Dynan, and Wayne Passmore, "Mortgage Refinancing in 2001 and Early 2002," *Federal Reserve Bulletin*, Vol. 88, No. 12, December 2002.

asset that can be borrowed against. Basically, homeowners can "liquefy" (turn into cash) the equity they have built up in their homes.

Since the late 1980s a combination of rising home values and decreasing interest rates has prompted many homeowners to refinance their mortgages and take out home equity loans. The macroeconomic effects of this phenomenon are examined by researchers at the Federal Reserve Bank of New York in a December 2003 article titled "After the Refinancing Boom: Will Consumers Scale Back Their Spending?" in the journal *Current Issues in Economics and Finance* (vol. 9, no. 12, http://www.newyorkfed.org/research/current_issues/ci9-12.pdf). The article reports that homeowners liquefied $450 billion of home equity in 2003. Table 4.2 shows the results of a Fed survey on how homeowners used liquefied home equity funds following refinancings in 2001 and early 2002. More than a third of the money (35%) was devoted to home improvements. Another 26% was used to repay other debts, and 16% went to consumer spending. Smaller shares were devoted to financial investments (11%), real estate or business investments (10%), and tax payments (2%).

Economists are encouraged by the use of home equity money for home improvements. This type of spending is considered an investment, because it adds value to the home. Many homeowners chose to use home equity funds to repay other debt. Because mortgage loans typically have lower interest rates than other loans, this exchange is beneficial. In addition, the interest paid on mortgage loans is tax deductible for most Americans, while interest paid on other types of loans is not deductible. Thus, conversion of "bad" types of debt—such as credit

cards—to mortgage debt has favorable consequences. As shown in Table 4.2, more than half of the loans obtained from 2001 and 2002 refinancings were taken by homeowners to repay other debts. On the other hand, some economists worry that homeowners who use home equity loans to pay off "bad" kinds of debt (such as credit card debt) may succumb to temptation and run up bad debt again. This could put them in a dire financial situation. They will no longer have their home equity to fall back on if their new debts become more than they can afford, and they might have to default on their loans. Home equity loans, like all mortgage loans, are secured by property. Thus, default on a home equity loan can result in loss of the home by the owner.

Mortgage Debt

As shown in Table 4.3, outstanding mortgage debt totaled $11.5 trillion in the third quarter of 2005. The vast majority of the debt ($8.8 trillion, or 77%) was for non-farm properties containing houses designed for one to four families.

There are two types of mortgages in common use: conventional mortgages and government-underwritten mortgages. Conventional mortgages are loans made by nongovernmental businesses, such as banks and finance companies. In third-quarter 2005 there were $10.7 trillion in outstanding conventional mortgage loans on nonfarm properties. This represents 95% of the total for nonfarm properties. Another $619 billion was in government-underwritten mortgages, including $359 billion in loans insured by the FHA and $203 billion in loans guaranteed by the Veterans Administration.

CONSUMER CREDIT

The Federal Reserve defines consumer credit as credit extended to individuals that does not include loans secured by real estate. In other words, mortgages are excluded from consumer credit. As shown in Figure 4.3, consumer credit topped $2 trillion during the first quarter of 2006. The amount has risen since 2001, when $1.8 trillion in credit was outstanding. The breakdown for first-quarter 2006 was $1.36 trillion in nonrevolving loans and $0.8 trillion in revolving loans. Nonrevolving debt includes loans for vehicles, boats, vacations, and student loans. Revolving debt is almost entirely comprised of credit card debt.

Figure 4.4 shows the breakdown of outstanding consumer debt by creditor as of April 2006. Nearly one-third of the total was owed to commercial banks. Pools of securitized assets (bundled debts sold as securities on the stock markets) accounted for 28% of the total. Finance companies held another 16% of the debt, while credit unions held 11%. The remaining creditors each accounted for 5% or less of the total.

TABLE 4.3

Mortgage debt outstanding by type of property and type of financing, 2001–third quarter 2005

[Billions of dollars]

End of year or quarter	All properties	Farm properties	Nonfarm properties				Nonfarm properties by type of mortgage					
							Government underwritten				Conventional[b]	
			Total	1- to 4-family houses	Multifamily properties	Commerical properties	Total[a]	1- to 4-family houses			Total	1- to 4-family houses
								Total	FHA insured	VA guaranteed		
2001	7,421.0	117.8	7,303.1	5,571.3	447.8	1,284.0	772.7	718.5	497.4	221.2	6,530.5	4,852.8
2002	8,243.0	125.5	8,117.5	6,244.1	486.7	1,386.7	759.3	704.0	486.2	217.7	7,358.2	5,540.2
2003	9,235.0	133.6	9,101.5	7,026.1	557.2	1,518.2	709.2	653.3	438.7	214.6	8,392.3	6,372.8
2004	10,463.2	141.7	10,321.5	8,013.7	609.0	1,698.8	661.5	605.4	398.1	207.3	9,660.0	7,408.4
2004:												
I	9,490.1	135.3	9,354.8	7,235.3	564.8	1,554.7	702.1	646.3	433.2	213.1	8,652.7	6,589.0
II	9,776.7	138.3	9,638.4	7,465.8	582.0	1,590.5	687.6	631.7	422.0	209.7	8,950.8	6,834.2
III	10,142.1	140.5	10,001.6	7,768.3	594.0	1,639.3	676.2	620.3	411.6	208.7	9,325.4	7,148.0
IV	10,463.2	141.7	10,321.5	8,013.7	609.0	1,698.8	661.5	605.4	398.1	207.3	9,660.0	7,408.4
2005:												
I	10,716.1	143.0	10,573.1	8,210.2	617.6	1,745.3	647.9	591.6	386.1	205.5	9,925.2	7,618.6
II	11,093.9	146.2	10,947.7	8,502.0	632.4	1,813.3	633.4	577.2	372.7	204.4	10,314.3	7,924.8
III[p]	11,499.7	148.3	11,351.4	8,821.5	641.6	1,888.3	619.1	562.5	359.3	203.2	10,732.3	8,259.0

[a]Includes FHA (Federal Housing Administration) insured multifamily properties, not shown separately.
[b]Derived figures. Total includes multifamily properties, not shown separately, and commercial properties not shown here but are the same as nonfarm properties—commercial properties.

SOURCE: Adapted from "Table B-75. Mortgage Debt Outstanding by Type of Property and of Financing, 1949–2005," in *Economic Report of the President*, U.S. Government Printing Office, February 2006, http://www.gpoaccess.gov/eop/2006/2006_erp.pdf (accessed June 17, 2006)

FIGURE 4.3

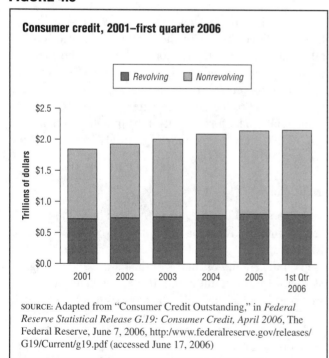

Consumer credit, 2001–first quarter 2006

SOURCE: Adapted from "Consumer Credit Outstanding," in *Federal Reserve Statistical Release G.19: Consumer Credit, April 2006*, The Federal Reserve, June 7, 2006, http://www.federalreserve.gov/releases/G19/Current/g19.pdf (accessed June 17, 2006)

FIGURE 4.4

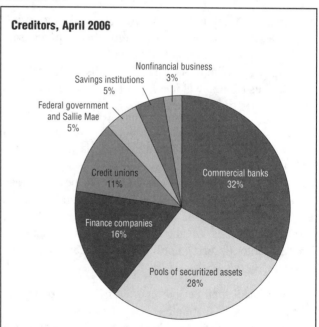

Creditors, April 2006

SOURCE: Adapted from "Major Holders," in *Federal Reserve Statistical Release G.19: Consumer Credit, April 2006*, The Federal Reserve, June 7, 2006, http://www.federalreserve.gov/releases/G19/Current/g19.pdf (accessed June 17, 2006)

Interest Rates on Consumer Loans

Consumer loans are not secured by real estate. Because they have a higher risk of default, consumer loans generally have higher interest rates than mortgage loans. Table 4.4 lists the average interest rates charged on various kinds of consumer loans from 2001 through 2005 and for the first quarter of 2006. It should be noted that borrowers with good credit histories would have likely received lower interest rates than these averages, while borrowers with poor credit histories would have been charged higher rates.

TABLE 4.4

Terms of credit at commercial banks and finance companies, 2001–first quarter 2006

[Percent except as noted, not seasonally adjusted]

Institution, terms, and type of loan	2001	2002	2003	2004	2005*	2006 Q1*
Commercial banks						
Interest rates						
48-mo. new car	8.50	7.62	6.93	6.60	7.08	7.39
24-mo. personal	13.22	12.54	11.95	11.89	12.05	12.18
Credit card plan						
All accounts	14.87	13.40	12.30	12.71	12.50	13.29
Accounts assessed interest	14.46	13.11	12.73	13.21	14.54	14.38
New car loans at auto finance companies						
Interest rates	5.65	4.29	3.40	4.36	5.46	5.34
Maturity (months)	55.1	56.8	61.4	60.5	60.0	61.8
Loan-to-value ratio	91	94	95	89	88	90
Amount financed (dollars)	22,822	24,747	26,295	24,888	24,133	24,926

Notes: Interest rates are annual percentage rates (APR) as specified by the Federal Reserve's Regulation Z. Interest rates for new-car loans and personal loans at commercial banks are simple unweighted averages of each bank's most common rate charged during the first calendar week of the middle month of each quarter. For credit card accounts, the rate for all accounts is the stated APR averaged across all credit card accounts at all reporting banks. The rate for accounts assessed interest is the annualized ratio of total finance charges at all reporting banks to the total average daily balances against which the finance charges were assessed (excludes accounts for which no finance charges were assessed). Finance company data are from the subsidiaries of the three major U.S. automobile manufacturers and are volume-weighted averages covering all loans of each type purchased during the month.
*Revised.

SOURCE: Adapted from "Terms of Credit at Commercial Banks and Finance Companies," in *Federal Reserve Statistical Release G.19: Consumer Credit, April 2006*, The Federal Reserve, June 7, 2006, http://www.federalreserve.gov/releases/G19/Current/g19.pdf (accessed June 17, 2006).

New Car Loans

Loans for the purchase of new cars (and other types of vehicles) are secured by the vehicle being purchased. In other words, the creditor can repossess the vehicle if the loan is in default. As a result of this collateral, the interest rates on new vehicle loans tend to be lower than on other types of consumer loans.

As of the first quarter of 2006, the average interest rate on a four-year loan from a commercial bank for the purchase of a new car was 7.39%. The interest rate charged by auto finance companies for a new car loan was lower, at 5.34%. According to the Federal Reserve, the latter rate is based on the rates charged by the finance companies of the "big three" automakers— General Motors Corp., Ford Motor Co., and Daimler-Chrysler AG.

The typical loan period reported by the auto finance companies was 61.8 months (just over five years). This is much longer than the three-year loan periods that were common for new car loans in the mid-1970s. Longer loan periods reflect longer car lifetimes. The average loan-to-value ratio reported by the auto finance companies for first quarter 2006 was 90%. This means that the average new car buyer borrowed 90% of the value of the new car being purchased. The remaining 10% would have been a down payment paid by the buyer in cash or via trade-in of another vehicle. The average amount financed during first quarter 2006 for a new car purchase was $24,926.

Personal Loans

Personal loans are generally unsecured loans based on the creditworthiness of the borrower. Lack of collateral makes personal loans more risky from the loaners' viewpoint; thus, interest rates are higher for personal loans than for car loans. (See Table 4.4.) In the first quarter of 2006 the average interest rate charged by commercial banks for a twenty-four-month personal loan was 12.2%. The rate varied from 11.9% to 13.2% between 2001 and 2005.

Credit Cards

As shown in Table 4.4, credit cards have the highest average interest rates of all types of consumer loans. Most credit card loans are unsecured and are granted based on the creditworthiness of the borrower. The higher risk factor for the creditor and the huge demand for credit cards contribute to the high interest rates that are charged.

The average interest rate charged by commercial banks on credit card loans was 14.4% during the first quarter of 2006. The rate varied from 12.7% to 14.5% between 2001 and 2005. Rates charged on credit cards issued by department and specialty stores can be much higher, however, according to Bankrate.com's Lucy Lazarony (http://moneycentral.msn.com/content/Banking/creditcardsmarts/P55860.asp). Lazarony notes that while these stores sometimes offer discounts and "rewards" for items charged on their cards, their interest rates can be more than 20%.

TABLE 4.5

Effects of different minimum monthly payments on credit card debt

Interest rate	Amount borrowed	Minimum monthly payment required	Months to pay off loan	Total interest paid	Total principal + interest paid
13%	$1,000	2%	148	$815	$1,815
18%	$1,000	2%	232	$1,931	$2,931
21%	$1,000	2%	397	$4,198	$5,198
13%	$1,000	4%	77	$322	$1,322
18%	$1,000	4%	87	$516	$1,516
21%	$1,000	4%	95	$665	$1,665

SOURCE: Created by Kim Masters Evans for Thomson Gale, 2006

REVOLVING CREDIT AND MINIMUM PAYMENTS. Credit card debt is an example of revolving debt, a type of debt that is not amortized. There is no preset schedule of payments that will eliminate the debt within a particular time frame. The creditor grants the borrower a total amount of credit at a particular interest rate. Although the interest rate may be fixed for a short introductory period, in general, credit card interest rates are variable.

Each month the borrower is billed for the outstanding balance on the credit card, which includes principal plus interest. The borrower can pay off the entire balance or a lesser amount down to the minimum payment required by the credit card issuer. Payment of any amount less than the total will result in additional finance charges on the remaining balance. This is an example of compound interest (interest charged on an amount that already includes built-up interest charges).

When credit cards were first introduced, it was common for creditors to require 5% or more of the balance as a minimum monthly payment. Minimum payment requirements were gradually reduced, until 2% was typical among most credit card issuers. Low required minimum payments, high interest rates, and the effect of compounding interest make it difficult for many consumers to pay off credit card debt. In 2003 federal banking regulators issued a recommendation that credit card issuers set minimum payments so that balances can be paid off in a "reasonable" period of time. The Bankruptcy Abuse Prevention and Consumer Protection Act of 2005 requires creditors to tell borrowers how long it will take to pay off their credit card debt if only minimum payments are made.

Table 4.5 illustrates the tremendous difference to the borrower between credit card debts paid off by differing minimum monthly payments. A $1,000 loan at 13% interest takes 148 months to pay off with 2% minimum monthly payments. The same loan takes only seventy-seven months to discharge if 4% of the balance is paid

each month. The higher monthly payment also results in far less interest being paid over the life of the debt ($322 compared with $815). Even greater savings are achieved when a minimum monthly sum of 4% is paid on credit card loans that charge 18% or 21% interest.

Student Loans

Student loans are loans obtained to pay for educational expenses, primarily at the college level. Although they are technically consumer loans, student loans are not for consumption purposes. They fund the advancement of skill and knowledge in individuals, likely increasing the potential for higher future income. Thus, student loans are considered a type of "human investment."

Because the federal government wishes to encourage secondary education, it plays a major role in ensuring that student loans are available. There are three major types of student loans:

- Low-interest loans provided by the government through the financial aid departments of participating schools; these loans are available to needy students through the Perkins Loan Program

- Loans provided directly to students by the government through the William D. Ford Federal Direct Loan Program

- Loans guaranteed by the federal government but provided to students by private lenders

According to the U.S. Department of Education, approximately $27.5 billion was disbursed via direct student loans during fiscal year 2005. This figure is up from $20 billion disbursed during fiscal year 2004. As of September 30, 2005, the total outstanding balance of federally guaranteed student loans held by lenders was $289 billion, up from $245 billion as of September 30, 2004 (http://www.ed.gov/about/reports/annual/2005report/pdf/3b6-notes.pdf).

CONSUMER OPINIONS ABOUT DEBT

In March 2005 the Gallup Organization, in conjunction with the credit marketing company Experian, began compiling a Personal Credit Index (PCI)—an index gauging consumer perceptions and intentions regarding personal credit. The first index value was arbitrarily set to one hundred. Periodic polls have been conducted to calculate a PCI for comparison to the original value. In April 2006 pollsters found that the PCI had declined to a value of eighty-four, indicating a more negative viewpoint about personal credit. Each PCI has two components—a rating by consumers of their present credit situation and a rating indicating their expectations about their future credit situation. The April 2006 PCI included a present situation rating of thirty-six and a future situation rating of forty-eight. Both ratings are down slightly from values reported earlier in 2006.

FIGURE 4.5

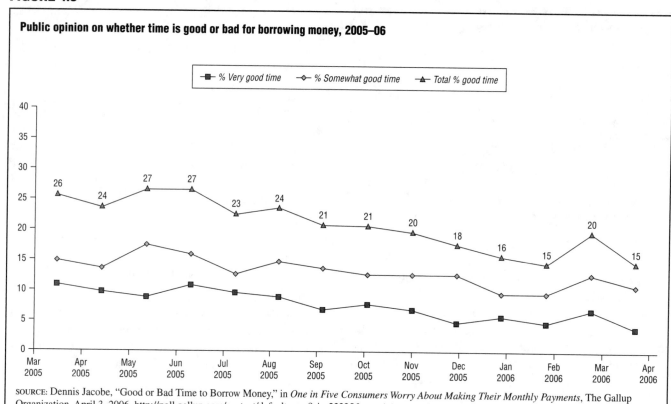

Public opinion on whether time is good or bad for borrowing money, 2005–06

Legend: ■ % Very good time   ◇ % Somewhat good time   ▲ Total % good time

SOURCE: Dennis Jacobe, "Good or Bad Time to Borrow Money," in *One in Five Consumers Worry About Making Their Monthly Payments*, The Gallup Organization, April 3, 2006, http://poll.gallup.com/content/default.aspx?ci=22225&pg=1 (accessed June 20, 2006). Copyright © 2006 by The Gallup Organization. Reproduced by permission of The Gallup Organization.

Figure 4.5 shows the results of a Gallup poll on consumer views about the appropriateness of current conditions for taking out loans. In April 2006 only 15% of those asked felt it was a "good time" to borrow money. This value is down from 24% reported in April 2005. Rising interest rates are most likely to blame for consumer pessimism about assuming more debt.

A Gallup survey conducted in April 2006 found that the average American household has three credit cards issued by banks, department stores, or retail chains. People earning $75,000 or more per year were more likely to have three or more credit cards than lower-wage earners. When asked about their payment habits, 42% of people said they pay off their credit card bills each month. (See Figure 4.6.) More than one-fourth of respondents (27%) usually carry over a balance from month to month. Only 11% of those asked usually pay only the minimum amount due each month. A small percentage (2%) reported they sometime pay less than the minimum amount required. According to Gallup, the average credit card balance was $5,960 for those respondents who carry a balance from month to month. Seventeen percent of these people reported they were "very" or "somewhat" worried about not being able to make the required minimum payments on their cards.

FIGURE 4.6

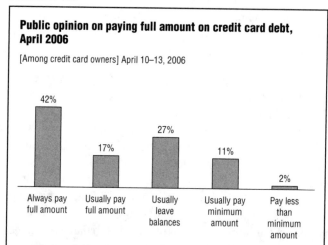

Public opinion on paying full amount on credit card debt, April 2006

[Among credit card owners] April 10–13, 2006

SOURCE: Joseph Carroll, "Pay Full Amount on Credit Cards?" in *Credit Card Owners' Average Balance Is More Than $3,000*, The Gallup Organization, May 19, 2006, http://poll.gallup.com/content/default .aspx?ci=22879&pg=1 (accessed June 2, 2006). Copyright © 2006 by The Gallup Organization. Reproduced by permission of The Gallup Organization.

PERSONAL BANKRUPTCIES

The word bankrupt is derived from the Italian phrase *banca rotta*, which translates literally as "bench broken," referring to the benches or tables used by merchants in outdoor markets in sixteenth-century Italy. Bankruptcy is

FIGURE 4.7

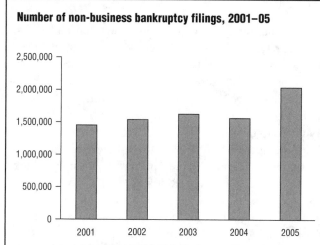

Number of non-business bankruptcy filings, 2001–05

SOURCE: Adapted from "Table F-2. U.S. Bankruptcy Courts: Business and Nonbusiness Bankruptcy Cases Commenced, by Chapter of the Bankruptcy Code, during the Twelve-Month Period Ended Dec. 31, 2005," in *Bankruptcy Statistics*, The U.S. Courts, December 2005, http://www.uscourts.gov/bnkrpctystats/bankrupt_f2table_dec2005.xls (accessed June 17, 2006)

- Chapter 13—A payment plan is developed under which debtors receiving regular income repay their creditors. Liquidation of assets is not required in most cases.

- Chapter 11—While similar to Chapter 13, Chapter 11 is reserved for individuals with "substantial" debts and assets.

In 2005 the vast majority (80%) of personal bankruptcy cases were filed under Chapter 7. Nearly 20% of filings were under Chapter 13, and less than 1% of cases were under Chapter 11 (http://www.uscourts.gov/bnkrpctystats/bankrupt_f2table_dec2005.xls).

Evolving Bankruptcy Law

The first federal bankruptcy laws were written in the early 1800s but were considered emergency measures to remain in effect for only short periods of time. The first comprehensive federal legislation was the National Bankruptcy Act of 1898, which was extensively amended during the 1930s and later replaced by the Bankruptcy Reform Act of 1978. This law was substantially amended by the Bankruptcy Reform Act of 1994. Major reforms in the law were enacted when the Bankruptcy Abuse Prevention and Consumer Protection Act of 2005 went into effect.

Because of different state laws regulating which assets and belongings a person could keep after a Chapter 7 filing, regulators and creditors believed that some people were using bankruptcy as a way to keep possessions without having to pay for them. The new federal law instituted measures intended to eliminate abuses and loopholes and increased the amount of paperwork and fees required from most filers.

Opponents of the new bill argued that it was designed to make more money for credit card companies and lenders and that it would be detrimental to ordinary people who chose bankruptcy as a last resort.

Bankruptcy Filers

In researching their book *The Two-Income Trap: Why Middle-Class Mothers and Fathers Are Going Broke* (2003), Elizabeth Warren and Amelia Warren Tyagi found that women and families with children at home were two of the fastest-growing groups filing for personal bankruptcy. Between 1981 and 1999, for example, the number of women who filed for bankruptcy went from about sixty-nine thousand to about five hundred thousand—a 662% increase.

Warren discussed the phenomenon of bankruptcy among middle-class American families in her article "Financial Collapse and Class Status: Who Goes Bankrupt?" (*Osgoode Hall Law Journal*, vol. 41, no. 1, 2003), writing of the importance of documenting who files for

a state of financial ruin. Under U.S. law people with more debts than they can reasonably hope to repay can file for personal bankruptcy. This results in a legally binding agreement between debtors and the federal government worked out in a federal bankruptcy court. The agreement calls for the debtors to "pay" as much as they can with whatever assets they have, and after a predetermined amount of time—usually a number of years—begin again with new credit. Depending on state law, certain belongings may be kept through the bankruptcy.

According to the American Bankruptcy Institute (http://www.abiworld.org/Content/NavigationMenu/Consumer_Education_Center/Frequently_Asked_Questions/General_Concepts/General_Concepts.htm#5), an official declaration of bankruptcy benefits individuals in the short term, because it puts a stop to all collection efforts by creditors. An "automatic stay" goes into effect that prevents creditors from calling, writing, or suing debtors covered by a bankruptcy plan.

Figure 4.7 shows the number of personal bankruptcy cases filed per year between 2001 and 2005. In 2005 just over two million individuals filed for bankruptcy, up from 1.5 million cases in 2001 and, according to the U.S. Courts, 872,438 cases in 1991 (http://www.uscourts.gov/bnkrpctystats/Bk2002_1990Calendar.pdf).

There are three types (or chapters) of personal bankruptcy under which individuals may file:

- Chapter 7—A liquidation plan is developed in which the debtor turns over certain assets that are sold and used to pay creditors.

bankruptcy: "Knowing who files for bankruptcy can signal information about successes and failures throughout the population, informing research, for example, on the economic progress of different social and racial subgroups, the heightened vulnerability of the elderly, or the economic risks facing divorced women or mothers of small children." In her study Warren found that an overwhelming majority of the people she interviewed who had filed for bankruptcy had at least some college education, worked in occupations that are typically rated high in status surveys, and were homeowners—the three factors that Warren used to identify membership in the American middle class. This finding contradicts the idea that people who declare bankruptcy tend to be poorly educated and economically disadvantaged from the outset. Additionally, the most common reasons people give for declaring bankruptcy are sudden financial setbacks, such as job loss, illness or injury, medical debt, or divorce, rather than long-term problems involving chronic overspending (although those cases do exist).

PREYING ON DEBTORS

Consumer demand for credit has led to enormous growth in businesses engaged in making loans, counseling debtors, and arranging debt management plans. Although these are legitimate enterprises, some businesses have aroused consumer ire and even run afoul of the law with practices considered abusive toward debtors.

Predatory Lending?

Most large creditors, such as banks and finance companies, only loan money to applicants who meet stringent requirements for creditworthiness, excluding people with low incomes and poor credit histories. This has led to the growth of "sub-prime" lenders—businesses that make loans to customers considered undesirable by traditional lenders. Because they are assuming higher risk, subprime lenders charge their customers higher interest rates and fees to loan money to them. Some consumers and legislators have accused these businesses of charging excessive fees and interest rates on loans—a practice called "predatory lending." Predatory lenders allegedly victimize poor people by imposing loan terms designed to maximize creditor profits and make it difficult for debtors to pay off their debt.

"Usury" is a word that centuries ago meant "interest" or "the charging of interest." In modern terminology it has come to mean the charging of excessive interest. Although there are state usury laws against the charging of excessive interest, this issue has not been addressed at the federal level. In fact, most banks are allowed to ignore state usury laws. Other lenders can avoid usury laws through a variety of means, such as charging large loan fees and forcing borrowers to take out expensive insurance policies.

Two particular types of loans are often called predatory: payday loans and refund anticipation loans (RALs). Borrowers obtain payday loans from establishments that agree to accept and hold personal checks until the borrower receives a paycheck. According to the Consumer Federation of America (CFA), the typical fee for a payday loan due in two weeks is $15 per $100 borrowed ("CFA Launches New Web Site on Payday Lending for Consumers," May 1, 2006, http://www.consumerfed.org/pdfs/PDL_Website_Press_Rel050306.pdf). RALs are also short-term loans that must be paid back within two weeks. Creditors loan RALs to people expecting refunds when their income taxes are filed. According to a CFA report, the typical loan fee for an RAL ranges from $29 to $120. The CFA estimates that more than twelve million taxpayers spent $1.6 billion in fees in 2004 to obtain RALs. The organization claims that RALs are targeted at uneducated minority populations that "are vulnerable to quick cash loan offers" ("Refund Anticipation Loans: Updated Facts and Figures," January 17, 2006, http://www.consumerfed.org/pdfs/RAL_2006_Early_info.pdf).

Credit Counseling and Debt Management Services

The explosive growth in consumer debt has resulted in a large number of organizations offering credit counseling and debt management services to debtors in financial difficulties. Consumer activists maintain that many of these organizations charge debtors large fees in return for little to no aid. In September 2003 a federal committee began investigating alleged abuses in the credit counseling industry. They published their findings in "Profiteering in a Non-Profit Industry: Abusive Practices in Credit Counseling" (April 13, 2005, http://frwebgate.access.gpo.gov/cgi-bin/getdoc.cgi?dbname=109_cong_rep orts&docid=f:sr055.109.pdf).

According to the report, credit counseling as an industry began in the 1960s with the help of large creditors, such as banks, concerned about rising bankruptcy rates. The early credit counseling agencies (CCAs) were locally based nonprofit organizations with trained counselors who met in person with debtors and provided advice on budgeting and paying off debt. CCAs could also arrange debt management plans for debtors in which creditors agreed to charge lower monthly minimum payments, lower interest rates, and waive outstanding late fees. The CCAs would collect the new monthly payments from the debtor and pay the creditors. Creditors supported the CCAs with contributions and participated in debt management plans in hopes that the debtors would avoid filing for bankruptcy. Some CCAs also charged small fees to the debtor for administrative costs. These reputable CCAs were members of the National Foundation for Credit Counseling, an organization known for its focus on standards and ethics.

The investigation found that a large number of new CCAs entered the industry beginning in the 1990s, operating in a much different way. Most are Internet-based, communicate with consumers solely by phone, and focus exclusively on enrolling debtors in debt management plans for large fees. Although officially nonprofit organizations, many of these new CCAs were found to have ties to for-profit businesses. The investigation concluded that many of the newer CCAs engage in deceptive practices and provide no actual counseling services to debtors.

The investigation coincided with a federal crackdown on CCAs. The Internal Revenue Service began revoking the tax-exempt status of CCAs found to be funneling money to for-profit businesses. The Federal Trade Commission (FTC) filed charges against some of the CCAs accused of wrongdoing. In January 2006 the founder of a large CCA called AmeriDebt agreed to pay the FTC a $35-million fine to avoid a trial. AmeriDebt had allegedly collected more than $170 million in fees from an estimated three hundred thousand customers who never received any credit counseling (Stephen Manning, "AmeriDebt Founder to Settle with the FTC," January 9, 2006, http://www.boston.com/business/articles/2006/01/09/ameridebt_founder_settles_with_the_ftc/). In June 2006 the CCA Credit Foundation of America agreed to pay more than $900,000 in fines to the FTC for making false claims about its debt management program and operating as part of a for-profit company ("Debt Management Telemarketers Settle FTC Charges," June 15, 2006, http://www.consumeraffairs.com/news04/2006/06/ftc_debt_management.html).

IDENTITY THEFT

Modern technology and compilation of personal and financial information in computer databases has made obtaining loans faster and easier than in the past. No longer are face-to-face meetings required between creditors and borrowers. Today loans can be secured through the mail, over the phone, and via the Internet. But this convenience has a price. It allows unscrupulous people to pretend to be someone else, to steal the identity of people with good credit histories and use it for criminal purposes.

As shown in Figure 4.8, the number of identity theft complaints reported to the FTC has skyrocketed from around 86,000 in 2001 to more than 250,000 complaints in 2005. According to the FTC publication *Consumer*

FIGURE 4.8

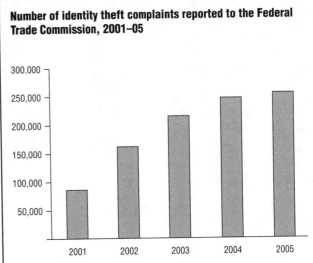

Number of identity theft complaints reported to the Federal Trade Commission, 2001–05

SOURCE: Adapted from "Sentinel Complaints by Calender Year," in *National and State Trends in Fraud and Identity Theft: January–December 2003, Three-Year Trend for Sentinel Complaints*, U.S. Federal Trade Commission, January 22, 2004, http://www.consumer.gov/sentinel/states03/3year_trends.pdf and *Consumer Fraud and Identity Theft Complaint Data: January–December 2005*, U.S. Federal Trade Commission, January 25, 2006, http://www.consumer.gov/sentinel/pubs/Top10Fraud2005.pdf (accessed June 17, 2006)

Fraud and Identity Theft Complaint Data, January–December 2005, the most common outcome of identity theft cases in 2005 was credit card fraud. More than one-fourth of the complaints filed (26%) were associated with credit card fraud. More than half of these cases occurred when consumers were opening new accounts with credit card issuers.

The FTC notes that the ten metropolitan areas—in descending order of number of complaints per one hundred thousand population—associated with the most reported cases of identity theft in 2005 were:

1. Phoenix-Mesa-Scottsdale, Arizona
2. Las Vegas-Paradise, Nevada
3. Riverside-San Bernardino-Ontario, California
4. Dallas-Fort Worth-Arlington, Texas
5. Los Angeles-Long Beach-Santa Ana, California
6. Miami-Fort Lauderdale-Miami Beach, Florida
7. San Francisco-Oakland-Fremont, California
8. Houston-Baytown-Sugar Land, Texas
9. San Diego-Carlsbad-San Marcos, California
10. San Antonio, Texas

CHAPTER 5
WORK AND WORKERS

When we are all in the business working together, we all ought to have some share in the profits—by way of a good wage, or salary, or added compensation.

—Henry Ford, *My Life and Work*, 1922

The American workforce plays a major role in the U.S. economy. Workers produce goods and provide services, the consumption of which drives the nation's gross domestic product (GDP) growth. But there is an age-old struggle between employers and employees over compensation. Businesses must compensate workers with pay and benefits that are high enough to attract and keep motivated employees, but not so high as to damage the profitability and growth of the business itself. On a macroeconomic scale, gainful employment of large numbers of workers is important to the overall health of the U.S. economy.

THE EMPLOYMENT SITUATION

The U.S. Department of Labor's Bureau of Labor Statistics (BLS) conducts a monthly survey of approximately 160,000 nonfarm businesses and government agencies with around 400,000 worksites around the country. Detailed information on employment, work hours, and payroll are obtained as part of the Current Employment Statistics (CES) program. These data are published monthly by the BLS in a news release titled "The Employment Situation."

The BLS defines the civilian labor force as including all civilian noninstitutionalized people age sixteen years or over who have a job or are actively looking for a job. People are considered to be employed during a given week if they meet any of the following criteria:

- They performed any work that week for pay or profit.

- They worked without pay for at least fifteen hours that week in a family-operated enterprise.

- They had a job but could not work that week due to illness, vacation, personal obligations, leave of absence, bad weather, or labor disputes.

People considered not to be in the labor force are those who do not have a job and are not looking for a job. This category includes many students, retirees, stay-at-home moms and dads, the mentally and physically challenged, and people in prison and other institutions, as well as those who are not employed but have become discouraged from looking for work. The unemployed are counted as those who do not have a job but have actively looked for a job during the prior four weeks and are available for work. Also included are people who did not work during a given week due to temporary layoffs.

Table 5.1 lists major findings from the CES for the first quarter of 2006. The civilian labor force averaged just over 150 million people at that time. Another seventy-seven million people were considered to not be in the labor force. Just over seven million people were counted as unemployed, giving an overall unemployment rate of 4.7%. The unemployment rates were much higher than this for minorities and teenagers. Of the nearly 135 million people employed in nonfarm occupations, more than 112 million (or 83%) held service-providing jobs. The other 17% (approximately twenty-two million employees) worked at goods-producing jobs, primarily in manufacturing. Table 5.1 also notes that average earnings for private-sector production or nonsupervisory workers during the quarter were $16.46 per hour, or $556.35 per week.

Employment and Unemployment as of May 2006

In May 2006 the BLS reported that 144 million people were employed in the United States. Nonfarm payroll employment totaled just over 135 million people (based on preliminary estimates). As shown in Figure 5.1, this value has steadily increased from June 2003, when it

TABLE 5.1

Labor market activity, first quarter 2006

[Numbers in thousands, seasonally adjusted]

Category	Quarterly averages 2006 I
Household data	**Labor force status**
Civilian labor force	150,405
Employment	143,324
Unemployment	7,081
Not in labor force	77,359
	Unemployment rates
All workers	4.7
Adult men	4.1
Adult women	4.2
Teenagers	15.5
White	4.1
Black or African American	9.2
Hispanic or Latino ethnicity	5.6
Establishment data	**Employment**
Nonfarm employment	134,722
Goods-producing[a]	22,363
Construction	7,483
Manufacturing	14,226
Service-providing[a]	112,359
Retail trade[b]	15,299
Professional and business services	17,161
Education and health services	17,584
Leisure and hospitality	12,954
Government	21,873
	Hours of work[c]
Total private	33.8
Manufacturing	41.0
Overtime	4.5
	Indexes of aggregate weekly hours (2002=100)[c]
Total private	104.2
	Earnings[c]
Average hourly earnings, total private	$16.46
Average weekly earnings, total private	556.35

[a]Includes other industries, not shown separately.
[b]Quarterly averages are calculated using unrounded data.
[c]Data relate to private production or nonsupervisory workers.
p=preliminary.

SOURCE: Adapted from "Table A. Major Indicators of Labor Market Activity, Seasonally Adjusted," in *News—The Employment Situation: May 2006*, U.S. Department of Labor, Bureau of Labor Statistics, June 2, 2006, http://www.bls.gov/news.release/pdf/empsit.pdf (accessed June 17, 2006)

FIGURE 5.1

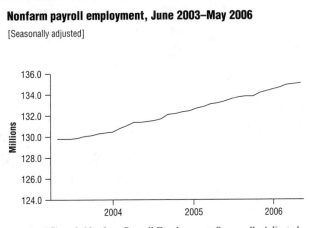

Nonfarm payroll employment, June 2003–May 2006

[Seasonally adjusted]

SOURCE: "Chart 2. Nonfarm Payroll Employment, Seasonally Adjusted, June 2003–May 2006," in *News—The Employment Situation: May 2006*, U.S. Department of Labor, Bureau of Labor Statistics, June 2, 2006, http://www.bls.gov/news.release/pdf/empsit.pdf (accessed June 7, 2006)

FIGURE 5.2

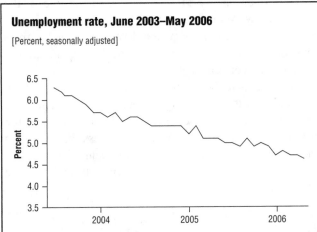

Unemployment rate, June 2003–May 2006

[Percent, seasonally adjusted]

SOURCE: "Chart 1. Unemployment Rate, Seasonally Adjusted, June 2003–May 2006," in *News—The Employment Situation: May 2006*, U.S. Department of Labor, Bureau of Labor Statistics, June 2, 2006, http://www.bls.gov/news.release/pdf/empsit.pdf (accessed June 7, 2006)

stood at around 130 million people. Figure 5.2 indicates that the unemployment rate declined over this same time period from more than 6% in June 2003 to 4.6% in May 2006.

The unemployment rate varied widely according to certain demographic factors in May 2006, as illustrated in Figure 5.3. Teenagers were unemployed at a rate of 14%. Racial and ethnic differences were significant; African-American workers had an unemployment rate of 8.9%, while those of Hispanic or Latino ethnicity had a rate of 5%. These values are higher than the 4.1% unemployment rate reported for white workers. There was virtually no difference by sex among adults; for adult men the rate was 4.2% and for adult women it was 4.1%.

Table 5.2 provides a breakdown on duration of unemployment as of May 2006. Approximately 2.5 million people had been unemployed for less than five weeks at that time. This represents 36% of all the unemployed. Another 2.2 million people (32%) had been unemployed for five to fourteen weeks, and 968,000 (14%) had been unemployed for fifteen to twenty-six weeks. Lastly, more than 1.3 million people (19%) had been unemployed for at least twenty-seven weeks.

A poll conducted by the Gallup Organization in May 2006 found that 41% of those asked felt it was a "good time to find a quality job." (See Figure 5.4.) This compares with 54% who believed that it was a "bad time to

FIGURE 5.3

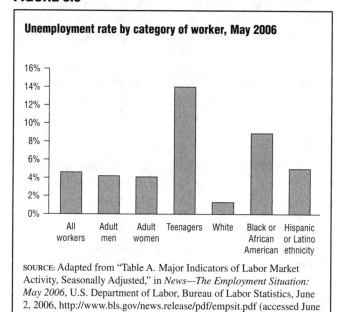

Unemployment rate by category of worker, May 2006

SOURCE: Adapted from "Table A. Major Indicators of Labor Market Activity, Seasonally Adjusted," in *News—The Employment Situation: May 2006*, U.S. Department of Labor, Bureau of Labor Statistics, June 2, 2006, http://www.bls.gov/news.release/pdf/empsit.pdf (accessed June 19, 2006)

TABLE 5.2

Unemployed persons by duration of unemployment, May 2005– May 2006

[Numbers in thousands, seasonally adjusted]

Duration	May 2006
Number of unemployed	
Less than 5 weeks	2,516
5 to 14 weeks	2,242
15 weeks and over	2,297
15 to 26 weeks	968
27 weeks and over	1,329
Average (mean) duration, in weeks	17.1
Median duration, in weeks	8.5
Percent distribution	
Total unemployed	100.0
Less than 5 weeks	35.7
5 to 14 weeks	31.8
15 weeks and over	32.6
15 to 26 weeks	13.7
27 weeks and over	18.8

Note: Data reflect revised population controls used in the household survey.

SOURCE: Adapted from "Table A-9. Unemployed Persons by Duration of Unemployment," in *News—The Employment Situation: May 2006*, U.S. Department of Labor, Bureau of Labor Statistics, June 2, 2006, http://www.bls.gov/news.release/pdf/empsit.pdf (accessed June 17, 2006)

find a quality job." The number of people who believe that the timing was right to find a good job has increased since the early 2000s.

JOBS

The federal government broadly characterizes jobs as being in the goods-providing or services-providing categories. Goods-providing industries include businesses

FIGURE 5.4

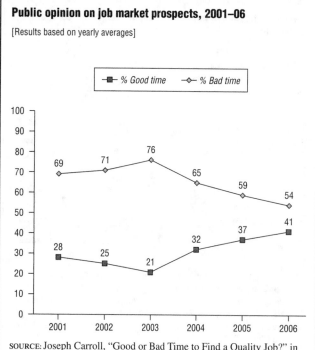

Public opinion on job market prospects, 2001–06

[Results based on yearly averages]

SOURCE: Joseph Carroll, "Good or Bad Time to Find a Quality Job?" in *Americans Remain More Positive about Job Market*, The Gallup Organization, June 6, 2006, http://www.galluppoll.com/content/?ci=23215 (accessed September 19, 2006). Copyright © 2006 by The Gallup Organization. Reproduced by permission of The Gallup Organization.

engaged in manufacturing, construction, mining, and natural resources. The service industry includes businesses whose main function is to provide a professional or trade service, rather than a product. Service-providing industries are extremely diverse and include businesses involved in retail and wholesale trade, professional and business services, education and health services, leisure and hospitality, government, and numerous other services.

Since the mid-twentieth century the service-providing industries have grown to dominate the U.S. economy. (See Figure 5.5.) In 1960 goods-producing industries employed around nineteen million people. This value has increased slowly over time, reaching twenty-two million in 2005. By comparison, the number of people employed in service-providing industries has skyrocketed from around thirty-five million in 1960 to 111 million in 2005.

Industry "Supersectors"

Jobs are categorized by the government using the North American Industry Classification System (NAICS; pronounced "Nakes"). Adopted in 1997, NAICS was devised by the U.S. Economic Classification Policy Committee in conjunction with Statistics Canada and the Instituto Nacional de Estadística, Geografía e Informática

FIGURE 5.5

Payroll employees in nonfarm occupations, selected years 1960–2005

☐ Goods producing   ■ Services

Millions of employees

SOURCE: Adapted from "Table B-1. Employees on Nonfarm Payrolls by Major Industry Sector, 1956 to Date," in *Employment Situation, Supplemental Files: Monthly Tables from Employment and Earnings (Establishment Data)*, U.S. Department of Labor, Bureau of Labor Statistics, June 2006, ftp://ftp.bls.gov/pub/suppl/EMPSIT.CESEEB1.txt (accessed June 19, 2006)

of Mexico, and is the standard classification system for businesses throughout North America. There are twelve major so-called "supersectors" tracked by the BLS that encompass all private and public jobs within the United States and businesses owned by U.S.-based companies operating in other countries.

The twelve supersectors are:

- Construction
- Education and health services
- Financial activities
- Government
- Information
- Leisure and hospitality
- Manufacturing
- Natural resources and mining
- Other services
- Professional and business services
- Transportation and utilities
- Wholesale and retail trade

Virtually every job can be placed into one of these categories. It should be noted that industry tracking focuses on the core mission of the business rather than on the particular tasks performed by employees. For example, jobs in public schools and government-owned hospitals are considered part of the government sector rather than education and health services.

Industry and job data in the following sections were obtained from *Industry at a Glance*, an online profile of American business maintained by the BLS at http://stats.bls.gov/iag/iaghome.htm.

CONSTRUCTION. The construction supersector includes all businesses that contribute to the development of land, roads, utilities, buildings, and such structures as bridges and dams. Included are firms that build new projects and those that provide maintenance, repairs, and alterations to existing structures. For the most part, such enterprises are managed from a central location with work performed elsewhere.

In 2005 construction employment accounted for 5% of all employment and 30% of employment in the goods-producing sectors, according to the BLS. More than 60% of goods-producing establishments were engaged in construction. This supersector employed nearly 7.3 million people in 2005, up from 5.5 million in 1996. Employment in construction increased steadily over that time period and has been predicted by the BLS to increase by 11.4% between 2004 and 2014. But the 2005 unemployment rate among people most recently employed in construction was 7.4%, higher than the overall unemployment rate of 5.1% for that year. Construction employment often fluctuates throughout the year, especially in areas of the country that experience severe winter weather.

EDUCATION AND HEALTH SERVICES. The education and health services supersector includes all instructional and training facilities, including private schools and universities, that are not funded by the government. Nongovernmental organizations that provide child day care, medical care, and social assistance are also included. Businesses of this type that are government owned (public schools and hospitals, for example) are considered part of the government sector.

In 2005 employment in education and health services accounted for 1.6% and 10.8%, respectively, of all employment. This supersector employed 17.3 million people in 2005, up from 13.7 million in 1996. Employment in these fields increased steadily over that time period and has been predicted by the BLS to increase by at least 30% between 2004 and 2014. This rate of increase is the highest projected for any industry. The 2005 unemployment rate among people most recently employed in education and health services was 3.4%.

FINANCIAL ACTIVITIES. The financial activities supersector includes the banking, insurance, and real estate industries, including businesses that, according to *Industry at a Glance*, facilitate "transactions involving the creation, liquidation, or change in ownership of financial assets." The real estate sector includes businesses that manage properties for others, appraise real estate, and facilitate property buying, selling, and leasing.

In 2005 employment in financial activities accounted for 4.5% of all employment. This supersector employed 8.1 million people in 2005, representing a steady increase from nearly seven million people in 1996. The BLS predicts that employment in this sector will increase by 10.5% between 2004 and 2014. The 2005 unemployment rate among people most recently employed in financial activities was 2.9%.

GOVERNMENT. The government sector encompasses all local, state, and federal government agencies as well as public schools and public hospitals. This includes law enforcement agencies, courts, and legislative assemblies but, for the purposes of industry tracking, does not include military personnel.

In 2005 employment in government accounted for 16.1% of all employment broken down as follows: federal (2.1% of total), state (3.5% of total), and local (10.5% of total). This supersector employed 21.8 million people in 2005, having increased steadily from 19.5 million in 1996. According to the BLS, employment in the government supersector should increase by 14.8% between 2004 and 2014. Growth in state and local government employment accounts for 11.3% of the increase. Only a 1.6% increase is projected for federal government employment. The 2005 unemployment rate among people most recently employed in government was 2.6%.

INFORMATION. The production and distribution of information falls under the information supersector of the American economy. This supersector includes book and software publishing, Internet service providers, and television broadcasting, as well as the motion picture and sound recording industries.

In 2005 employment in the information industry accounted for 2.4% of all employment. This supersector employed nearly 3.1 million people in 2005, up slightly from 2.9 million people in 1996. Employment in this field increased through the late 1990s before peaking in the early 2000s and then declining. The BLS expects employment in this sector to increase by 11.6% between 2004 and 2014. The 2005 unemployment rate among people most recently employed in the information industry was 5%.

LEISURE AND HOSPITALITY. The leisure and hospitality supersector contains businesses in the arts, entertainment, recreation, spectator sports, accommodation, and food service industries. This includes performance venues, gambling outlets, golf courses, amusement parks, arcades, hotels and other lodging sites, food service establishments, and privately funded exhibit spaces and historic sites.

In 2005 employment in leisure and hospitality accounted for 9.6% of all employment, broken down as follows: accommodation and food services (8.2%) and arts, entertainment, and recreation (1.4%). This supersector employed 12.8 million people in 2005, up steadily from nearly 10.8 million people in 1996. Employment in this field has been predicted by the BLS to increase by 17.7% between 2004 and 2014. The 2005 unemployment rate among those most recently employed in leisure and hospitality was 7.8%.

MANUFACTURING. An organization is considered part of the manufacturing supersector if its primary business is to transform raw materials into new products through mechanical, physical, or chemical processes. Manufacturing covers many separate industries, including aerospace, apparel, computers, automobiles, pharmaceuticals, printing, steel, and textiles, among others, and provides products that contribute and support all other economic sectors.

In 2005 employment in manufacturing accounted for 11% of all employment and 62% of goods-producing employment. This supersector employed 10.1 million people in 2005, down from more than seventeen million people in 1996. Employment in this field remained relatively steady through the late 1990s and then declined sharply in the early 2000s before leveling off between 2003 and 2005. The BLS predicts that manufacturing employment will continue to decrease by 5.4% through 2014. The 2005 unemployment rate among people most recently employed in manufacturing was 4.9%.

NATURAL RESOURCES AND MINING. The natural resources and mining supersector includes all agriculture, forestry, fishing, hunting, and mining enterprises. Farms engaged in growing crops and raising animals are included in this sector, as are lumber and fishing operations, coal mining, petroleum and natural gas extraction, and other mining and quarrying activities.

In 2005 employment in natural resources and mining made up 1.3% of all employment and approximately 7.3% of goods-producing employment. This supersector employed 625,000 people in 2005. Employment in this field has remained relatively flat since 1996 and has been predicted by the BLS to decrease by 10.7% through 2014. This is the largest projected decrease of any industry. The 2005 unemployment rate among those most recently employed in agriculture, forestry, fishing, and hunting was 8.3%, while the rate among people most recently employed in the mining industries was 3.1%.

OTHER SERVICES. This supersector includes such jobs as repairing equipment and machinery, promoting or administering religious activities, operating dry cleaning and laundry services, conducting personal care, death care, and pet care services, and supplying photo processing services, temporary parking, and dating services. People who work in grant making and advocacy are also included in this category.

In 2005 employment in the other services category accounted for 3.3% of all employment. This supersector employed nearly 5.4 million people in 2005, up from around 4.5 million people in 1996. Employment in this field increased steadily over that time period and has been predicted by the BLS to increase by 11.8% between 2004 and 2014. The 2005 unemployment rate among people most recently employed in other services was 4.8%.

PROFESSIONAL AND BUSINESS SERVICES. Professional and business services include legal, accounting, architectural, engineering, advertising, marketing, translation, and veterinary services. This sector also includes those who manage companies and all of the administrative support needed for a business to operate. In addition, security, surveillance, cleaning, and waste disposal services are tracked in this sector.

In 2005 employment in professional and business services accounted for 12.6% of all employment broken down as follows: professional, scientific, and technical services (5.2%); management of companies and enterprises (1.3%); and administrative and support and waste management and remediation services (6.1%). This supersector employed nearly 16.9 million people in 2005, up from fewer than fourteen million people in 1996. Employment in this field increased dramatically during the late 1990s before undergoing a mild decline in the early 2000s. Following a leveling off period in 2002 and 2003, employment began to rise again. Employment has been predicted by the BLS to increase by 27.8% through 2014. The 2005 unemployment rate among people most recently employed in professional and business services was 6.2%.

TRANSPORTATION, WAREHOUSING, AND UTILITIES. The transportation, warehousing, and utilities supersector includes businesses that transport passengers or cargo by air, rail, water, road, or pipeline. The sector also includes businesses that provide storage of goods and that support transportation activities. Also tracked in this sector are private enterprises that generate, transmit, or distribute such utilities as electric power, natural gas, and water.

In 2005 employment in transportation, warehousing, and utilities made up 3.5% of all employment, broken down as follows: transportation and warehousing (3.1%; 4.3 million employees) and utilities (0.4%; 557,600 employees). Employment in transportation and warehousing has increased slightly since 1996, when approximately four million people were employed. The utilities sector has lost employees since 1996, when 639,600 people were employed. Employment has been predicted by the BLS to increase by 11.9% in the transportation and warehousing sector and decrease by 1.3% in the utilities sector through 2014. The 2005 unemployment rate among people most recently employed in transportation, warehousing, and utilities was 4.1%.

WHOLESALE AND RETAIL TRADE. The wholesale and retail supersector encompasses private businesses that trade in products that they do not produce. Wholesalers buy large quantities of finished goods from manufacturers and sell the goods in smaller lots to businesses engaged in retail trade. Retailers then offer the goods for sale to consumers at an increased price, usually figured as a percentage of the wholesale cost. Goods in this sector are classified as durable (expected to last longer than three years) or nondurable (expected to need replacement within three years). Consumer goods in the durable sector include motor vehicles, furniture, household appliances, sporting goods, and toys. Durable goods are also sold to other businesses—for example, to the manufacturing or construction sector, including such items as machinery, equipment, metals, and construction materials. Examples of nondurable goods include paper products, drugs, apparel, groceries, books, flowers, and tobacco products. While the traditional notion of a retail establishment includes at least one store location, many retailers in the early twenty-first century operate via Internet and/or catalog sales without stores.

In 2005 employment in wholesale and retail trade accounted for 16% of all employment, broken down as follows: wholesale trade (4.4%, or 5.7 million employees) and retail trade (11.6%, or 15.2 million employees). Employment in this field has increased slightly since 1996 and has been predicted by the BLS to increase by 8.4% for wholesale trade and by 11% for retail trade between 2004 and 2014. The 2005 unemployment rate among those most recently employed in wholesale and retail trade was 5.4%.

JOB SUPERSECTOR EMPLOYMENT AS OF MAY 2006. Table 5.3 provides a breakdown of the number of employees working in each nonfarm job sector as of May 2006. At that time more than 135 million people were listed on nonfarm payrolls. Government employed nearly twenty-two million people, making it the largest job sector. Other major sectors include professional and business services (17.2 million employees), retail trade (15.2 million employees), health services (14.8 million employees), and manufacturing (14.2 million employees).

Table 5.3 also shows the changes in employment in each sector between May 2005 and May 2006. Natural resources and mining had the largest increase in employment, at 8.7%. Modest gains were achieved in construction (up 3.5%), financial activities and professional and business services (both up 2.7%), and health services (up 2.4%). Several job sectors lost employees over the year:

TABLE 5.3

Employees on nonfarm payrolls, May 2006

Job sector	Thousands of employees, May 2006	Change from May 2005
Government	21,916	0.7%
Professional & business services	17,243	2.7%
Retail trade	15,236	−0.1%
Health services	14,823	2.4%
Manufacturing	14,230	−0.1%
Leisure & hospitality	12,995	1.7%
Financial activities	8,322	2.7%
Construction	7,512	3.5%
Wholesale trade	5,850	1.9%
Other services	5,413	0.5%
Transportation & warehousing	4,399	1.2%
Information	3,055	−0.3%
Educational services	2,876	2.2%
Natural resources & mining	674	8.7%
Utilities	561	0.9%
Total	**135,106**	**1.4%**

Note: Individual sectors do not sum to total due to rounding.

SOURCE: Adapted from "Table B-1. Employees on Nonfarm Payrolls by Industry Sector and Selected Industry Detail," in *News—The Employment Situation: May 2006*, U.S. Department of Labor, Bureau of Labor Statistics, June 2, 2006, http://www.bls.gov/news.release/pdf/empsit.pdf (accessed June 19, 2006)

information (down 0.3%); manufacturing (down 0.1%); and retail trade (down 0.1%).

LABOR UNIONS

Although many historians trace the origins of labor unions to medieval guilds (organized groups of tradespeople and artisans in the Middle Ages), the modern labor movement is more directly linked to the trade unions of the early Industrial Revolution, when working conditions in factories and mines were barely tolerable and employees began to join together to demand reasonable work hours, safe conditions, and decent wages. Unions have often had tense relationships with both employers and government; at times they have been banned altogether, and the struggle between labor and employers has sometimes resulted in violence.

Labor unions have had a significant impact on the American workforce and labor policy. Unions are often able to secure higher wages and increased benefits for their members. The BLS reported in "Union Members in 2005" that 15.7 million wage and salary workers were union members in 2005. This represents 12.5% of all wage and salary workers. The percentage is unchanged from 2004, but it is significantly lower that the peak of 20.1% reached in 1983. According to the report, more than a third (36.5%) of government workers were unionized in 2005, compared with only 7.8% of private industry workers. Local governments have the most highly unionized employees, particularly teachers, police officers, and firefighters. The highest rates of union membership in the private industries are found in the transportation and utilities, information, construction, and manufacturing sectors (*Union Members Summary*, January 20, 2006, http://www.bls.gov/news.release/union2.nr0.htm).

Despite their successes on behalf of American workers, contemporary labor unions continue to face opposition from employers, and often from employees, who question whether the benefits of being associated with a union are worth the costs. Union members are required to go on strike when the union has an unresolved grievance against an employer, and striking union members receive only a fraction of their income in strike pay. Workers who are part of a union may also find themselves facing fines for not abiding by the union bylaws.

For employers, unions can pose other problems. Business operations can be greatly interrupted by unresolved negotiations, whether or not they lead to a strike. Further, due to the increased expenses associated with employing union members, a company's products or services might become less competitively priced in the marketplace. If sales are lost to foreign or nonunion competitors, companies may be forced to lay off employees or even go out of business.

COMPENSATION OF AMERICAN WORKERS

Compensation has two components: pay and benefits. Pay includes wages (which is the term used primarily for pay made on an hourly, weekly, or monthly basis) and salaries (which is pay calculated on an annual basis). Benefits provided by employers include paid time off from work, various insurance and retirement plans, and other programs designed to attract and keep employees.

Table 5.4 shows the wage and salary disbursements and supplements paid by employers in 2004, 2005, and calculated for 2006 based on first-quarter 2006 values. It is estimated that more than $7.3 trillion was to be paid out in compensation in 2006, up from $6.7 trillion in 2004 and $7.1 trillion in 2005. In addition, nearly $1.5 trillion in supplements was estimated to be contributed by employers in 2006, primarily for employee pensions and insurance funds. In 2004 and 2005 these supplements totaled about $1.3 trillion and $1.4 trillion, respectively.

Income

The U.S. Census Bureau reported in *Income, Poverty, and Health Insurance Coverage in the United States: 2004* (August 2005, http://www.census.gov/prod/2005pubs/p60-229.pdf) that the median U.S. household income in 2004 was $44,389. Although this value is higher than the median of $43,318 reported in 2003, there is actually no difference when inflation is considered.

Incomes differed by householder characteristics, such as age, education, work experience, and race or ethnic

TABLE 5.4

Personal income, 2004–first quarter 2006

[Billions of dollars, seasonally adjusted at annual rates]

	2004	2005*	2006 Q1*
Personal income	9,713.3	10,237.7	10,593.7
Compensation of employees, received	6,687.6	7,113.1	7,329.5
Wage and salary disbursements	5,389.4	5,712.3	5,867.4
Private industries	4,450.0	4,740.7	4,876.2
Goods-producing industries	1,049.9	1,117.4	1,142.1
Manufacturing	687.7	720.0	726.3
Services-producing industries	3,400.1	3,623.3	3,734.2
Trade, transportation, and utilities	899.7	953.9	975.4
Other services-producing industries	2,500.4	2,669.5	2,758.7
Government	939.5	971.6	991.2
Supplements to wages and salaries	1,298.1	1,400.8	1,462.1
Employer contributions for employee pension and insurance funds	895.5	975.0	1,022.9
Employer contributions for government social insurance	402.7	425.8	439.1

*Revised. Revisions include changes to series affected by the introduction of revised wage and salary estimates for the fourth quarter of 2005.

SOURCE: Adapted from "Table 2. Personal Income and Its Disposition (Years and Quarters)," in *Personal Income and Outlays: 2006 (BEA 06–21)*, U.S. Department of Commerce, Bureau of Economic Analysis, May 26, 2006, http://www.bea.gov/bea/newsrelarchive/2006/pi0406.pdf (accessed June 19, 2006)

FIGURE 5.6

Poll respondents on receipt of pay raises during previous year, 1999–2005

HAVE YOU, PERSONALLY, RECEIVED A PAY RAISE FROM YOUR EMPLOYER IN THE PAST 12 MONTHS?

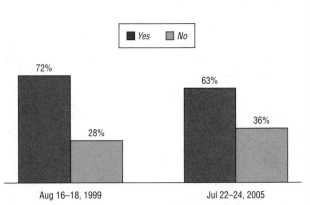

SOURCE: Raksha Arora, "Have you, personally, received a pay raise from your employer in the past 12 months?" in *Consumers Fall Behind on Getting Ahead*, The Gallup Organization, September 20, 2005, http://poll.gallup.com/content/default.aspx?ci=18679 (accessed June 20, 2006). Copyright © 2005 by The Gallup Organization. Reproduced by permission of The Gallup Organization.

origin. For example, the median annual income of householders ages fifteen to twenty-four years was $27,586, compared with $61,111 for those ages forty-five to fifty-four years. White non-Hispanic householders had a median annual income of $48,977 in 2004. This was less than the median income of Asian-American householders ($57,518) but greater than that of African-American householders ($30,134).

RAISES. Because of price inflation, the cost of paying for goods and services increases each year for consumers. If workers do not receive a comparable increase in pay, it becomes more difficult for them to maintain their standard of living. In July 2005 the Gallup Organization conducted a poll in which workers were asked about whether they had received a pay raise from their employers in the previous twelve months and, if so, how that pay raise affected their financial situation. As shown in Figure 5.6, a majority of respondents (63%) had received a pay raise during the previous year. This value compares with 72% recorded when the same question was asked by Gallup in August of 1999. Nearly half of the people who reported receiving a pay raise in the 2005 survey believed they had "lost ground" financially over the previous year in the face of rising prices. (See Figure 5.7.) A like amount reported they had "gained ground" financially. Five percent of those receiving raises reported no change in their financial situation. Among all employed adults contacted for the 2005 poll (those who received raises and those who did not), two-thirds believed they had "lost ground," while 30% felt they had "gained ground" over the previous year.

FIGURE 5.7

Public opinion on pay raises received and financial impact, July 2005

THINKING ABOUT THE AMOUNT OF YOUR PAY RAISE IN COMPARISON TO RISING PRICES, WOULD YOU SAY YOU HAVE GAINED GROUND FINANCIALLY OR HAVE LOST GROUND FINANCIALLY IN THE LAST YEAR?

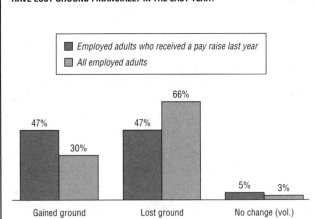

SOURCE: Raksha Arora, "Thinking about the amount of your pay raise in comparison to rising prices, would you say you have gained ground financially or have lost ground financially in the last year?" in *Consumers Fall Behind on Getting Ahead*, The Gallup Organization, September 20, 2005, http://poll.gallup.com/content/default.aspx?ci=18679 (accessed June 20, 2006). Copyright © 2005 by The Gallup Organization. Reproduced by permission of The Gallup Organization.

Benefits

In order to attract and keep the best employees and earn a level of loyalty from them, many U.S. employers offer benefits and incentives. The BLS tracks the avail-

FIGURE 5.8

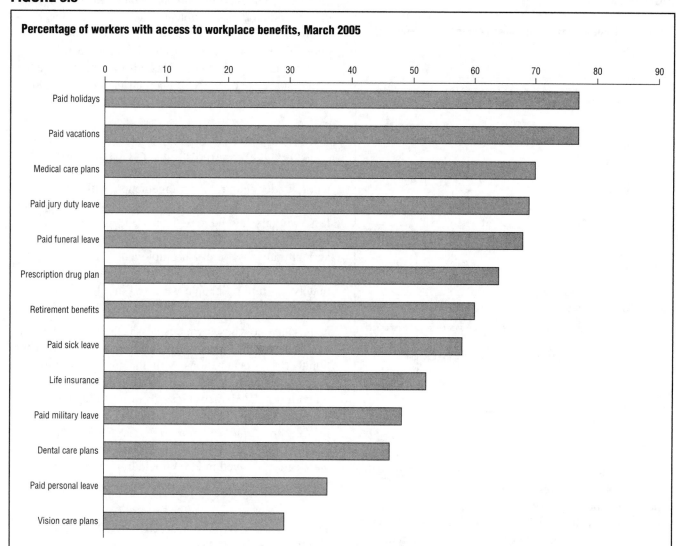

Percentage of workers with access to workplace benefits, March 2005

SOURCE: Adapted from "Table 1. Percent of Workers with Access to Retirement and Healthcare Benefits, by Selected Characteristics, Private Industry, National Compensation Survey, March 2005," and "Table 4. Percent of Workers with Access to Life Insurance and Disability Benefits, by Selected Characteristics, Private Industry, National Compensation Survey, March 2005," and "Table 18. Percent of Workers with Access to Selected Leave Benefits, by Selected Characteristics, Private Industry, National Compensation Survey, March 2005," in *National Compensation Survey: Employee Benefits in Private Industry in the United States, March 2005 (Summary 05–01)*, U.S. Department of Labor, Bureau of Labor Statistics, August 2005, http://www.bls.gov/ncs/ebs/sp/ebsm0003.pdf (accessed June 19, 2006)

ability of employee benefits using national surveys. In August 2005 the agency published *National Compensation Survey: Employee Benefits in Private Industry in the United States, March 2005*. The results are illustrated in Figure 5.8.

As of March 2005, a large majority of employees (77%) in private industry had access to paid holidays and vacations. These were the most commonly offered benefits. Other benefits available to more than two-thirds of the workforce were medical care plans (70%), paid jury duty leave (69%), and paid funeral leave (68%). More than half of employees also had access to prescription drug plans, retirement benefits, paid sick leave, and life insurance. Less commonly offered benefits include paid

military leave, dental care plans, paid personal leave, and vision care plans.

In general, employees working for larger companies—those with more than one hundred employees—and union members had the highest access to company benefits.

MEDICAL INSURANCE. Typically, the total cost of monthly health insurance coverage is split between employers and employees, with employers paying the largest portion. As shown in Figure 3.8 in Chapter 3, the price of medical care grew at a faster rate between 1996 and 2005 than the price of all other consumer expenses. Due to rising health care costs, medical insurance has become a costly benefit for both employers and employees.

FIGURE 5.9

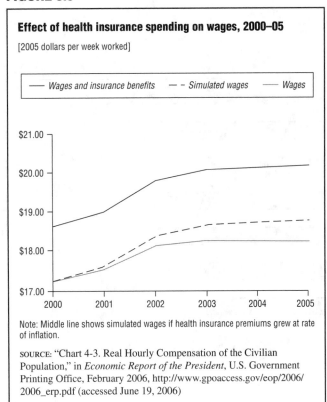

Effect of health insurance spending on wages, 2000–05

[2005 dollars per week worked]

— Wages and insurance benefits   – – Simulated wages   — Wages

Note: Middle line shows simulated wages if health insurance premiums grew at rate of inflation.

SOURCE: "Chart 4-3. Real Hourly Compensation of the Civilian Population," in *Economic Report of the President*, U.S. Government Printing Office, February 2006, http://www.gpoaccess.gov/eop/2006/2006_erp.pdf (accessed June 19, 2006)

The BLS estimates that rising expenses for health insurance premiums are depressing wages. In other words, employers are paying lower wages than they otherwise would, because they are devoting so much money to providing health care coverage. As shown in Figure 5.9, paid hourly wages have remained relatively flat since 2002, while the price of insurance benefits has increased. As a result, a disparity has developed between actual wages and the wages that could have been paid if health insurance premiums had grown at the same rate as inflation over this time period.

NONTRADITIONAL WORK ARRANGEMENTS

Working from Home

In September 2005 a BLS report indicated that 20.7 million people worked from home at least once per week as of May 2004 ("Work at Home Summary," September 22, 2005, http://www.bls.gov/news.release/homey.nr0.htm). This represents approximately 15% of the total nonagricultural workforce, a value virtually unchanged from May 2001. The data were collected as part of a special supplement to the monthly Current Population Survey. Nearly two-thirds of the at-home workers in 2004 were wage and salary earners. The remainder was self-employed.

With technological advances such as Internet access, e-mail, and teleconferencing, working at home has become a viable option for many types of jobs. As

employees conduct much of their daily work from home offices, employers are able to save on operating costs. Many employers will pay for computers, additional telephone lines, and even utilities to allow their employees to work from home offices. This allows them to reduce office space, one of the higher costs for an employer, especially in large metropolitan markets.

Self-Employment

Self-employed workers are not on the payroll of a company. They may own or operate small businesses or work under contract arrangements with companies. According to the BLS, the number of self-employed U.S. workers has increased over the past few decades. In 1970 just over five million people working in non-agricultural jobs were self-employed. By the mid-1990s the number had reached around nine million. Approximately 9.5 million people were self-employed in 2005.

For the purposes of its statistical findings, the BLS counts anyone whose own business is their primary source of income as self-employed, whether or not they are incorporated. The occupations with the most self-employed individuals are managerial operations and sales- and marketing-related activities. But self-employment is common in other businesses as well. The BLS estimated in *Career Guide to Industries: 2006–07 Edition* that approximately 1.9 million construction industry workers were self-employed in 2004, including more than 40% of painters, paperhangers, and flooring installers.

FOREIGN WORKERS IN THE UNITED STATES

Relatively high wages and favorable working conditions have attracted workers from around the world to the United States. There are two broad categories of foreign workers: those who have entered the country legally with the proper paperwork to pursue work and those who have entered illegally. Legal workers are tracked by the U.S. Citizenship and Immigration Service (USCIS), formerly the Immigration and Naturalization Service.

Legal Foreign Workers

The U.S. Department of Labor issues a limited number of certifications to foreign workers to work in the United States on a temporary or permanent basis under the following programs:

- Permanent Labor Certification—Allows a foreign worker to work permanently in the United States

- H-1B Specialty (Professional) Workers—Temporary certification for workers in occupations requiring highly specialized knowledge with at least a bachelor's degree or equivalent

- H-2A Temporary Labor Certification (Seasonal Agricultural)—For workers engaged in agricultural labor or services of a temporary or seasonal nature working for employers anticipating a shortage of U.S. workers

- H-2B Temporary Labor Certification (Nonagricultural)—For nonagricultural laborers working for employers anticipating a shortage of U.S. workers; the need can be a one-time occurrence, seasonal, peak load, or intermittent

- D-1 Crewmembers Certification—For longshoremen hired to work at U.S. ports; there are numerous restrictions, one of which is that there cannot be a strike or lockout ongoing that keeps U.S. longshoremen from working

According to the DOL, "certification may be obtained in cases where it can be demonstrated that there are insufficient qualified U.S. workers available and willing to perform the work at wages that meet or exceed the prevailing wage paid for that occupation in the area of intended employment."

The U.S. Department of Homeland Security's Office of Immigration Statistics (OIS) tracks the number of foreign workers entering the United States and publishes related data in annual reports. The latest report available on nonimmigrant (temporary) foreign workers is "Estimates of the Nonimmigrant Population in the United States: 2004," published in June 2006 (http://www.uscis.gov/graphics/shared/statistics/publications/NIM_2004.pdf). The report notes that there were approximately 700,000 temporary workers in the United States in 2004. Legal permanent residents are foreigners who have obtained "green cards" and have been granted permanent residency in the United States. According to the OIS report "U.S. Legal Permanent Residents: 2005," published in April 2006, approximately 247,000 foreigners were granted employment-based legal permanent residency during 2005 (http://www.uscis.gov/graphics/shared/statistics/publications/USLegalPermEst_5.pdf).

Temporary foreign workers maintain the citizenship of their native countries, and after fulfilling their contracts with U.S. employers they typically return to their own countries. Immigrant workers are people who have come to the United States through legal channels and intend to become citizens, obtaining jobs while they are waiting for their naturalization (the process of becoming a U.S. citizen) to be finalized.

Illegal Foreign Workers

The issue of illegal immigration has become a heated topic, particularly in 2006. Much of the debate centers on the economic effect of undocumented workers—foreign workers who have entered the United States illegally. Some people claim that undocumented workers take jobs away from Americans and place a large burden on government-provided social programs. Others believe that undocumented workers are willing to take jobs that Americans do not want—low paying, labor-intensive jobs with no benefits and little to no chance for advancement.

Employers are required by law to verify that new hires are U.S. citizens or foreigners with legal working status who are eligible to work in the United States. Job applicants have to show identification and documentation, including a Social Security card. But the authenticity of these documents cannot be verified immediately. Thus, well-meaning businesses may unknowingly hire and train illegal workers who have used fake documentation to obtain jobs. According to the *Christian Science Monitor*, as of December 2003 the Social Security Administration had $374 billion in funds that could not be matched to valid Social Security numbers. It is believed that much of the money was paid into the system by illegal workers using fake Social Security numbers ("Jobs and Illegal Immigrants," December 4, 2003, http://www.csmonitor.com/2003/1204/p08s03-comv.htm).

In 2005 the *New York Times* estimated that illegal immigrants pay up to $7 billion per year into the Social Security system (Eduardo Porter, "Illegal Immigrants Are Bolstering Social Security with Billions," April 5, 2005). This represents approximately 1% of the total $700 billion paid into the system during 2005 by all workers.

There is little doubt that some businesses purposely hire illegal workers or at least ignore questionable paperwork in order to get inexpensive labor. In April 2006 the Associated Press reported on what it calls "an underground employment network" in the United States that encourages and facilitates the employment of illegal immigrants from Mexico and Central and South America ("Many Illegal Immigrants Have Jobs in U.S. before Crossing Border," April 16, 2006, http://www.foxnews.com/story/0,2933,191889,00.html). The article notes that lax enforcement of laws prohibiting the hiring of illegal workers has allowed the network to flourish. Many critics maintain that the federal government's focus on terrorism and national security has diminished attention on issues related to undocumented workers. Others believe that businesses willing to hire the workers are to blame. Like many factors in the U.S. economy, the issue of undocumented workers is driven by supply and demand factors. As one analyst notes in the article: "It continues to be clear who controls immigration; it's not governments, but rather the market."

POLITICAL DEBATE AND PUBLIC PROTEST. An August 2006 report from the Department of Homeland Security estimated that there were around eleven million illegal immigrants in the United States at the beginning of 2006 ("Estimates of the Unauthorized Immigrant Population Residing in the United States, January 2005"). Illegal immigration has become a politically charged and divisive issue. In late 2005 the U.S. Congress and Senate began drafting immigration reform bills designed to deal with the problem. Both bodies called for tighter border security. The Senate bill would allow many illegal immigrants already in the country the opportunity to obtain U.S. citizenship under certain conditions. This so-called amnesty provision has received harsh criticism from some politicians, but it has been advocated by the administration of President George W. Bush. A much tougher bill drafted in the House contained provisions that would make illegal immigrants felons. (It is a felony to enter the U.S. illegally, but illegal immigrants that are already in the United States face only civil penalties when caught.)

In December 2005 passage of the House bill caused a firestorm of controversy, particularly among the nation's Hispanic and Latino populations. In March 2006 demonstrations were held in major cities around the country to protest the proposed legislation. According to a *New York Times* report, "hundreds of thousands" of demonstrators participated in marches across the country (Linda Chavez, "American Dreams, Foreign Flags," March 30, 2006.) Another massive demonstration was held on May 1, 2006, in honor of "May Day," or International Worker's Day—a day historically used by activists to push for workers' rights. Organizers called for immigrants to skip work and forego shopping as part of a one-day economic boycott designed to illustrate their presence and financial clout. Media reports estimated that hundreds of thousands of immigrants and supporters participated in the event.

As of August 2006, the House and Senate bills were "in conference," meaning that a commission was working to combine the bills into one piece of legislation acceptable to both bodies. Due to the large differences in the bills, analysts have predicted that an acceptable compromise will probably not be possible in the near future.

AMERICAN JOBS GOING TO FOREIGN COUNTRIES

One consequence of the globalization of American business has been "offshoring"—the transfer of jobs from the United States to other countries. This can occur when an entire business establishment, such as a factory or service center, is relocated to another nation or when certain jobs within a business are transferred to a foreign company. The latter is also an example of outsourcing—a business practice in which certain tasks within a company are contracted out to another firm. (Outsourcing may or may not involve sending work to another country.) During the 1990s outsourcing became a popular means of reducing costs for some companies. Noncore functions,

such as payroll management or housekeeping, are common examples in which outsourcing can be cost effective. Offshoring is controversial, because jobs move outside of the United States, primarily to developing countries where labor costs are much cheaper.

Critics say that offshoring harms the U.S. economy by putting Americans out of work. Others claim that relocation of some operations to foreign countries has a very limited effect on domestic employment. They argue that offshoring leads to lower prices for consumer and investment goods, with the ultimate effect of raising real wages (wages that are adjusted for changes in the price of consumer goods) and living standards in the United States.

In 2004 the BLS published data on the relationship between extended mass layoffs and overseas job relocations. An extended mass layoff is defined as an event in which at least fifty initial claims for unemployment benefits are filed against an establishment during a five-week period. According to a BLS press release issued June 10, 2004, the layoffs of 4,633 workers during the first quarter of 2004 were associated with job relocations to other countries (http://www.bls.gov/news.release/reloc.nr0.htm). This number represents just 1.9% of the total of 239,361 private-sector nonfarm workers who were separated from their jobs for at least thirty-one days during the quarter. Overseas relocations within the same company accounted for 2,976 lost jobs, while 1,657 jobs were lost to overseas workers employed by different companies.

In December 2004 a study published by Duke University's Fuqua School of Business in conjunction with Archstone Consulting found that offshoring had been very cost effective for large U.S. companies. Researchers studied the offshoring experiences of ninety large companies with average annual revenues of $21 billion. A large majority (72%) of offshore implementations had met or bettered expected costs savings. As a result, companies indicated great willingness to pursue additional offshoring opportunities. The report notes that the functions most often offshored were information technology (66%), finance and accounting (60%), engineering services (44%), and research (32%). Eighty percent of offshored operations had been transferred to India ("Fortune 500 Reap Early Cost Benefits from Offshoring Initiatives," December 10, 2004, http://www.fuqua.duke.edu/admin/extaff/news/fortune_offshore_dec_2004.htm). A combination of relatively low costs and a large number of well-educated workers who speak English has made India a popular location to offshore work.

A 2005 report published in *The McKinsey Quarterly* estimates that approximately 274,000 software and business-process jobs were moved from the United States to India between 2000 and 2003 ("Don't Blame Trade for U.S. Job Losses," http://www.mckinseyquarterly.com/article_page.aspx?ar=1559&L2=19&L3=67). The article notes that "although the costs were substantial for the displaced employees, a job shift of this size is small compared with the 2.1 million service jobs created every year during the 1990s and minor compared even with the net annual job increase of about 327,000 from 2000 to 2003."

PROTECTING AMERICAN WORKERS

The United States has enacted comprehensive labor laws to ensure that workplaces are operated safely and workers are treated fairly. These include relatively strict laws to protect American workers from discrimination on the basis of gender, age, race, ethnicity, religion, sexual orientation, and other factors.

The Fair Labor Standards Act

The Fair Labor Standards Act (FLSA) offers protection for full- and part-time workers in private and government jobs, covering minimum wages, overtime pay, employer record keeping, and child labor. The FLSA also established the standard forty-hour workweek. Local fire and police employees typically are not covered by the FLSA. It was passed in 1938 and has been amended many times over the years.

THE MINIMUM WAGE. The FLSA established a federal hourly minimum wage that U.S. employers must honor for many nonsupervisory, nonfarm, private sector, and government employees. Most states have their own minimum wage as well. In states with minimum wages that differ from the federal, the employer must pay the higher of the two. As of May 2006, the federal minimum wage was $5.15 per hour.

There are numerous exceptions to the minimum wage law. Employers may apply for subminimum wage certificates for disabled workers, full-time students, workers under age twenty who are in their first ninety days of employment, workers who receive tips, and student-learners (usually high school students). Lawmakers reasoned that exempting employers from paying the minimum wage to certain workers—the disabled and students, for example—encourages them to hire more of those workers who may otherwise be at a disadvantage. Employers may not, however, displace other workers in order to hire those subject to the subminimum wage. Other workers exempt from the minimum wage include certain professional and administrative employees, certain workers in the fishing industry, certain seasonal employees, babysitters, and certain farm workers.

The BLS tracks the number of hourly wage earners in the United States based on the results of the Current Population Survey. According to *Characteristics of Minimum Wage Workers: 2005* (May 2006, http://www. bls.gov/cps/minwage2005.htm), there were 479,000 workers paid the federal minimum wage of $5.15 per hour during 2005. Another 1.4 million workers earned less than the minimum

wage. The total number of workers earning minimum wage or less accounted for 2.5% of the nearly seventy-six million people earning hourly wages that year.

Women, people under age twenty-five, part-time workers, and those without a college degree were the groups most likely to earn the minimum wage or less. Jobs in the service sector—particularly those related to food service—had the highest rate (about 8% of the total) of workers making $5.15 or less per hour. In some cases, however, those who work in food and beverage service jobs also earn tips, which supplement their hourly wages.

The minimum wage policy is not without controversy. Advocates for low-income workers believe the minimum wage should be increased on a regular basis to keep up with the effects of inflation. The current minimum wage of $5.15 per hour has been in effect since 1997. But, according to the BLS, inflation has increased at a rate of around 2.5% per year over this time period. (See Figure 2.3 in Chapter 2.) Opponents of the minimum wage assert that wage levels should be determined by market conditions and supply and demand factors. They argue that forcing businesses to pay a higher minimum wage discourages new hiring of low-income workers.

In October 2005 the Senate rejected a proposal to raise the minimum wage to $6.25 per hour. In August 2006 another bill, which would have raised the minimum wage to $7.25 per hour gradually over three years, was rejected by Senate Democrats because Republicans had tied a permanent reduction in the estate tax, as well as a total of $38 billion in other tax breaks, to the wage increase.

Meanwhile, state and local governments began taking action in response to public disappointment about low wages. In July 2006 the Chicago city council approved an ordinance requiring "big-box" retailers—stores that are larger than ninety thousand square feet run by companies doing more than $1 billion in business annually—to increase their minimum wage to $10 per hour by 2010 and spend no less than $3 per hour on employee benefits. In August 2006 the State of California announced an agreement struck between state legislators and California governor Arnold Schwarzenegger to raise the state's minimum wage from $6.75 to $8 per hour over two years.

CHILD LABOR LAWS. In an agricultural economy children typically begin working on the family farm or are apprenticed out to other farms at early ages. In the American colonial period children as young as three whose parents couldn't afford to support them were apprenticed out to work. This was the case in the United States until the early nineteenth century, when the Industrial Revolution permanently changed the American economy and way of life. Because they were considered easier to manage, less likely to unionize, and could be paid far less than adults, children became desirable as workers in the industrial economy, particularly in factories, mines, cotton fields, and the textile industry.

With no laws to regulate children's work, and no mandatory school attendance, the use of children as a cheap labor source became a widely accepted practice. Children as young as six worked thirteen-hour days, six days per week. They frequently suffered from hunger and malnutrition, work-related injuries, and diseases. Although social reformers began to campaign for child labor laws in the mid-nineteenth century, and the National Child Labor Committee was formed in 1904, it was not until the passage of the FLSA in 1938 that child labor in the United States was finally regulated by the federal government.

The FLSA prohibits employers from hiring children under the age of sixteen, although fourteen- and fifteen-year-olds are allowed to work at nonmining, nonmanufacturing jobs as long as the hours worked do not interfere with time spent in school and are not hazardous to the young person's health and well-being. The FLSA also prohibits anyone under age eighteen from working at jobs considered dangerous. Babysitting, delivering newspapers, and working in the entertainment industry are all specifically exempted from the provisions of the FLSA, and children of migrant farm workers often are not protected by the legislation because of the transient nature of their families' lives.

Occupational Safety and Health Administration

The Occupational Safety and Health Administration (OSHA) was formed in 1971 to institute and monitor safety regulations in the workplace. Focusing mainly on industries with high rates of work-related injuries and illnesses, OSHA works directly with employers and employees to ensure that health and safety standards are followed.

According to the BLS, there were 5,703 fatal work injuries during 2004, an increase of 2% from 2003. The most frequent events blamed for the deaths were highway incidents, falls, being struck by objects, and workplace homicides. The industries with the highest number of fatal work injuries were construction; transportation and warehousing; agriculture, forestry, fishing, and hunting; government; and manufacturing ("National Census of Fatal Occupational Injuries: 2004," August 25, 2005, http://stats.bls.gov/news.release/pdf/cfoi.pdf).

The BLS reported 4.3 million nonfatal work injuries and illnesses in the private sector in 2004, down slightly from 4.4 million in 2003. Illnesses accounted for 249,000 of the cases in 2004. The industry sectors with the largest number of nonfatal work injuries were manufacturing, health care and social assistance, retail trade, construction, and leisure and hospitality ("Workplace Injuries and Illnesses in 2004," November 17, 2005, http://stats.bls.gov/iif/oshwc/osh/os/osnr0023.pdf).

Whistleblower Protection Laws

A whistleblower is a person who reports unlawful activity in the workplace to the authorities. At one time whistleblowers were subject to demotion, threats, harassment, and firing if their reports were discovered by their employers, who wanted to prevent public scandals and avoid facing criminal and civil charges. But in 1989 the federal government passed the Whistleblower Protection Act to protect employees who report evidence of criminal wrongdoing in the workplace. In May 2002 President Bush signed the Notification and Federal Employee Antidiscrimination and Retaliation (NoFEAR) Act, which strengthened protections for whistleblowers by requiring federal agencies to be accountable for violations of whistleblower laws. Some states have their own additional whistleblower protection laws.

Equal Employment Opportunity Commission

The Equal Employment Opportunity Commission (EEOC) enforces federal workplace discrimination laws. It is composed of five commissioners and a general counsel who are appointed by the U.S. president and approved by the Senate. In addition to its enforcement role, the EEOC has a training institute to educate employers on workplace discrimination and help them comply with the laws. The federal antidiscrimination laws that fall under the EEOC's watch are:

- The Equal Pay Act of 1963 (EPA), which protects men and women who perform approximately equal work in the same workplace from gender-based wage discrimination

- Title VII of the Civil Rights Act of 1964, which prohibits employment discrimination based on race, color, religion, sex, or national origin, including sexual harassment and discrimination against pregnant women

- The Age Discrimination in Employment Act of 1967 (ADEA), which protects individuals who are forty years of age or older. The ADEA applies to both employees and job applicants

- Titles I and V of the Americans with Disabilities Act of 1990 (ADA), which prohibit employment discrimination against qualified individuals with disabilities in the private sector, as well as in state and local governments (the ADA applies to people with both physical and mental impairments)

- Sections 501 and 505 of the Rehabilitation Act of 1973, which prohibit discrimination against qualified individuals with disabilities who work in the federal government

- The Civil Rights Act of 1991, which, among other things, provides monetary damages in cases of intentional employment discrimination

CHAPTER 6
AMERICAN BUSINESSES

The business of America is business.

—President Calvin Coolidge, 1925

Businesses are diverse in America. They range in size from the huge multinational corporation employing thousands of people to the self-employed individual. They include large and small businesses, home-based businesses, Internet-based businesses, and corporate and family farms. Businesses are a vital part of the American economic engine. They supply goods and services to the world. Consumption of business output is the primary driver behind the growth of the nation's gross domestic product (GDP). Businesses also provide opportunities for employment, wealth-building, and investment.

Capitalism encourages business growth. However, businesses can become so large and powerful that they trigger concern about lack of competition within an industry. Corporate fraud and accounting scandals have eroded the public's trust in the integrity of "big business." American society also has certain expectations regarding the effects of business on the environment, local development, and public welfare and well-being.

HISTORICAL DEVELOPMENTS

When the first colonists arrived in America, they traded in furs and food with the native peoples and exchanged American resources for goods from other countries. The primary industries were agriculture, timber harvesting, and ship building. Manufacturing gradually grew in importance as the United States became an independent country and underwent the Industrial Revolution. As shown in Figure 1.2 in Chapter 1, agriculture accounted for 22% of national income in 1869. Other major sectors were trade and manufacturing (15% each), services (14%), and finance, insurance, and real estate (12%). The U.S. Census Bureau reports that by 1929 the contribution of agriculture to national income had shrunk to only 12%, while manufacturing had grown to 22%. By

the mid-1950s agriculture accounted for only 5% of national income, while manufacturing had grown to 31%. (See Figure 1.9 in Chapter 1.)

Over the next half century, the United States underwent a gradual change from dependence on manufacturing as its primary business to reliance on service industries. As shown in Figure 1.9 in Chapter 1, services accounted for only 10% of national income in the mid-1950s. By the beginning of the twenty-first century, service industries dominated the American business world.

LEGAL STRUCTURES OF BUSINESSES

For legal and tax purposes, all businesses must be structured as one of several legally defined forms: sole proprietorships, business partnerships, corporations, or limited liability companies (LLC). Each offers both advantages and disadvantages to the business owner.

Sole Proprietorships

In a sole proprietorship one person owns and operates the whole business. Because the business and its owner are considered a single entity under the law, the owner assumes all of the risk but also reaps all of the benefits of the business. If the business fails, the sole proprietor may have to cover the losses from his or her personal assets, but if the business succeeds, he or she keeps all of the profits. Sole proprietors can pay lower taxes than those who head corporations or other forms of small businesses. Still, because almost all credit decisions are based on the owner's assets and credit history, it is often difficult for businesses set up under this structure to borrow enough money to expand as rapidly as other kinds of businesses.

Business Partnerships

A business partnership has two or more co-owners. As in a sole proprietorship, members of a business partnership are legally recognized as one and the same with their company, meaning that they are personally responsible for the company's debts and other liabilities. Most partnerships start with the partners signing agreements that specify their duties in the business. Many states allow for "silent partners," who invest start-up capital but have little role in the company's day-to-day affairs. (Start-up capital is the money used to start a new business.) A significant drawback of this form of business is that each of the partners is responsible for every other partner's actions. If a partner loses or steals money from the company, the other partners will have a legal responsibility to pay that debt.

There are three kinds of business partnerships: A general partnership is the simplest form, in which profits and liability are equally divided among partners or divided according to the terms of the signed agreement; a limited partnership allows partners to have limited liability for the company but also limited decision-making rights; and a joint venture, while similar legally to a general partnership, is used only for single projects or short periods of time.

Corporations

A corporation is an entity recognized by the state and federal governments as entirely separate from its owner or owners. As such, a corporation can be taxed and sued, and it can enter into contractual agreements. Because it is an individual legal entity, a corporation allows its owners to have less personal liability for debts and lawsuits than a sole proprietorship or partnership. Owners of corporations are considered shareholders, and they may elect a board of directors to oversee management of the company.

While corporations are commonly thought of as large companies with hundreds or thousands of employees and publicly traded stock, this is not always the case. Owners of small businesses frequently incorporate as their business expands. All corporate owners must file "articles of incorporation" with their state governments. For smaller businesses these forms are simple to fill out and file. One option is to file with the Internal Revenue Service (IRS) as a subchapter S corporation. In an S corporation the owner must pay him- or herself wages like any other employee, but the structure also offers substantial tax flexibility. All corporations that are publicly traded have C corporation status. This means they have nearly unrestricted ownership and they are subject to corporate taxes, paying at both the corporate and stockholder levels.

Limited Liability Company

The limited liability company is a combination of a corporation and a partnership in which the owners (or shareholders) have less personal liability for the company's debts and legal issues and also have the benefit of simpler tax filings and more control over management issues.

THE ROLE OF SMALL BUSINESS IN A COMPLEX ECONOMY

Many people perceive the American economy as being dominated by large businesses, like McDonald's and Microsoft. While it is true that many of the world's largest companies are headquartered in the United States, according to the U.S. Census Bureau's 2002 economic census, 57.4 million of America's 115 million workers were employed at companies with fewer than five hundred employees in 2001.

The size of what is considered a small business varies by industry, and size standards are determined by the Small Business Administration's Office of Size Standards, which issues standards according to a business's number of employees or its average annual receipts. The more generally accepted definition of a small business, however, is one that employs fewer than five hundred people at any one time. Table 6.1 provides a breakdown of business sizes in 2003. More than 5.7 million firms each employed less than five hundred workers. The payroll for the 57.4 million employees working in these small businesses was nearly $1.82 trillion, representing 45% of the total payroll for that year.

Home-Based Businesses

Small businesses operated out of a person's home may be organized as any of the legal business structures. In 2003, 53% of all small businesses in the United States were home-based. Of those, 60% were in service industries, 16% in construction, 14% in retail trade, and the remaining 10% in a variety of other sectors, including finance, communications, manufacturing, and transportation. About 91% of home-based businesses were sole proprietorships; 5% were subchapter S corporations; and 4% were partnerships. Almost all (91%) home-based businesses as of 2003 had no employees, and less than half operated on a full-time basis. In fact, owners of home-based businesses reported working approximately twenty-six to thirty-five hours per week, about ten hours per week less than owners of companies that operated outside the home ("The Small Business Economy: A Report to the President," U.S. Small Business Administration Office of Advocacy, 2004, http://www.sba.gov/advo/research/sb_econ2004.pdf).

The Small Business Administration

The Small Business Administration (SBA) was created in 1953 with the passage of the Small Business Act. The SBA's purpose is to support small businesses by offering financial and counseling assistance and ensuring that small businesses can compete against large companies in receiving government contracts. Since the SBA

TABLE 6.1

Business sizes, 2003

Employment size of firm	Firms	Establishments	Employment	Annual payroll ($1,000)
Total	5,767,127	7,254,745	113,398,043	4,040,888,841
0*	770,299	772,325	—	38,404,329
1–4	2,734,133	2,738,027	5,768,407	158,836,735
5–9	1,025,497	1,037,709	6,732,132	187,418,785
10–14	408,652	426,057	4,778,791	139,988,796
15–19	211,735	229,370	3,551,022	106,572,773
20–24	130,748	147,885	2,852,748	86,889,769
25–29	86,801	102,096	2,330,691	71,139,268
30–34	62,645	76,995	1,996,287	61,789,875
35–39	47,122	60,521	1,737,450	53,959,859
40–44	36,272	49,025	1,518,598	47,903,548
45–49	28,696	40,918	1,345,981	42,723,644
50–74	83,102	132,061	5,005,188	160,330,470
75–99	39,670	77,606	3,400,046	110,532,661
100–149	37,602	96,124	4,546,020	150,937,401
150–199	17,966	61,968	3,086,877	103,422,448
200–299	16,998	82,066	4,117,449	138,692,471
300–399	7,790	53,607	2,686,114	91,122,920
400–499	4,473	37,731	1,993,769	67,828,110
500–749	5,678	66,672	3,432,914	121,816,473
750–999	2,730	42,137	2,354,268	84,346,542
1,000–1,499	2,721	57,395	3,312,888	123,432,170
1,500–2,499	2,246	73,668	4,314,523	167,423,764
2,500+	3,551	792,782	42,535,880	1,725,376,030
<20	5,150,316	5,203,488	20,830,352	631,221,418
<50	5,542,600	5,680,928	32,612,107	995,627,381
<100	5,665,372	5,890,595	41,017,341	1,266,490,512
<500	5,750,201	6,222,091	57,447,570	1,818,493,862

*Employment is measured in March, thus some firms (start-ups after March, closures before March, and seasonal firms) will have zero employment and some annual payroll. Excludes farms.

SOURCE: "Employer Firms, Establishments, Employment, and Annual Payroll, Small Firm Size Classes, 2003," in *Firm Size Data*, U.S. Small Business Administration, Office of Advocacy, 2003, http://www.sba.gov/advo/research/us_03ss.pdf (accessed June 22, 2006)

was established, it has granted some form of aid to almost twenty million small businesses. As of 2003, the SBA offered more loans than any other single financial backer in the United States: 219,000 loans worth approximately $45 billion.

BIG BUSINESS: FUELING THE AMERICAN AND GLOBAL ECONOMIES

While small businesses have a significant impact on the U.S. economy and represent more than 99% of U.S. employers, large corporations still dominate the business world. According to the Census Bureau, in 2002 fifty-six million people were employed by the 16,845 U.S. companies with more than five hundred employees, with 30.5 million of them working at companies with more than ten thousand employees. The total payroll for these large businesses was more than $2.16 trillion, compared with $1.77 trillion for all U.S. small businesses.

According to the business magazine *Forbes* (http://www.forbes.com/2006/03/29/06f2k_worlds-largest-public-companies_land.html), the two companies with the highest sales in 2005 were American-owned: Exxon Mobil Corp. ($328 billion in sales and 83,700 employees) and Wal-Mart ($312 billion in sales and 1.7 million employees). Overall,

the two thousand top-grossing public companies in the world in 2005 employed sixty-eight million people and had sales of approximately $24 trillion.

Multinational Corporations

Many large businesses operate in more than one country, through subsidiaries or part ownership of foreign companies. These companies are called multinational or transnational corporations. Generally through mergers and acquisitions, a large company can grow beyond the boundaries of a single nation, buying and taking over companies in other countries to form a global network of subsidiaries. For example, Exxon Mobil, which was formed in 1999 by the merger of the two oil companies Exxon and Mobil, is headquartered in Irving, Texas, but it operates affiliated companies in at least forty countries on six continents.

Drawbacks to Economic Dependence on Big Business

Although it is unlikely that the entire U.S. economy could be affected by a downturn in a single business or industry, local and regional economies often suffer greatly when one kind of business—the automobile industry, for example—experiences a period of slow growth and poor performance.

One of the most notorious instances of a local economy depending too heavily on a single large company happened when the automotive company General Motors, the primary employer in Flint, Michigan, closed eleven plants in 1986 and laid off approximately forty thousand people throughout the 1970s and 1980s, resulting in a 25% unemployment rate and massive poverty by the late 1980s. Flint's rates of suicide, murder, alcoholism, and domestic violence reached unprecedented highs during this period. While the case of Flint and General Motors is extreme, it does illustrate the widespread economic and social problems that can come with a high degree of dependence on a single large corporation or industry.

In 2005 and 2006 the state of Michigan continued to experience an unemployment rate higher than the national average—7% as of August 2006, although that rate was due in part to seasonal layoffs that occur every summer in the auto industry (Kathy Barks Hoffman, "Michigan Jobless Rate up to 7%," Associated Press, August 16, 2006). Still, with General Motors losing $8.6 billion in 2005 (Bill Vlasic and Brett Clanton, "Simply Staggering," *Detroit News*, January 27, 2006) and Ford Motor Company announcing in August 2006 that it would cut production by 21%—with plant closings, layoffs, and pay and benefit cuts also planned (Joann Muller, "Ford Motor: It Only Gets Uglier," August 18, 2006, http://www.forbes.com/markets/2006/08/18/ford-output-update-cz_jm_0818output.html)—the regional economy was not expected to recover quickly or easily.

BUSINESS AND POLITICS

Large companies often have strong ties to the government. They have the resources to be able to donate millions of dollars to political campaigns to elect sympathetic lawmakers and to otherwise encourage the passage of pro-business legislation. Likewise, lawmakers, eager to have companies locate facilities in their constituencies to boost local economies, may support policies that favor business interests to the detriment of other programs. Members of Congress may be more inclined to pass pro-business laws if their region has benefited from a large corporation's presence, or if they or their party have received campaign contributions from such a company. This raises concerns that big businesses may be able to convince the government to favor their interests at the expense of the interests of other businesses, or even the population as a whole.

ECONOMIC PERFORMANCE

The businesses of America produce goods and provide services that are purchased by consumers. Consumption of business output is the major driving force behind the nation's GDP growth.

The U.S. Department of Commerce's Bureau of Economic Analysis (BEA) compiles data on the contributions made to GDP by various industries. One measure of output is called "real value added." This is defined as gross output minus the consumption of intermediate inputs. For example, the real value added to the economy by a manufacturer is calculated using the market value of the goods sold minus the cost of producing the goods.

Figure 6.1 shows the BEA breakdown of GDP growth per year by industry category for 2002 through 2005 and averaged over the period of 1995 through 2000. In 2005 the nation's GDP increased by 3.5%. Service-providing businesses grew by 4.1%, while goods-producing businesses had a 2.6% increase. As detailed in Table 6.2, the growth in the service-providing industry during 2005 was due to strong performance by information services (with a 7.4% increase) and professional, scientific, and technical services (with a 7% increase). The leading performers in the goods-producing sector were manufacturing (particularly the manufacture of computer and electronic products) and construction. Growth in these industries offset declines suffered in mining and agriculture businesses.

Table 6.2 indicates the incredibly strong growth during the late 1990s of a business sector the BEA calls information-communications-technology-producing industries. These are businesses that produce computers and electronic products, publish software and other materials, and provide services related to information and data processing and computer systems design. This sector had an annual growth rate of 22.1% between 1995 and 2000. After a downturn in 2002 the sector rebounded, experiencing growth rates of 6.7% in 2003, 12.9% in 2004, and 11.9% in 2005, according to the BEA.

Agriculture

The U.S. Department of Agriculture's National Agricultural Statistics Service (NASS) performs a Census of Agriculture every five years. The most recent census was conducted in 2002. According to the results, there were just over two million farms and ranches operating in 2002. The NASS defines a farm/ranch as an establishment from which at least $1,000 in agricultural products is produced or sold (or normally would be produced or sold) during a year (http://www.nass.usda.gov/census/census02/quickfacts/index.htm). Although less than 10% of farm/ranch establishments were owned by corporations or business partnerships in 2002, these farms accounted for nearly half of all sales and government payments.

As indicated in Table 6.3, the number of farms in America declined dramatically during the twentieth century, from 5.7 million in 1900 to 2.1 million in 2000. Likewise farming's share of the nation's workforce decreased from 41% to only 2%. However, the average farm size increased from 146 acres to 441 acres. This

FIGURE 6.1

Annual percent changes in real value added by industry, 1995–2005

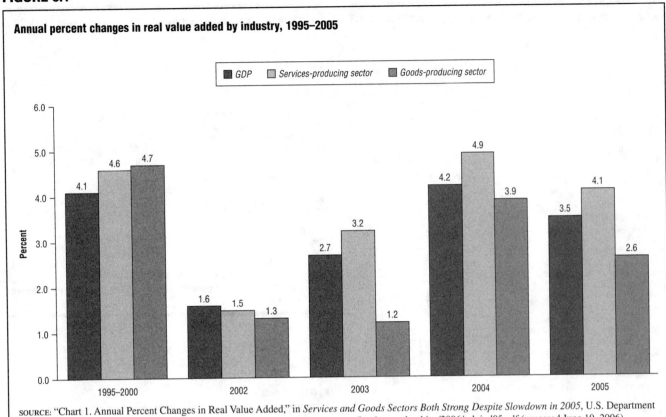

SOURCE: "Chart 1. Annual Percent Changes in Real Value Added," in *Services and Goods Sectors Both Strong Despite Slowdown in 2005*, U.S. Department of Commerce, Bureau of Economic Analysis, April 27, 2006, http://www.bea.gov/bea/newsrelarchive/2006/gdpind05.pdf (accessed June 19, 2006)

growth, combined with advances in agricultural science and technology, has resulted in an increase in farm output, even as farming's contribution to the nation's GDP has diminished. (See Figure 6.2 for a comparison of these measures between 1950 and 2000).

As shown in Table 6.2, the agriculture, forestry, fishing, and hunting sector experienced a downturn during 2005; real value added declined by 4.4%. This follows several years of positive moderate growth.

Nonagricultural Businesses

Table 6.4 shows results from the 2002 Economic Census performed by the U.S. Census Bureau. The agency conducts an economic census every five years. The table provides an economic overview of nonagricultural industry sectors with employee payrolls. The sectors are listed from largest to smallest in terms of value of sales, receipts, or shipments. Also included for each sector are the number of establishments, number of paid employees, and annual payroll.

Wholesale trade had $4.6 trillion in sales, receipts, or shipments during 2002. Wholesalers buy large quantities of finished goods from manufacturers and sell the goods in smaller lots to businesses engaged in retail trade. Retailers then offer the goods for sale to consumers at an increased price. There were more than one million

retail establishments operating in 2002. While the traditional notion of a retail establishment includes at least one store location, many retailers operate via the Internet and/or catalog sales, instead of or in addition to their physical locations.

The manufacturing sector had the highest annual payroll in 2002 at $576 billion. Nearly 14.7 million people were employed in this sector, the second-highest number of the sectors listed. The health care and social assistance sector was the top employer with just over fifteen million paid employees.

Corporate Profits

One of the economic indicators tracked by the BEA is called corporate profits. This is a measure of the income generated by corporations from the current production of goods and services. Because only current production is counted, corporate profits do not include capital gains, such as inventory profits.

Table 6.5 lists the corporate profits by industry for the years 2003 through 2005 and the change from 2004 to 2005. Corporate profits totaled almost $1.4 trillion in 2005, up by $190 billion from 2004. Domestic industries accounted for $1.1 trillion, or 85%, of the total in 2005. These values include adjustments for inventory valuation and capital consumption (depreciation).

TABLE 6.2

Percent change in real value added by industry group, 1995–2005

[Percent change]

	2005	Average annual rate of change, 1995–2000
Gross domestic product	3.5	4.1
Private industries	3.8	4.6
Agriculture, forestry, fishing, and hunting	−4.4	6.5
Mining	−2.6	−1.1
Utilities	0.4	1.3
Construction	2.7	3.0
Manufacturing	4.0	5.4
Durable goods	5.7	8.9
Nondurable goods	1.6	0.4
Wholesale trade	1.2	7.2
Retail trade	2.9	6.5
Transportation and warehousing	3.7	4.4
Information	7.4	8.0
Finance, insurance, real estate, rental, and leasing	4.1	4.4
Finance and insurance	6.7	6.5
Real estate and rental and leasing	2.5	3.1
Professional and business services	5.9	5.3
Professional, scientific, and technical services	7.0	6.9
Management of companies and enterprises	0.3	1.3
Administrative and waste management services	6.9	4.1
Educational services, health care, and social assistance	4.3	1.4
Educational services	0.8	2.1
Health care and social assistance	4.8	1.3
Arts, entertainment, recreation, accommodation, and food services	4.1	3.7
Arts, entertainment, and recreation	2.1	3.1
Accommodation and food services	4.8	3.9
Other services, except government	2.4	0.1
Government	1.1	1.2
Federal	1.1	-0.4
State and local	1.2	2.0
Addenda:		
Private goods-producing industries[a]	2.6	4.7
Private services-producing industries[b]	4.1	4.6
Information-communications-technology-producing industries[c]	11.9	22.1

[a]Consists of agriculture, forestry, fishing, and hunting; mining; construction; and manufacturing.
[b]Consists of utilities; wholesale trade; retail trade; transportation and warehousing; information; finance, insurance, real estate, rental, and leasing; professional and business services; educational services, health care, and social assistance; arts, entertainment, recreation, accommodation, and food services; and other services, except government.
[c]Consists of computer and electronic products within durable-goods manufacturing; publishing industries (includes software) and information and data processing services within information; and computer systems design and related services within professional, scientific, and technical services.

SOURCE: Adapted from "Table 1. Percent Changes in Real Value Added by Industry Group," in *Services and Goods Sectors Both Strong Despite Slowdown in 2005 (BEA 06-16)*, U.S. Department of Commerce, Bureau of Economic Analysis, April 27, 2006, http://www.bea.gov/bea/newsrelarchive/2006/gdpind05.pdf (accessed June 19, 2006)

Among domestic industries, corporations engaged in financial services had the highest corporate profits in 2005. These businesses had profits of $347 billion (including only the inventory valuation adjustment). Similarly, the manufacturing sector had corporate profits of nearly $208 billion during 2005. Corporate profits were positive for all subsectors but one—the manufacture of motor vehicles, bodies and trailers, and parts.

TABLE 6.3

Historical changes in agriculture sector, selected years 1900–2000

	1900	1930	1945	1970	2000
Number of farms (millions)	5.7	6.3	5.9	2.9	2.1
Average farm size (acres)	146	151	195	376	441
Average number of commodities produced per farm	5.1	4.5	4.6	2.7	1.3
Farm share of population (percent)	39	25	17	5	1
Rural share of population (percent)	60	44	36[b]	26	21
Farm share of workforce (percent)	41	22	16	4	2
Farm share of GDP (percent)	na	8	7	2	1[c]
Off-farm labor[a]	na	100 days	27%	54%	93%

na=not available.
[a]Off-farm labor measures the extent to which members of farm households work in other sectors besides farming: 1930, average number of days worked off-farm; 1945, percent of farmers working off-farm; 1970 and 2000, percent of farm households with off-farm income.
[b]Data for 1950.
[c]Data for 2002.

SOURCE: "Table 8-1. 100 Years of Structural Change in U.S. Agriculture," in *Economic Report of the President*, U.S. Government Printing Office, February 2006, http://www.gpoaccess.gov/eop/2006/2006_erp.pdf (accessed June 22, 2006)

FIGURE 6.2

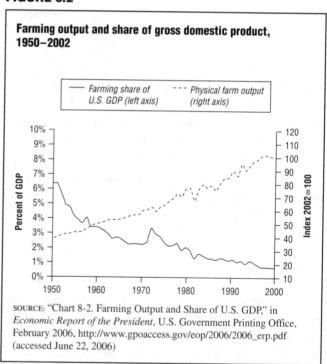

Farming output and share of gross domestic product, 1950–2002

SOURCE: "Chart 8-2. Farming Output and Share of U.S. GDP," in *Economic Report of the President*, U.S. Government Printing Office, February 2006, http://www.gpoaccess.gov/eop/2006/2006_erp.pdf (accessed June 22, 2006)

Figure 6.3 shows the percentage change in year-over-year growth in corporate profits for the second quarter of 2002 through the first quarter of 2006. Corporate profits for first-quarter 2006 were up nearly 24% compared with the first quarter of 2005. This was the highest one-year growth rate recorded since 2002.

TABLE 6.4

Economic statistics by industry, 2002

NAICS code	Description	Establishments	Sales, receipts or shipments ($1,000)	Annual payroll ($1,000)	Paid employees
42	Wholesale trade	435,521	4,634,755,112	259,653,080	5,878,405
31–33	Manufacturing	350,828	3,916,136,712	576,170,541	14,699,536
44–45	Retail trade	1,114,637	3,056,421,997	302,113,581	14,647,675
52	Finance & insurance	440,268	2,803,854,868	377,790,172	6,578,817
62	Health care & social assistance	704,526	1,207,299,734	495,845,829	15,052,255
23	Construction	710,307	1,196,555,587	254,292,144	7,193,069
51	Information	137,678	891,845,956	194,670,163	3,736,061
54	Professional, scientific, & technical services	771,305	886,801,038	376,090,052	7,243,505
72	Accommodation & food services	565,590	449,498,718	127,554,483	10,120,951
56	Administrative & support & waste management & remediation service	350,583	432,577,580	206,439,329	8,741,854
22	Utilities	17,103	398,907,044	42,417,830	663,044
48–49	Transportation & warehousing	199,618	382,152,040	115,988,733	3,650,859
53	Real estate & rental & leasing	322,815	335,587,706	60,222,584	1,948,657
81	Other services (except public administration)	537,576	307,049,461	82,954,939	3,475,310
21	Mining	24,087	182,911,093	21,173,895	477,840
71	Arts, entertainment, & recreation	110,313	141,904,109	45,169,117	1,848,674
55	Management of companies & enterprises	49,308	107,064,264	178,996,060	2,605,292
61	Educational services	49,319	30,690,707	10,164,378	430,164

Notes: Table includes only establishments of firms with payroll. Nonemployers are shown separately.

SOURCE: Adapted from "Summary Statistics by 2002 NAICS, United States: All Sector Totals," in *2002 Economic Census*, U.S. Census Bureau, November 7, 2005, www.census.gov/econ/census02/data/us/US000.HTM (accessed April 13, 2006)

Industry Outlook

Table 6.6 is a list of the industries expected to undergo the greatest growth or decline in output through 2014. The list was compiled by the Bureau of Labor Statistics (BLS). The BLS expects phenomenal growth from businesses engaged in the manufacture of computers and peripheral equipment. This business is expected to increase its output by nearly $1.2 trillion between 2004 and 2014. Strong performance is also expected from the wholesale trade industry, with an increase of more than $840 billion predicted over the same time period.

Industries expected to suffer declining output include tobacco manufacturers, natural gas distributors, and manufacturers of certain apparel items.

FEDERAL REGULATION OF BUSINESS

Historically, U.S. economic philosophy has been to let the market operate with a minimum of government interference. This does not mean, however, that American businesses go unregulated. Many local, state, and federal laws exist to protect the public and the economy from dangerous, unfair, or fraudulent activities by businesses. Major federal programs that oversee business activities are described below:

• Federal Trade Commission (FTC)—Created in 1914 with the passage of the Federal Trade Commission Act. Originally intended to combat the rise of business monopolies, the FTC grew to become the U.S. government's consumer protection agency, addressing consumer issues such as identity theft, false advertising, telemarketing and Internet scams, and anticompetition moves by businesses.

• Consumer Product Safety Commission (CPSC)—Established in 1973 to protect the American public from unreasonable risks of serious injury or death from consumer products. Through a combination of voluntary and mandatory safety standards, the CPSC tries to prevent dangerous products from entering the market. If a product is found to be dangerous after it has already been sold to consumers, the CPSC has the duty to inform the public and the power to force a recall of the product if it is deemed necessary.

• Equal Employment Opportunity Commission (EEOC)—Established in 1965, the EEOC is the primary federal agency responsible for preventing discrimination in the workplace. Its original purpose was to investigate violations of the Civil Rights Act of 1964, which prohibited discrimination in the workplace on the basis of race, color, national origin, sex, and religion. Over the years its powers have been expanded and it has been given responsibility to enforce other antidiscrimination laws.

• Employment Standards Administration (ESA)—One of the largest branches of the Department of Labor, the ESA is charged with enforcing a wide variety of labor laws dealing with minimum wage requirements, overtime pay standards, child labor protections, and unpaid leaves of absence. It also provides oversight of federal contractors with regards to employment issues.

TABLE 6.5

Level of corporate profits and change from preceding period, by industry, 2003–05

[Billions of dollars]

	Level			Change from preceding period
	2003	**2004**	**2005**	**2005**
Corporate profits with inventory valuation and capital consumption adjustments	1,031.8	1,161.5	1,351.9	190.4
Domestic industries	855.8	976.6	1,146.3	169.7
Financial	330.9	322.7	347.7	25.0
Nonfinancial	524.9	653.9	798.6	144.7
Rest of the world	176.0	184.9	205.6	20.7
Receipts from the rest of the world	255.7	309.5	334.2	24.7
Less: Payments to the rest of the world	79.7	124.6	128.5	3.9
Corporate profits with inventory valuation adjustment	923.9	1,019.7	1,406.8	387.1
Domestic industries	747.9	834.8	1,201.2	366.4
Financial	313.0	300.6	347.0	46.4
Federal Reserve banks	20.2	20.3	26.8	6.5
Other financial	292.8	280.3	320.3	40.0
Nonfinancial	434.9	534.2	854.2	320.0
Utilities	11.4	12.1	27.4	15.3
Manufacturing	80.7	118.9	207.9	89.0
Durable goods	−4.1	34.8	55.9	21.1
Fabricated metal products	8.5	10.3	12.4	2.1
Machinery	1.4	1.0	4.7	3.7
Computer and electronic products	−16.1	−3.2	5.0	8.2
Electrical equipment, appliances, and components	1.9	.3	4.5	4.2
Motor vehicles, bodies and trailers, and parts	−11.6	−3.4	−22.2	−18.8
Other durable goods	11.9	29.9	51.6	21.7
Nondurable goods	84.8	84.0	152.0	68.0
Food and beverage and tobacco products	23.5	24.0	39.8	15.8
Petroleum and coal products	23.6	31.0	70.2	39.2
Chemical products	20.8	13.5	21.4	7.9
Other nondurable goods	16.9	15.6	20.7	5.1
Wholesale trade	56.3	63.5	93.9	30.4
Retail trade	87.7	90.0	115.2	25.2
Transportation and warehousing	8.1	8.4	28.2	19.8
Information	−1.9	17.0	51.1	34.1
Other nonfinancial	192.4	224.3	330.4	106.1
Rest of the world	176.0	184.9	205.6	20.7

Note: Estimates in this table are based on the 1997 North American Industry Classification System (NAICS).

SOURCE: Adapted from "Table 12. Corporate Profits by Industry: Level and Change from Preceding Period," in *Gross Domestic Product: Fourth Quarter 2005 (Final); Corporate Profits: Fourth Quarter 2005*, U.S. Department of Commerce, Bureau of Economic Analysis, March 30, 2006, http://www.bea.gov/bea/newsrelarchive/2006/gdp405f.pdf (accessed June 19, 2006)

- The Environmental Protection Agency (EPA)—Develops and enforces federal environmental regulations. The EPA keeps track of industrial pollutants and regularly updates its compliance codes for individual sectors and industries.

- The Food and Drug Administration (FDA)—Works to ensure that the food, drugs, and cosmetics sold in the United States are safe and effective. It establishes safety and sanitation standards for manufacturers of these goods, as well as quality standards that the goods themselves must meet. FDA scientists must prove that certain products, especially drugs, are safe and effective before they can be sold in the United States, and it can force products off the market if they are later discovered to be dangerous. In addition, the FDA ensures that the labeling of food, drugs, and cosmetics is complete and truthful.

- The Occupational Safety and Health Administration (OSHA)—Establishes and enforces workplace safety stan-

dards. One or more OSHA standards covers almost every workplace in the United States.

Other Agencies

Besides the organizations listed above, there are a number of other government agencies that regulate specific industries or aspects of the economy. Some of them are well known, while many others may be virtually unknown to people outside the fields they regulate. A few examples are:

- The Federal Communications Commission (FCC) regulates the telecommunications industry, including all television, radio, satellite, cable, and wire services in the United States and its territories.

- The Federal Energy Regulatory Commission (FERC) regulates the national transmission network for oil, natural gas, and electricity.

FIGURE 6.3

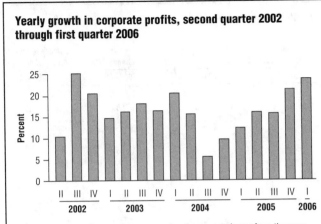

Yearly growth in corporate profits, second quarter 2002 through first quarter 2006

Note: Corporate profits growth is measured as the percent change from the same quarter one year ago.

SOURCE: "Year–over–Year Growth in Corporate Profits," in *GDP Growth Revised Up in First Quarter*, U.S. Department of Commerce, Bureau of Economic Analysis, May 25, 2006, http://www.bea.gov/bea/newsrelarchive/2006/gdp106p_fax.pdf (accessed June 19, 2006)

- The Federal Maritime Commission regulates the waterborne foreign commerce of the United States.

- The National Highway Traffic Safety Administration regulates automobile design and safety.

- The Office of Surface Mining regulates surface coal mining.

- The Securities and Exchange Commission (SEC) regulates the stock market.

Government Regulation and Deregulation

Since the late 1970s the federal and many state governments have lessened their restrictions on certain industries. Called deregulation, this process allows industries to set their own standards and control their own systems of pricing and other business functions. For example, beginning in 1938 the airline industry was regulated by a federal body called the Civil Aeronautics Board (CAB), which controlled airlines' schedules, flying routes, and prices. In order to stimulate competition in the industry, Congress passed the Airline Deregulation Act (PL 95–504) in 1978. The industry experienced a flood of new airlines offering low fares to compete with the established airlines. Although deregulation has actually caused some problems with larger airlines having too much control (or monopolizing) the industry and with overly crowded flight routes, most economists agree that the end result has been an air transportation system that offers some of the lowest costs and safest flights in its one-hundred-year history. Other industries that have experienced some degree of deregulation include electric utilities, telephone services, trucking, railroads, and banking.

MARKET POWER—MONOPOLIES AND MONOPSONIES

One of the foundations of a capitalistic economy is competition. Competition for customers among sellers theoretically ensures that buyers receive the lowest price. If an industry becomes dominated by one seller, lack of competition allows that entity to set prices in the marketplace—a situation known as monopolization. The federal government has long fought against monopolization in most U.S. industries. In 1890 the U.S. Congress passed the Sherman Antitrust Act to strengthen competitive forces in the economy. Section 2 of the law states: "Every person who shall monopolize, or attempt to monopolize, or combine or conspire with any other person or persons, to monopolize any part of the trade or commerce among the several States, or with foreign nations, shall be deemed guilty of a felony."

A monopsony is a different situation, in which the power lies with one buyer. This arrangement can occur if one company wields enormous power over the suppliers in that industry. Lack of other customers forces the suppliers to meet the price and quota demands of the monopsonist. Monopsony is an obscure economic concept to most Americans. But changing market forces in the retail industry are drawing attention to the possible existence and consequences of monopsony in some business sectors.

The Microsoft Monopoly?

In 1993 the Department of Justice began an investigation of software company Microsoft based on allegations that the company was engaging in unfair competition. Microsoft's Windows program already dominated the operating systems market. By bundling Web browsers and other applications with Windows, Microsoft made it difficult for other companies to compete in the market for these other applications as well.

In 1994 Microsoft reached an agreement with the Department of Justice, and the company agreed to stop bundling other products with Windows. In 1998 Microsoft was accused of violating its agreement, and the Department of Justice and the attorneys general of twenty states brought an antitrust suit against it. Microsoft reached a settlement in the case but still faced a number of class-action lawsuits. (A class-action lawsuit is one that is filed by a large group of people, all of whom accuse a single company of engaging in the same illegal acts against them.)

During the 2000s Microsoft fought and lost antitrust cases brought against it in Japan, South Korea, and Europe. In 2004 a European court ordered Microsoft to pay a fine of $613 million for violating the European Union's competition law. The company was also ordered to offer for sale a modified version of Windows that does not

TABLE 6.6

Top 10 industries with the fastest growing and most rapidly declining output growth, 2004 and 2014

2002 NAICS	Industry description	Billions of chained (1996) dollars		Change 2004–14	Average annual rate of change 2004–14
		2004	2014		
	Fastest growing				
3341	Computer and peripheral equipment manufacturing	171.8	1,367.6	1,195.8	23.1
42	Wholesale trade	971.0	1,812.5	841.5	6.4
55	Management of companies and enterprises	397.4	681.4	284.0	5.5
523	Securities, commodity contracts, and other financial investments and related activities	296.2	565.4	269.2	6.7
3342	Communications equipment manufacturing	92.2	318.8	226.7	13.2
5112	Software publishers	101.1	281.2	180.0	10.8
533	Lessors of nonfinancial intangible assets (except copyrighted works)	122.7	291.8	169.1	9.0
516, 518, 519	Internet and other information services	119.9	271.8	152.0	8.5
5415	Computer systems design and related services	154.6	305.4	150.8	7.0
5416	Management, scientific, and technical consulting services	148.8	271.7	123.0	6.2
	Most rapidly declining				
3122	Tobacco manufacturing	42.5	25.7	−16.8	−4.9
2212	Natural gas distribution	59.6	45.8	−13.8	−2.6
3152	Cut and sew apparel manufacturing	43.9	32.8	−11.2	−2.9
3132	Fabric mills	20.4	14.0	−6.5	−3.7
3333	Commercial and service industry machinery manufacturing	25.9	22.3	−3.6	−1.5
3313	Alumina and aluminum production and processing	35.2	31.7	−3.6	−1.1
3133	Textile and fabric finishing and fabric coating mills	11.2	8.4	−2.8	−2.8
3315	Foundries	29.3	26.5	−2.8	−1.0
3151	Apparel knitting mills	8.0	5.6	−2.4	−3.5
3131	Fiber, yarn, and thread mills	10.0	7.8	−2.2	−2.4

SOURCE: Adapted from Jay M. Berman, "Table 6. Industries with the Fastest Growing and Most Rapidly Declining Output Growth, 2004–14," in "Industry Output and Employment Projections to 2014," *Monthly Labor Review*, vol. 128, no. 11, November 2005, http://www.bls.gov/opub/mlr/2005/11/art4full.pdf (accessed June 26, 2006)

include a media player and to share certain communications protocols with competitors. In July 2006 the European Commission levied a $357 million fine against Microsoft for failing to fully comply with the 2004 ruling. Microsoft immediately appealed the fine, claiming that it has acted in good faith to meet the requirements imposed by the European Commission in 2004.

The Wal-Mart Monopsony?

During the early 2000s the mega-retailer Wal-Mart became the subject of much media attention for its business practices. In November 2003 the *Los Angeles Times* published a three-part series on Wal-Mart. Part two, titled "Scouring the Globe to Give Shoppers an $8.63 Polo Shirt" (by Nancy Cleeland, Evelyn Iritani, and Tyler Marshall), describes the relentless push at Wal-Mart for suppliers to lower costs. One textile producer summed up Wal-Mart's power: "They control so much of retail that they can put someone into business or take someone out of business if they choose to."

In November 2004 the Public Broadcasting System (PBS) series *Frontline* aired an episode titled "Is Wal-Mart Good for America?" The show traces the rise of Wal-Mart as a major force in the retail industry and describes the power that the company developed over its suppliers. One commentator noted, "Wal-Mart used its buying power and its information about consumer buying habits to force vendors into squeezing their costs and keeping their profit margins low. Over time, some suppliers—especially middle-sized and smaller firms—were bankrupted" (Sam Hornblower, "Always Low Prices").

At that time Wal-Mart employed 1.2 million employees and served one hundred million shoppers per week at more than three thousand stores around the country. The company had sales of $256 billion in 2003 and accounted for approximately 8% of total U.S. retail sales (excluding automobiles).

Wal-Mart's relatively small share of retail sales is one factor that helps the company avoid antitrust charges. A December 2003 article by *New York Times* columnist Steve Lohr asserts that Wal-Mart's emphasis on low prices to consumers is another factor ("Discount Nation: Is Wal-Mart Good for America?"). This view is shared by *Washington Post* columnist Peter J. Solomon. In the March 2004 article "A Lesson from Wal-Mart," Solomon notes that "federal regulators have refrained from pursuing monopsony antitrust action against Wal-Mart for putting the squeeze on its suppliers, because of the price benefits to consumers."

CORPORATE BEHAVIOR AND RESPONSIBILITY

Businesses play a vital role in the economic well-being of the United States. In addition to economic performance, Americans also expect businesses to behave in a legally and socially responsible manner. There is no public or political consensus on the exact social responsibilities of businesses. But it is recognized that the decisions and practices of company officials, particularly of large corporations, affect not only employees and investors but also the communities in which businesses are located. Fraud and corruption at the corporate level can adversely impact large numbers of people. Likewise, poor performance by businesses in meeting environmental, health, or consumer-protection standards has detrimental effects on society at large.

Corporate Scandals

ENRON. Based in Houston, Texas, Enron was an international broker of commodities such as natural gas, water, coal, and steel. In August 2000 Enron's stock rose to an all-time high of $90 per share. But the company was incurring more and more debt because its contracts outstripped its ability to deliver. To hide its liabilities, Enron created a web of partnerships; the idea was to transfer debt so it would not show on the company's books. Enron's accounting firm, Arthur Andersen, helped the company hide its debts and shredded key documents. With debts transferred to other entities, Arthur Andersen and Enron could overstate the value of the company, and its stock continued to perform well.

Enron eventually had to pay the debts either with cash or with stock, which would create a huge loss that the company could not hide. Enron Vice President Sherron Watkins discovered the accounting discrepancy in the summer of 2001, becoming the key whistleblower when she sent a memo about the problem to CEO Kenneth Lay. In October 2001 Enron announced part of the loss—$638 million in the third quarter of 2001, with a loss in shareholder equity of $1.2 billion—and its stock price plummeted. The company announced that it was being investigated by the SEC for possible conflicts of interest with its many partnerships. In November 2001 Enron stock dropped to less than a dollar per share, and in December the company filed for bankruptcy. Four thousand employees were laid off at that time.

Shortly before announcing the income overstatement, Enron executives took two additional steps. First, some of them sold their stock so they could get their money out before the stock lost all its value. Second, the company imposed a freeze on employee sales of the stock shares in their 401(k) plans. So when the news broke and employees tried to sell their stock to save what they could of their retirement savings funds, they found that they were stuck with worthless stock in a bankrupt company. Thousands of people lost their jobs, along with their health care, retirement funds, and, in many cases, life savings. While investors both in and outside the company lost tens

of billions of dollars, Enron wrote $55 million in bonus checks for company executives the day before it declared bankruptcy.

In 2002 Enron's accounting firm, Arthur Andersen, was found guilty of obstruction of justice charges; two years later the company also lost its appeal of the original ruling.

In December 2005 former accounting officer Richard Causey pleaded guilty to securities fraud and agreed to cooperate with authorities in exchange for a plea deal providing a five- to seven-year prison term and a $1.25 million fine. In May 2006, after a lengthy trial, former CEO Jeffrey Skilling and Enron founder Kenneth Lay were found guilty on various counts of fraud and conspiracy. Lay died six weeks later from a heart attack. Skilling was scheduled to be sentenced in October 2006. Dozens of other people were charged in the Enron scandal; a complete list is published by the *Houston Chronicle* ("The Fall of Enron," 2006, http://www.chron.com/news/specials/enron/background.html#scorecard).

WORLDCOM. In 2002 the federal government began investigating the accounting practices of WorldCom, the second-largest long-distance telephone company in the United States and the world's largest Internet service provider. Eventually, an $11 billion scandal was uncovered. The company filed for bankruptcy—the largest such filing in U.S. history to date. The stock held by investors was worthless, and thousands of former employees lost their jobs, pensions, benefits, and severance pay.

Company executives were indicted on fraud charges; several agreed to testify against former CEO Bernard J. Ebbers in exchange for lighter sentences. In March 2005 Ebbers was convicted of all nine charges against him. He received a sentence of twenty-five years in prison.

TYCO. In 2002 Tyco International Ltd. became embroiled in a series of scandals centered on the company's CEO, L. Dennis Kozlowski, and its CFO, Mark Swartz. Both men resigned and were sued by Tyco in connection with $600 million in loans, salary, and fringe benefits they allegedly took from the company without board approval. The government indicted the men for grand larceny and securities fraud, among other criminal charges.

Kozlowski and Swartz were first tried in September 2003. Particularly at issue during the trial was Kozlowski's extravagant lifestyle. Prosecutors told of Kozlowski throwing his wife a $2.1 million birthday party paid for in part by Tyco, living in a $19 million Manhattan duplex bought for him by the company, and purchasing a $6,000 shower curtain, all while Tyco investors lost millions because of his stock manipulations. The case was declared a mistrial in April 2004 when a juror, suspected of communicating with defense attorneys, was named in

FIGURE 6.4

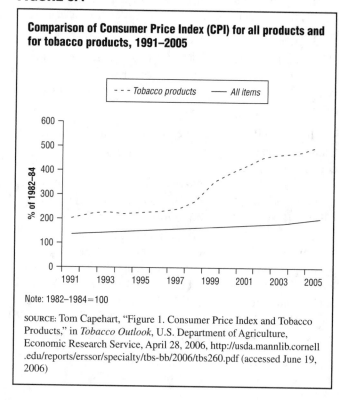

Comparison of Consumer Price Index (CPI) for all products and for tobacco products, 1991–2005

Note: 1982–1984=100

SOURCE: Tom Capehart, "Figure 1. Consumer Price Index and Tobacco Products," in *Tobacco Outlook*, U.S. Department of Agriculture, Economic Research Service, April 28, 2006, http://usda.mannlib.cornell .edu/reports/erssor/specialty/tbs-bb/2006/tbs260.pdf (accessed June 19, 2006)

FIGURE 6.5

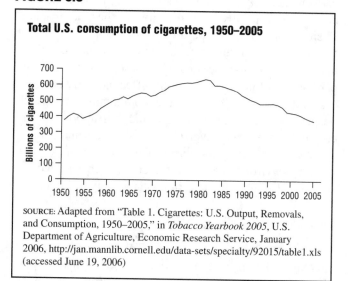

Total U.S. consumption of cigarettes, 1950–2005

SOURCE: Adapted from "Table 1. Cigarettes: U.S. Output, Removals, and Consumption, 1950–2005," in *Tobacco Yearbook 2005*, U.S. Department of Agriculture, Economic Research Service, January 2006, http://jan.mannlib.cornell.edu/data-sets/specialty/92015/table1.xls (accessed June 19, 2006)

the media and subsequently received threatening letters and phone calls. In 2005 the men were retried, found guilty, and sentenced to up to twenty-five years in prison.

Big Tobacco—An Industry under Attack

In the 1990s many state governments brought lawsuits against the nation's major tobacco firms to recoup taxpayer money spent treating sick smokers under state Medicaid programs. In 1998 a settlement was reached in which the companies affected agreed to pay a total of $246 billion spread amongst the governments of all fifty states. The payments are to be made over a twenty-five-year period. The settlement also required the tobacco companies to change their advertising methods and reduce their political lobbying efforts.

In 1999 the federal government filed its own lawsuit (*United States v. Philip Morris*) against the tobacco companies alleging that the defendants had engaged in a decades-long scheme to "defraud the American public" regarding the safety of cigarette smoking. The case centered on internal documents obtained from tobacco companies that seemed to demonstrate that the companies were well aware that nicotine was addictive and cigarette smoking caused lung cancer. The trial began in 2004 and lasted for nine months. As of July 2006, the federal judge who presided over the case had not given a ruling on the findings. But rulings by other courts during 2005 mean that the government cannot pursue a $280 billion penalty that it was seeking from the tobacco companies.

The lawsuits represent an unusual occurrence in American history, because the government has brought financial pressure on an entire industry. Rising costs of doing business in an unfavorable climate have led tobacco companies to raise prices. Figure 6.4 compares the consumer price index (CPI) for all items and for tobacco products between 1991 and 2005. Price inflation for tobacco products has outpaced the general inflation rate over this period, particularly since 1999. On the flip side of the supply-demand relationship, consumption of cigarettes has dropped dramatically. This is likely due to a combination of price pressure and greater public awareness about the dangers of smoking. As shown in Figure 6.5, total U.S. consumption of cigarettes peaked in the 1980s at around 640 billion cigarettes per year. Since then, consumption has plummeted; only 378 billion cigarettes were purchased in 2005, based on preliminary estimates.

Public Perception of Big Business

In June 2006 the Gallup Organization conducted a poll to gauge public confidence in various institutions. As shown in Figure 6.6, the military garnered the highest rating, with 73% of those asked expressing a great deal or quite a lot of confidence in the military. Big business received a much lower rating. Only 18% of respondents had a great deal or quite a lot of confidence in big business.

An earlier Gallup poll conducted in February and March of 2006 found that 65% of respondents felt that major corporations should have less influence in the United States. This value is up from 52% who felt that way in January 2001. Nearly three-quarters of those asked said that big business has "too much influence" over the decisions made by the administration of President George W. Bush (*Big Business*, The Gallup Organization, http://poll.gallup.com/content/default.aspx?ci=5248&pg =1&VERSION=p).

FIGURE 6.6

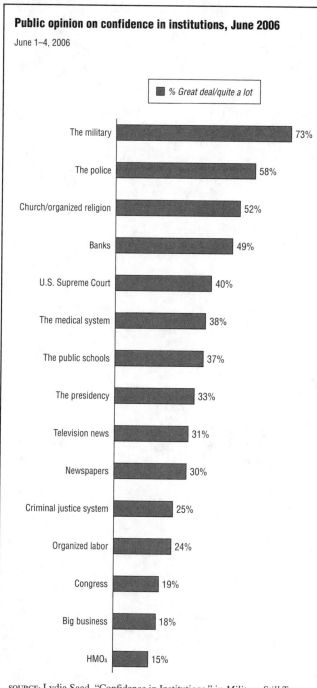

Public opinion on confidence in institutions, June 2006

June 1–4, 2006

■ % Great deal/quite a lot

The military	73%
The police	58%
Church/organized religion	52%
Banks	49%
U.S. Supreme Court	40%
The medical system	38%
The public schools	37%
The presidency	33%
Television news	31%
Newspapers	30%
Criminal justice system	25%
Organized labor	24%
Congress	19%
Big business	18%
HMOs	15%

SOURCE: Lydia Saad, "Confidence in Institutions," in *Military Still Tops in Public Confidence*, The Gallup Organization, June 7, 2006, http://poll.gallup.com/content/default.aspx?ci=23227&pg=1 (accessed June 21, 2006). Copyright © 2006 by The Gallup Organization. Reproduced by permission of The Gallup Organization.

CHAPTER 7
SAVING AND INVESTING

If you would be wealthy, think of saving as well as of getting.

—Benjamin Franklin

Saving and investing are two sides of the same coin. The purpose of saving is to put aside money for use in the future. Saved money can actually make money if it is put into a bank account that earns interest. This is basically a low-risk investment with a low rate of return, but it does preserve the money for the future. Investing is another matter. It means exchanging money for assets that may or may not go up in value over time. Investments that go up in value reap profits for the investor, and those profits can be modest or extravagant. Investments that go down in value are another story. Some or even all of the original money invested is lost. Thus, investing entails risk, particularly in a market-driven economy where fluctuations in supply and demand determine the profitability of investments. At a macroeconomic level, the U.S. economy thrives on investing—it provides money for business growth and government expenses. From a microeconomic standpoint, Americans are urged to save and/or gainfully invest some of their earnings to ensure that they have a safety net in the event of a personal financial crisis and to sustain them after they retire.

PERSONAL SAVING RATE

The personal saving rate is a government-measured rate that tracks how much money Americans have available for saving and investing. It is calculated by the U.S. Department of Commerce's Bureau of Economic Analysis (BEA) using data from numerous sources on income, taxes, government revenues and expenses, and personal expenses. The rate is actually a ratio of two BEA measures: personal saving to disposable personal income (DPI). DPI is defined as personal income (wages, salaries, etc.) minus tax and nontax payments made to the government. Personal saving is determined by subtracting personal outlays

(which are 97% personal consumption expenditures) from DPI. Thus, personal saving is the money left over. This value is divided by the DPI to show what percentage of DPI is available for saving and investing.

Because the personal saving rate is based on so many other calculated variables, any small errors in the dependent variables will be exaggerated in the rate itself. In addition, the BEA excludes from its definition of income certain wealth components like capital gains (which is an increase in the value of an asset). As a result, the agency admits that the personal saving rate "gives an incomplete picture of household savings behavior." However, it is useful for tracking changes over time.

Table 7.1 shows the amounts and derivations of personal saving for the years 1959 through 2005. Personal saving was -$41.6 billion in 2005 based on preliminary estimates. It peaked in 1992 at $366 billion. A negative amount of personal saving in 2005 seems to indicate that Americans spent more than they made in income. Figure 7.1 shows the personal saving rate for first quarter 2000 through first quarter 2006. The rate was positive through the first quarter of 2005 and negative in each subsequent quarter.

DEFINING INVESTMENTS

In the broadest sense any money expenditure that returns a profit is considered an investment. Thus, the cost of a college education would be considered an investment, because it will likely increase earnings potential in the future. In this discussion investments are limited to tangible assets (such as cash or real estate) and intangible financial assets (such as stock, bonds, and other securities).

SAVING ACCOUNTS

Savings accounts are accounts held at financial institutions in which customers can deposit money for

TABLE 7.1

Disposition of personal income, 1959–2005

[Billions of dollars, except as noted; quarterly data at seasonally adjusted annual rates]

Year or quarter	Personal income	Less: personal current taxes	Equals: disposable personal income	Less: personal outlays				Equals: personal saving
				Total	Personal consumption expenditures	Personal interest payments*	Personal current transfer payments	
1959	392.8	42.3	350.5	323.9	317.6	5.5	0.8	26.7
1960	411.5	46.1	365.4	338.8	331.7	6.2	.8	26.7
1961	429.0	47.3	381.8	349.6	342.1	6.5	1.0	32.2
1962	456.7	51.6	405.1	371.3	363.3	7.0	1.1	33.8
1963	479.6	54.6	425.1	391.8	382.7	7.9	1.2	33.3
1964	514.6	52.1	462.5	421.7	411.4	8.9	1.3	40.8
1965	555.7	57.7	498.1	455.1	443.8	9.9	1.4	43.0
1966	603.9	66.4	537.5	493.1	480.9	10.7	1.6	44.4
1967	648.3	73.0	575.3	520.9	507.8	11.1	2.0	54.4
1968	712.0	87.0	625.0	572.2	558.0	12.2	2.0	52.8
1969	778.5	104.5	674.0	621.4	605.2	14.0	2.2	52.5
1970	838.8	103.1	735.7	666.2	648.5	15.2	2.6	69.5
1971	903.5	101.7	801.8	721.2	701.9	16.6	2.8	80.6
1972	992.7	123.6	869.1	791.9	770.6	18.1	3.1	77.2
1973	1,110.7	132.4	978.3	875.6	852.4	19.8	3.4	102.7
1974	1,222.6	151.0	1,071.6	958.0	933.4	21.2	3.4	113.6
1975	1,335.0	147.6	1,187.4	1,061.9	1,034.4	23.7	3.8	125.6
1976	1,474.8	172.3	1,302.5	1,180.2	1,151.9	23.9	4.4	122.3
1977	1,633.2	197.5	1,435.7	1,310.4	1,278.6	27.0	4.8	125.3
1978	1,837.7	229.4	1,608.3	1,465.8	1,428.5	31.9	5.4	142.5
1979	2,062.2	268.7	1,793.5	1,634.4	1,592.2	36.2	5.9	159.1
1980	2,307.9	298.9	2,009.0	1,807.5	1,757.1	43.6	6.8	201.4
1981	2,591.3	345.2	2,246.1	2,001.8	1,941.1	49.3	11.4	244.3
1982	2,775.3	354.1	2,421.2	2,150.4	2,077.3	59.5	13.6	270.8
1983	2,960.7	352.3	2,608.4	2,374.8	2,290.6	69.2	15.0	233.6
1984	3,289.5	377.4	2,912.0	2,597.3	2,503.3	77.0	16.9	314.8
1985	3,526.7	417.4	3,109.3	2,829.3	2,720.3	90.4	18.6	280.0
1986	3,722.4	437.3	3,285.1	3,016.7	2,899.7	96.1	20.9	268.4
1987	3,947.4	489.1	3,458.3	3,216.9	3,100.2	93.6	23.1	241.4
1988	4,253.7	505.0	3,748.7	3,475.8	3,353.6	96.8	25.4	272.9
1989	4,587.8	566.1	4,021.7	3,734.5	3,598.5	108.2	27.8	287.1
1990	4,878.6	592.8	4,285.8	3,986.4	3,839.9	116.1	30.4	299.4
1991	5,051.0	586.7	4,464.3	4,140.1	3,986.1	118.5	35.6	324.2
1992	5,362.0	610.6	4,751.4	4,385.4	4,235.3	111.8	38.3	366.0
1993	5,558.5	646.6	4,911.9	4,627.9	4,477.9	107.3	42.7	284.0
1994	5,842.5	690.7	5,151.8	4,902.4	4,743.3	112.8	46.3	249.5
1995	6,152.3	744.1	5,408.2	5,157.3	4,975.8	132.7	48.9	250.9
1996	6,520.6	832.1	5,688.5	5,460.0	5,256.8	150.3	52.9	228.4
1997	6,915.1	926.3	5,988.8	5,770.5	5,547.4	163.9	59.2	218.3
1998	7,423.0	1,027.0	6,395.9	6,119.1	5,879.5	174.5	65.2	276.8
1999	7,802.4	1,107.5	6,695.0	6,536.4	6,282.5	181.0	73.0	158.6
2000	8,429.7	1,235.7	7,194.0	7,025.6	6,739.4	204.7	81.5	168.5
2001	8,724.1	1,237.3	7,486.8	7,354.5	7,055.0	212.2	87.2	132.3
2002	8,881.9	1,051.8	7,830.1	7,645.3	7,350.7	196.4	98.2	184.7
2003	9,169.1	999.9	8,169.2	7,996.3	7,709.9	183.2	103.3	172.8
2004	9,713.3	1,049.1	8,664.2	8,512.5	8,214.3	186.7	111.5	151.8
2005ᵖ	10,238.2	1,206.9	9,031.3	9,072.8	8,745.9	206.4	120.5	−41.6

*Consists of nonmortgage interest paid by households.
ᵖPreliminary.

SOURCE: Adapted from "Table B-30. Disposition of Personal Income, 1959–2005," in *Economic Report of the President*, U.S. Government Printing Office, February 2006, http://www.gpoaccess.gov/eop/2006/2006_erp.pdf (accessed June 26, 2006)

safekeeping. Deposits up to $100,000 per customer are insured at most financial institutions by an independent government agency—the Federal Deposit Insurance Corporation (FDIC). FDIC insurance ensures depositors that their money will be repaid even if the financial institution goes out of business.

The Survey of Consumer Finances (SCF) is a survey conducted every three years by the Federal Reserve (the Fed) in cooperation with the Internal Revenue Service to collect detailed financial information on American families. The most recent SCF was conducted in 2004. According to the February 2006 issue of *Federal Reserve Bulletin*, less than half of American families (47.1%) had a savings account in 2004 ("Recent Changes in U.S. Family Finances: Evidence from the 2001 and 2004 Survey of Consumer Finances").

Variations on savings accounts include money market deposit accounts (which allow limited withdrawals in

FIGURE 7.1

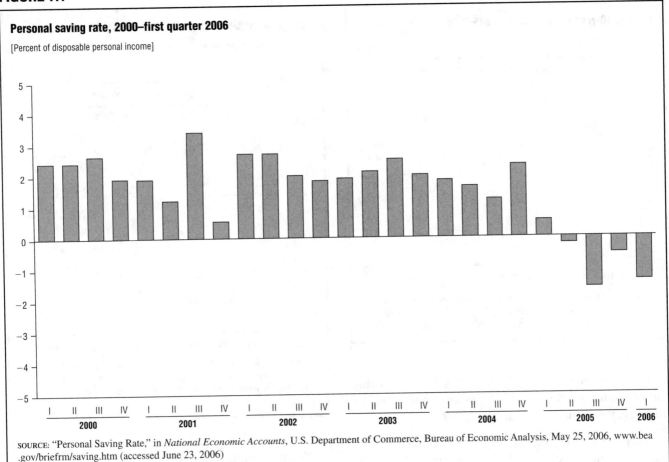

Personal saving rate, 2000–first quarter 2006

[Percent of disposable personal income]

SOURCE: "Personal Saving Rate," in *National Economic Accounts*, U.S. Department of Commerce, Bureau of Economic Analysis, May 25, 2006, www.bea .gov/briefrm/saving.htm (accessed June 23, 2006)

some circumstances) and certificates of deposit (CDs). CDs are savings accounts in which money is placed for a predetermined amount of time, commonly one to five years, in exchange for payment of a set interest rate throughout that time period. There are penalties for early withdrawal of the money.

GOVERNMENT SECURITIES

The government issues a variety of securities with the purpose of earning revenue. Local and state governments sell bonds to raise funds for public projects, such as road improvement or school construction. A bond is basically an IOU from the government that promises to pay back the borrowed amount plus interest at a specified future date (the maturity date). The federal government also sells bonds (called savings bonds) through the U.S. Treasury Department.

Savings bonds are not marketable securities. They can only be sold or redeemed by the Treasury Department. Treasury bills (T-bills) are short-term securities that mature within a few days or up to twenty-six weeks. The customer purchases a T-bill for less than its face value and then receives face value at maturity. For example, a customer might pay $90 upfront for a $100 T-bill.

When the T-bill matures, the customer will receive the $100. T-bills can be bought and sold in other markets. Treasury notes (T-notes) have maturity periods lasting two, three, five, and ten years. They earn a fixed rate of interest every six months. T-notes can be sold by the customer before the maturity date.

Figure 7.2 shows the annual percent yield between 1995 and 2005 on a ten-year T-note and a ninety-one-day T-bill. The interest paid on the ten-year T-note has been higher than that paid on the short-term T-bill due to the longer maturity period of the T-note.

HOMEOWNERSHIP AS AN INVESTMENT

One of the largest investments made by most Americans is the purchase of a home. Because real estate tends to appreciate in value, buying a home is considered a relatively low-risk investment. During the mid-1980s interest rates began a downward trend in response to rate cuts by the Fed. The result was a boom in home purchases and refinancings that has lasted into the early 2000s. Figure 7.3 shows the sales rate for newly built and existing single-family homes from 1997 through the spring of 2006. Annual sales of newly built homes reached 1.23 million units in May 2006, up from less

FIGURE 7.2

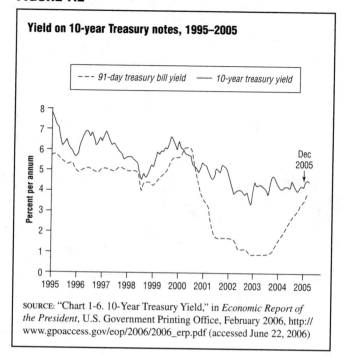

Yield on 10-year Treasury notes, 1995–2005

SOURCE: "Chart 1-6. 10-Year Treasury Yield," in *Economic Report of the President*, U.S. Government Printing Office, February 2006, http://www.gpoaccess.gov/eop/2006/2006_erp.pdf (accessed June 22, 2006)

FIGURE 7.3

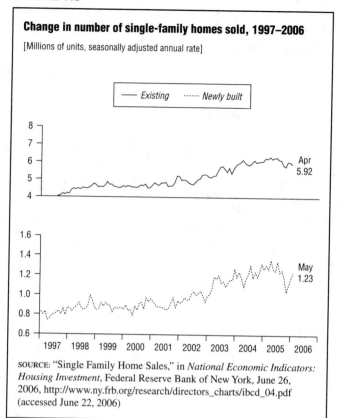

Change in number of single-family homes sold, 1997–2006

[Millions of units, seasonally adjusted annual rate]

SOURCE: "Single Family Home Sales," in *National Economic Indicators: Housing Investment*, Federal Reserve Bank of New York, June 26, 2006, http://www.ny.frb.org/research/directors_charts/ibcd_04.pdf (accessed June 22, 2006)

than 800,000 units in 1997. Annual sales of existing homes totaled nearly six million as of April 2006, up from less than four million units in 1997.

Figure 7.4 shows the vacancy rates for owner homes and rental units between 1995 and early 2006. The vacancy rate of owner homes was less than 2% for most of the time period. In contrast, the rental vacancy rate soared to almost 10.5% in the early 2000s. It has since trended downward but remains high by historical standards. Economists agree that high vacancy rates are generally an indicator of a sluggish economy.

Housing Price Index

The Office of Federal Housing Enterprise Oversight (OFHEO) is a federal financial regulator. It was established as an independent entity within the Department of Housing and Urban Development by the Federal Housing Enterprises Financial Safety and Soundness Act of 1992. The OFHEO House Price Index (HPI) provides an indicator of home appreciation (increase in home value) by measuring average price changes in repeat sales or refinancings of the same properties over time.

Figure 7.5 shows the OFHEO House Price Index for the country as a whole and for individual states as of fourth-quarter 2005. Nationwide home prices appreciated by 13.3% since fourth-quarter 2004. The ten states with the highest percent changes were:

- Arizona—35.5%
- Florida—27.8%
- Hawaii—24.4%

- Washington, DC—23.4%
- Maryland—21.9%
- California—21.5%
- Oregon—20.1%
- Virginia—20%
- Idaho—19%
- Washington—18.8%

In general, states in the Midwest had the lowest percent changes in home values. Figure 7.6 shows nationwide HPI values from 1995 through early 2006. House values have climbed dramatically over that time, reflecting a boom in the housing market. A slight downturn occurred in late 2005 and early 2006.

A Housing Bubble?

Dramatic increases in the Housing Price Index have led some analysts to warn about a housing market bubble in the United States. This is a condition in which homes become overvalued due to overconfidence by exuberant investors. As described in Chapter 1, a stock market bubble in Internet-based companies grew and then burst around the year 2000, causing major losses for some investors. Unfortunately, a bubble is only obvious after the fact, when investments suddenly plummet in value and it becomes apparent that they were overvalued.

FIGURE 7.4

Vacancy rates for rental units and owned homes, 1995–2006

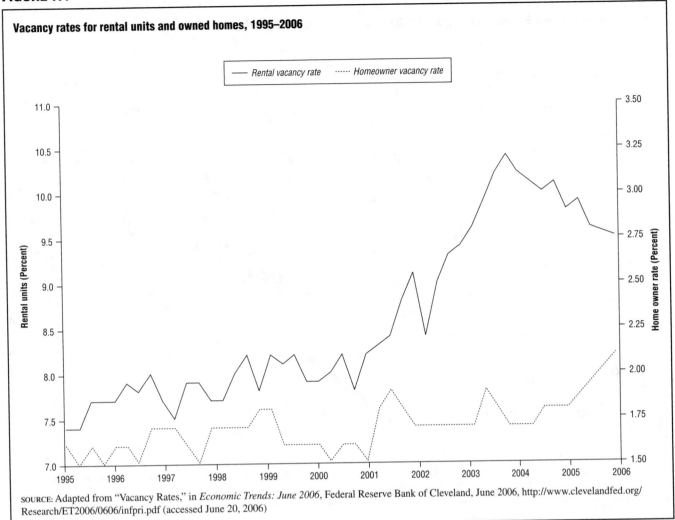

SOURCE: Adapted from "Vacancy Rates," in *Economic Trends: June 2006*, Federal Reserve Bank of Cleveland, June 2006, http://www.clevelandfed.org/
Research/ET2006/0606/infpri.pdf (accessed June 20, 2006)

Appreciating home prices and decreasing interest rates combined to make the housing market very attractive to investors during the 1990s and early 2000s. "Flipping" is a practice in which a home is purchased as a short-term investment, rather than for living purposes. During a housing boom homes can be bought and resold quickly for a handsome profit. Likewise, homeowners who want to move may wait for a boom to peak before selling or sell quickly and rent in anticipation of lower home prices after the bubble bursts. The gamble for all parties involved is the difficulty of predicting when a boom will end and prices will fall.

In 2005 the FDIC conducted a study to quantify housing booms and busts that have occurred since 1978. The FDIC defined a boom as occurring when inflation-adjusted home prices in an area increased by 30% or more during any three-year period. Using this criterion, the FDIC identified dozens of metropolitan areas around the country that have experienced temporary housing booms that could be described as unsustainable bubbles. Geographically, they were concentrated in California and

the Northeast. However, the study found that most housing bubbles did not burst, but slowly deflated following a period of price stagnation. Cases in which housing bubbles did burst were associated with local economic downturns, independent of the housing market ("U.S. Home Prices: Does Bust Always Follow Boom?," February 10, 2005, http://www.fdic.gov/bank/analytical/fyi/2005/021005fyi.html).

In December 2005 the *Wall Street Journal* noted that the U.S. housing market was cooling in many parts of the country due to rising interest rates and waning investor interest (Ruth Simon, "Investors Retreat from Housing Market," December 7, 2005, http://online.wsj.com/public/article/SB113392311667515894-v7ZPwGcry2bT7zPObFt9kC0j3hY_20051213.html?mod=mktw). This assessment became a common one as 2006 progressed and regional housing markets continued to decline. In August 2006 a *New York Times* article predicted that the housing market would undergo a "painful" correction, particularly on the East and West coasts and in the Southwest, where home price appreciation has been the greatest (Vikas Bajaj, "For

FIGURE 7.5

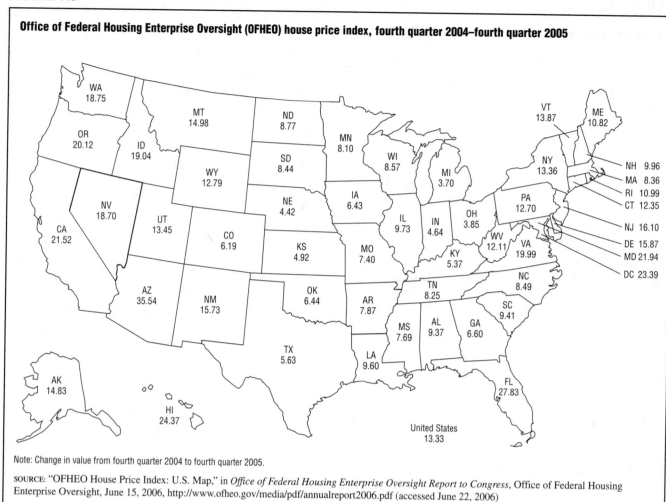

Office of Federal Housing Enterprise Oversight (OFHEO) house price index, fourth quarter 2004–fourth quarter 2005

WA 18.75
OR 20.12
MT 14.98
ID 19.04
ND 8.77
MN 8.10
WI 8.57
MI 3.70
VT 13.87
ME 10.82
NY 13.36
NH 9.96
MA 8.36
RI 10.99
CT 12.35
WY 12.79
SD 8.44
IA 6.43
PA 12.70
NV 18.70
UT 13.45
NE 4.42
IL 9.73
IN 4.64
OH 3.85
NJ 16.10
DE 15.87
CA 21.52
CO 6.19
KS 4.92
MO 7.40
KY 5.37
WV 12.11
VA 19.99
MD 21.94
DC 23.39
AZ 35.54
NM 15.73
OK 6.44
AR 7.87
TN 8.25
NC 8.49
SC 9.41
MS 7.69
AL 9.37
GA 6.60
TX 5.63
LA 9.60
FL 27.83
AK 14.83
HI 24.37
United States 13.33

Note: Change in value from fourth quarter 2004 to fourth quarter 2005.

SOURCE: "OFHEO House Price Index: U.S. Map," in *Office of Federal Housing Enterprise Oversight Report to Congress*, Office of Federal Housing Enterprise Oversight, June 15, 2006, http://www.ofheo.gov/media/pdf/annualreport2006.pdf (accessed June 22, 2006)

Housing, A Finger in the Wind," August 10, 2006, http://www.nytimes.com/2006/08/10/business/10housing.html?ex=1312862400&en=6ba6164f8fef2e87&ei=5090&partner=rssuserland&emc=rss).

Home Mortgages

The Fed compiles home mortgage data on a quarterly and annual basis. These values are published in tabular form in "L.218 Home Mortgages" as part of the *Federal Reserve Statistical Release Z.1: Flow of Funds Accounts of the United States*. The Fed includes only mortgages secured by one-to-four-family properties, including owner-occupied condominium units. Mortgage types include first and second mortgages, home equity lines of credit, mortgages held by households under seller-financings arrangements, and construction and land development loans associated with one-to-four-family residences.

Table 7.2 lists outstanding mortgage amounts reported by the Fed as annual amounts for 1999 through 2004 and on a quarterly basis for 2005 and the first quarter of 2006. As of the end of the first quarter of 2006, there was nearly $9.5 trillion in outstanding mortgages. The

vast majority of this amount—$8.9 trillion, or 94% of the total—was devoted to the household sector. Another $481 billion in mortgages was attributed to nonfarm, noncorporate businesses. Nearly $31 billion was devoted to nonfinancial corporate businesses.

SECURITIES AND COMMODITIES

Securities markets (stocks, bonds, and mutual funds) and commodities markets (raw materials and foreign currencies and securities) in the United States are used by corporations to raise money for their business operations and by individuals and banks to build wealth and, in some cases, pay for retirement. These markets have fueled periods of astounding economic growth (called bull markets), but they have also been at the center of downturns (called bear markets) and disastrous economic crashes, creating the need for an extensive regulatory system. Despite regulations, however, the markets occasionally see high-profile scandals involving major figures in the business world.

Securities are financial assets that give holders ownership or creditor rights in a particular organization. The

FIGURE 7.6

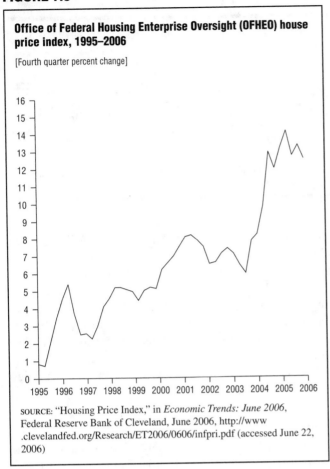

Office of Federal Housing Enterprise Oversight (OFHEO) house price index, 1995–2006

[Fourth quarter percent change]

SOURCE: "Housing Price Index," in *Economic Trends: June 2006*, Federal Reserve Bank of Cleveland, June 2006, http://www .clevelandfed.org/Research/ET2006/0606/infpri.pdf (accessed June 22, 2006)

word usually refers to stocks (also sometimes called equities), but there are other types of securities that can be bought and sold on the open market, including bonds and mutual funds. Commodities are tangible products—usually raw materials—that are bought and sold in bulk, as well as financial instruments such as foreign currencies and securities of U.S. and foreign governments. Commodities can refer either to the material itself or to a contract to buy the item in the future.

Stocks

To raise money to operate and expand a company, its owners will often sell part of the company. A company that wants to raise money this way must first organize itself as a legal corporation. At that time, it creates shares of stock, which are small units of ownership in the company. These shares of stock can then be sold to raise funds for the company. Those who own them are called shareholders in the company. They have the right to attend shareholder meetings, inspect corporate documents, and vote on certain matters that affect the company. Shareholders also may have preemptive rights, which means they are able to buy new shares before they are offered to the public so that existing shareholders can maintain their percentage of ownership in a company.

Not all corporations offer their shares for sale to the public. When a company chooses to do so, its first sale of shares is called an initial public offering (IPO). IPO stock is purchased by investors at a price set by the company. The money paid for each share of stock is then available to the company for its business operations. In return, shareholders can receive benefits in two forms: dividends and appreciation. Dividends are a portion of the company's profits distributed to shareholders. Not all companies that issue stock pay dividends. Those that do usually pay them every quarter (a quarter is three consecutive months of the year; there are four quarters in a fiscal year), and, while each share of stock might earn only a few pennies in dividends, the total amounts to individual or institutional investors who hold large amounts of shares can be enormous. Appreciation is a gradual increase in the value of a share over time. If a corporation prospers, a shareholder can sell his or her share to someone else for a higher price than he or she originally paid for it. There is no guarantee that a stock will appreciate, however; it is quite possible it will depreciate (decrease in value) over time instead.

TYPES OF SHAREHOLDERS. Corporations can offer different types of shares, called either common or preferred shares, with each type providing the shareholder a different set of rights. According to Ameritrade (http://www.ameritrade.com/educationv2/fhtml/stocksfunds/ prevscom), owners of common stock shares can be paid dividends in cash, property, or more stock. Cash dividends are investment earnings that are paid to the shareholder in the form of cash; they are taxed in the year in which they are paid out by a corporation to the shareholder. Property dividends are earnings usually paid in the form of the issuing company's products or services. Stock dividends are earnings paid in more shares of a company's stock. Although cash dividends are the type of stock earning most often issued to common shareholders, a corporation may decide to stop paying dividends on a temporary basis if the company is experiencing financial instability. Additionally, if a company files for bankruptcy, owners of common stock are the last to be paid, after all creditors and owners of preferred stock. Common stock shareholders, however, do have certain rights within a company, such as the right to vote for board members and officers, which preferred stock owners do not have.

Preferred stock shareholders do earn guaranteed dividends, the values of which are set in advance and pay indefinitely unless the stock is retired or recalled. There are four different kinds of preferred stock. Cumulative preferred stock accumulates whether or not a company has suspended paying dividends, and the preferred shareholder is paid the accumulated earnings once the company begins paying dividends again. Cumulative preferred stock owners receive their dividends before common

TABLE 7.2

Amounts of home mortgages for 1–4 family properties, 1999–first quarter 2006

[Billions of dollars; amounts outstanding end of period, not seasonally adjusted]

	1999	2000	2001	2002	2003	2004	2005 Q1	Q2	Q3	Q4	2006 Q1
Total liabilities	**4673.9**	**5075.2**	**5571.3**	**6244.2**	**7024.1**	**8029.9**	**8233.5**	**8530.3**	**8872.3**	**9175.5**	**9455.5**
Household sector	4410.3	4770.1	5221.4	5844.0	6679.5	7604.5	7794.4	8074.6	8389.4	8682.9	8943.6
Nonfinancial corporate business	11.5	13.5	15.6	16.2	18.0	22.1	23.4	25.2	26.9	28.8	30.9
Nonfarm noncorporate business	252.1	291.6	334.4	383.9	326.5	403.3	415.7	430.4	456.1	463.9	481.1

SOURCE: Adapted from "Table L.218. Home Mortgages," in *Federal Reserve Statistical Release Z.1: Flow of Funds Accounts of the United States*, The Federal Reserve, June 8, 2006, http://www.federalreserve.gov/releases/z1/current/z1.pdf (accessed June 20, 2006)

stock owners receive theirs. Noncumulative preferred stock does not accumulate over temporary dividend suspensions, and its owners do not receive dividend earnings before common stock shareholders. Participating preferred stocks allow shareholders to earn additional dividends when a company's profits exceed expectations. Convertible preferred stock can be changed into common stock if its owner wants to take advantage of common stock appreciation.

Although both common and preferred shareholders can lose the money that they paid for their shares, as well as whatever money the shares may have earned since the initial purchase, they have what is called "limited liability," meaning they cannot be held financially responsible for any lawsuits filed against the company. This limited liability is one of the most important characteristics of stock ownership. Without limited liability, people would not want to become part-owners of the corporation, and the corporation would therefore have trouble raising the money it needs to operate and expand.

PRICING SHARES. When a corporation creates shares, it determines the price per share for the initial public offering. From then on the price of each share depends on the public's perception of how well the corporation is doing. The more profit a corporation makes, the higher the price per share is likely to be. The challenge for investors, of course, is that shareholders cannot predict the future, and stock prices have a tendency to fluctuate up and down over time. A variety of events can influence a stock's price, from the release of a popular new product to news that a company's CEO (chief executive officer) is being investigated for fraud.

The market for stocks sold by shareholders to other shareholders is called the secondary stock market. It would be almost impossible for all shareholders to find buyers for their shares on their own when they choose to sell. To make it easier for shareholders to buy and sell shares, companies affiliate with a particular stock exchange that handles share transactions. In the United States the two most prominent exchanges are the New York Stock Exchange (NYSE) and the NASDAQ (originally known as the National Association of Securities Dealers Automated Quotations but now called by its acronym). The NYSE and NASDAQ are themselves publicly traded companies. The United States also hosts the American Stock Exchange, Boston Stock Exchange, Chicago Stock Exchange, Pacific Exchange in San Francisco, and the Philadelphia Stock Exchange. Additionally, there are stock exchanges in most countries throughout the world.

Bonds

Another way for a company to raise money is to borrow it. Companies can borrow from banks, just like individuals, but they can also borrow by issuing bonds, which are written promises to pay the bondholder back with interest. Bonds have a face value, called par, and that amount defines the amount of the debt.

A bond offers returns to holders in two ways. The organization that issued the bond pays interest to the holder, and the holder can redeem the bond after a certain period of time. That is, the holder can sell the bond back to the organization for its face value. The issuing organization will either make regular interest payments on the bond or initially sell the bond at a much lower price than the face value. After a certain amount of time (often many years), the holder can redeem the bond for face value.

Bonds differ from shares of stock in several important respects. First, any organization can issue bonds, whereas only corporations can issue stock. For that reason, unincorporated businesses and federal, state, and local governments use bonds to raise money. Second, bonds provide no ownership interest in the company. The organization's only obligation to the bondholder is to pay the debt and interest. Bonds are usually less risky for the purchaser than stocks, because the organization is legally obligated to pay the debt, whereas if a corporation has financial difficulties, it is not permitted to pay anything to shareholders until it has paid off its creditors.

However, the rate of return on investment for stocks is generally higher than on bonds to compensate for the higher risk factor. Like stocks, though, bonds are traded by investors for prices that may be very different from the par value. Investors who buy bonds are buying the right to receive the interest payments and to redeem the bond.

The price of a bond depends on a number of factors, including the organization's creditworthiness and the interest rate. Generally, the better the organization's credit rating, the higher the price of the bond. If the organization begins to have financial problems that could impact its ability to repay the bonds, the price of those bonds will go down. One of the best-known rating companies for bonds is Standard and Poor's, which rates issuing organizations on a scale ranging from AAA to D.

Bonds may be short-term or long-term. Long-term bonds are riskier than short-term, and therefore tend to pay higher interest rates.

Mutual Funds

Most investors try to diversify investments; that is, they put money into a number of different types of investments rather than just one or two (a person's total investments are called his or her portfolio). That way, even if one investment loses money, another may make enough profit to compensate for the loss.

For small investors, however, it can be difficult to diversify. It takes time to evaluate different investments, and small investors may only be able to afford to buy one or two shares of each stock. Most brokers have a minimum purchase requirement higher than what the average investor can afford. Mutual funds were developed to solve such problems for small investors. In a mutual fund the money of multiple investors is pooled and then invested in stocks, bonds, or both. The managers of the mutual fund then buy and sell the stocks and bonds on behalf of the investors. By combining their money, small investors are able to diversify.

Unlike the prices of stocks and bonds, the price of a mutual fund is determined by the fund manager rather than by the open market. This price, called net asset value, is based on the fund manager's estimation of the fund's value at a particular time. Mutual funds may be purchased either directly from the fund manager or through a broker or other intermediary. The latter is more expensive, because the investor will be required to pay fees. Mutual funds provide income to investors in two ways. First, if the mutual fund sells stocks or bonds at a profit or receives dividends or interest payments on bonds, these gains can be paid to investors as distributions. Second, the price of the mutual fund itself may go up, in which case investors can sell their mutual funds for more than they paid.

Some people are willing to take a fair amount of risk when they invest, hoping that they will make more money. Usually, the riskier the investment is, the higher the potential return on it is. Others would rather get a smaller return but know that their money is invested in a safer vehicle. Different types of mutual funds have been developed to meet the needs of these different types of investors. Mutual funds differ just as investors do in how much risk they want to take. Some mutual funds invest more conservatively than others. The safest type of mutual fund—and the one that pays the lowest interest—is a money-market fund, which invests in short-term bonds such as T-bills.

Commodities

The term "commodity," in the narrow sense used here, means a contract to buy or sell something that will be available in the future. (In a broader sense, anything that can be bought or sold is a commodity.) These sorts of agreements are traded in commodities exchanges. Two important exchanges in the United States are the Chicago Board of Trade and the Kansas City Board of Trade.

There are two basic types of commodities. Futures are standardized contracts in which the seller promises to deliver a particular good to the buyer at a specified time in the future, at which point the buyer will pay the seller the price called for in the contract. Options on futures (which are usually simply called options) are more complicated. Depending on their exact terms, they establish the right of the buyer of the option to either buy or sell a futures contract for a specified price. Options that establish the right to buy a futures contract are "call options." Those that establish the right to sell a futures contract are "put options." In either case, the buyer of the option only has a limited time in which he can exercise his right, but he is also free not to exercise the right at all.

The meaning of a commodities contract has changed over the years. Raw materials and agricultural commodities have been traded through commodities exchanges since the mid-nineteenth century. More recently, commodities markets have expanded to include trading in foreign currencies, U.S. and foreign government securities, and U.S. and foreign stock indexes.

Because contracts are made before the goods are actually available, commodities are by their very nature speculative. Buyers purchase commodities because they think that their value may increase over time, while the sellers think their value may decrease. For example, the seller of a grain futures contract may believe that there will be a surplus of grain that will drive down prices, while the buyer thinks that a shortage of grain will drive prices up. It is the speculative nature of commodities that makes them interesting to investors. Even if they have no need for the goods that the commodities contracts represent, speculative investors can make a profit by buying the commodities contracts at low prices and then selling them to others when prices rise. Commodities respond differently than stocks and bonds to market forces such as inflation; therefore, they can be a valuable part of a diversified portfolio. However, they are riskier and more difficult to understand.

INVESTMENT OPTIONS

Thanks to retirement investment options including 401(k) plans—funds that workers can contribute to on a before-tax basis and that grow tax-free until the money is withdrawn—a large percentage of Americans are now stock-market investors. Because Social Security retirement benefits are relatively low compared with a person's career income, and the long-term solvency of Social Security continues to be in question, retirement funds are essential to the baby-boom and later generations as they approach retirement age.

Historically, stocks have appreciated faster than inflation has increased, allowing people to build greater wealth than if they attempted to save money in traditional accounts. Investments can also serve as collateral for certain loans. Therefore, although Wall Street might seem far away, it provides small investors the opportunity to build wealth and prepare for retirement far more effectively than they otherwise could.

The stock market has also made it easier for employers to contribute to their employees' retirement funds. This is because many employers contribute company stock, instead of cash, to their employees' retirement accounts.

As shown in Table 7.3, retirement accounts are the most commonly held type of financial asset. Nearly half (49.7%) of all families surveyed in 2004 had a retirement account. Another 20.7% held stocks, while 17.6% had savings bonds, and 1.8% had bonds of other types.

According to the Investment Company Institute (ICI), retirement assets totaled $14.5 trillion in 2005, up 7% from 2004. The ICI reports that retirement assets accounted for more than one-third of all household financial assets during 2005 (*The U.S. Retirement Market, 2005* http://www.ici.org/stats/res/fm-v15n5.pdf).

GOVERNMENT REGULATION OF THE MARKET SYSTEM

Prices of stocks, bonds, and commodities fluctuate naturally, which generally is not cause for concern. However, when fluctuations are created as a result of greed or corruption, or by the creation of artificial and unsustainable conditions, the results can be disastrous. Such was the case in 1929, when the market crashed and ushered in the period known as the Great Depression. The exact causes of the stock market crash of 1929 and the ensuing depression are very complex and reach far beyond U.S. borders. But certain conditions related to the American stock market were significant contributors to the economic disaster. The federal government under President Franklin D. Roosevelt, who served from 1933 to 1945, passed a number of laws designed to prevent the sort of abuses of the market that led to the Great Depression, laws that form the basis for the modern market regulatory system.

An Unregulated System

At the time of the 1929 crash, the stock market was largely unregulated. In the months before the crash there were signs that the system was beginning to collapse under its own weight, but the industrialists who owned most of the real wealth fed millions of dollars into the market to stabilize it. They were successful for a time, but at last the artificial conditions created through margin buying (the buying of many market shares at a deflated value) and wild speculation brought the whole system down. Most people lost all, or nearly all, of the money they had invested in the stock market.

Regulation of Securities

Beginning in 1933, Congress enacted a series of laws designed to regulate the securities markets. The Securities Act of 1933 (sometimes referred to as the Truth in Securities law) was a reaction against the events that had led up to the stock market crash of 1929. Its purpose was relatively simple: to protect investors by ensuring that they receive full information on the securities offered for sale to the public, and to prohibit fraud in such sales. The Securities Act set up a system whereby most corporations that wanted to offer shares for sale to the public had to register their securities; the registration information was then made available to the public for review. The required registration forms—still in use today—contain information on the company's management and business structure and the securities it is offering for sale, as well as financial statements drafted by independent accountants. This system is intended to protect investors by making available any information they may need to make informed decisions about their investments, although the truth or accuracy of the information is not guaranteed.

With the passage of the Securities Exchange Act in 1934 Congress established the Securities and Exchange Commission (SEC), which regulates the entire American securities industry. The SEC expanded the Securities Act of 1933 to require more stringent reporting of publicly traded companies and all other entities involved in securities transactions, including stockbrokers, dealers, transfer agents, and exchanges. Additionally, large companies with more than $10 million in assets and five hundred shareholders are required to file regular reports with the

TABLE 7.3

Family holdings of financial assets, 2004

Family characteristic	Transaction accounts	Certificates of deposit	Savings bonds	Bonds	Stocks	Pooled investment funds	Retirement accounts	Cash value life insurance	Other managed assets	Other	Any financial asset
					Percentage of families holding asset						
All families	**91.3**	**12.7**	**17.6**	**1.8**	**20.7**	**15.0**	**49.7**	**24.2**	**7.3**	**10.0**	**93.8**
Percentile of income											
Less than 20	75.5	5.0	6.2	*	5.1	3.6	10.1	14.0	3.1	7.1	80.1
20–39.9	87.3	12.7	8.8	*	8.2	7.6	30.0	19.2	4.9	9.9	91.5
40–59.9	95.9	11.8	15.4	*	16.3	12.7	53.4	24.2	7.9	9.3	98.5
60–79.9	98.4	14.9	26.6	2.2	28.2	18.6	69.7	29.8	7.8	11.2	99.1
80–89.9	99.1	16.3	32.3	2.8	35.8	26.2	81.9	29.5	12.1	11.4	99.8
90–100	100.0	21.5	29.9	8.8	55.0	39.1	88.5	38.1	13.0	13.4	100.0
Age of head (years)											
Less than 35	86.4	5.6	15.3	*	13.3	8.3	40.2	11.0	2.9	11.6	90.1
35–44	90.8	6.7	23.3	.6	18.5	12.3	55.9	20.1	3.7	10.0	93.6
45–54	91.8	11.9	21.0	1.8	23.2	18.2	57.7	26.0	6.2	12.1	93.6
55–64	93.2	18.1	15.2	3.3	29.1	20.6	62.9	32.1	9.4	7.2	95.2
65–74	93.9	19.9	14.9	4.3	25.4	18.6	43.2	34.8	12.8	8.1	96.5
75 or more	96.4	25.7	11.0	3.0	18.4	16.6	29.2	34.0	16.7	8.1	97.6
Race or ethnicity of respondent											
White non-Hispanic	95.5	15.3	21.1	2.5	25.5	18.9	56.1	26.8	9.2	10.2	97.2
Nonwhite or Hispanic	80.6	6.0	8.5	*	8.0	5.0	32.9	17.4	2.1	9.4	85.0
Current work status of head											
Working for someone else	92.2	9.8	20.1	.8	19.6	13.5	57.1	21.8	5.4	9.5	94.5
Self-employed	94.4	14.2	18.7	4.3	31.6	22.3	54.6	29.8	7.6	15.1	96.1
Retired	90.4	20.2	11.4	3.5	19.0	16.2	32.9	29.7	12.8	8.4	93.6
Other not working	76.2	7.9	14.5	*	14.3	10.2	24.9	10.7	*	11.5	79.6
Housing status											
Owner	96.0	15.9	21.2	2.6	25.8	19.2	60.2	30.1	9.6	9.6	97.5
Renter or other	80.9	5.6	9.5	.2	9.1	5.7	26.2	11.0	2.0	10.9	85.5
Percentile of net worth											
Less than 25	75.4	2.2	6.2	*	3.6	2.0	14.3	7.7	*	6.9	79.8
25–49.9	92.0	6.5	13.2	*	9.3	7.2	43.1	19.3	2 3	9.5	96.1
50–74.9	98.0	16.0	22.7	*	21.0	12.5	61.8	30.1	8.8	10.2	99.4
75–89.9	99.7	24.2	28.5	3.2	39.1	32.4	77.6	36.7	15.6	11.2	100.0
90–100	100.0	28.8	28.1	12.7	62.9	47.3	82.5	43.8	21.0	16.4	100.0
					Median value of holdings for families holding asset (thousands of 2004 dollars)						
All families	**3.8**	**15.0**	**1.0**	**65.0**	**15.0**	**40.4**	**35.2**	**6.0**	**45.0**	**4.0**	**23.0**
Percentile of income											
Less than 20	.6	10.0	.4	*	6.0	15.3	5.0	2.8	22.0	2.5	1.3
20–39.9	1.5	14.0	.6	*	8.0	25.0	10.0	3.9	50.0	2.0	4.9
40–59.9	3.0	10.0	.8	*	12.0	23.0	17.2	5.0	36.0	2.5	15.5
60–79.9	6.6	18.0	1.0	80.0	10.0	25.5	32.0	7.0	35.0	4.0	48.5
80–89.9	11.0	20.0	.8	26.7	15.0	33.5	70.0	10.0	50.0	5.0	108.2
90–100	28.0	33.0	2.0	160.0	57.0	125.0	182.7	20.0	100.0	20.0	365.1
Age of head (years)											
Less than 35	1.8	4.0	.5	*	4.4	8.0	11.0	3.0	5.0	1.0	5.2
35–44	3.0	10.0	.5	10.0	10.0	15.9	27.9	5.0	18.3	3.5	19.0
45–54	4.8	11.0	1.0	30.0	14.5	50.0	55.5	8.0	43.0	5.0	38.6
55–64	6.7	29.0	2.5	80.0	25.0	75.0	83.0	10.0	65.0	7.0	78.0
65–74	5.5	20.0	3.0	40.0	42.0	60.0	80.0	8.0	60.0	10.0	36.1
75 or more	6.5	22.0	5.0	295.0	50.0	60.0	30.0	5.0	50.0	22.0	38.8
Race or ethnicity of respondent											
White non-Hispanic	5.0	16.0	1.0	80.0	18.0	45.0	41.0	7.0	45.0	5.0	36.0
Nonwhite or Hispanic	1.5	12.0	.6	*	5.3	18.0	16.0	5.0	40.0	2.5	5.0
Current work status of head											
Working for someone else	3.1	10.0	.7	25.0	10.0	25.0	30.0	5.4	50.0	3.0	20.5
Self-employed	10.0	20.0	1.9	130.0	25.0	60.0	60.0	10.5	42.0	6.0	53.2
Retired	4.2	25.0	3.0	90.0	45.0	75.0	47.0	5.0	45.0	10.0	26.5
Other not working	2.0	8.0	2.0	*	5.0	15.9	31.0	8.4	*	3.0	5.0
Housing status											
Owner	6.0	20.0	1.0	65.0	20.0	50.0	46.0	7.0	45.0	6.0	47.9
Renter or other	1.1	7.0	.7	130.0	4.5	10.0	11.0	3.0	42.0	2.0	3.0

TABLE 7.3

Family holdings of financial assets, 2004 [CONTINUED]

Family characteristic	Transaction accounts	Certificates of deposit	Savings bonds	Bonds	Stocks	Pooled investment funds	Retirement accounts	Cash value life insurance	Other managed assets	Other	Any financial asset
				Median value of holdings for families holding asset (thousands of 2004 dollars)							
Percentile of net worth											
Less than 25	5	2.0	.3	*	1.9	2.0	2.9	.8	*	.7	1.0
25–49.9	2.0	5.8	.5	*	3.5	7.4	11.8	4.0	9.4	2.0	9.9
50–74.9	5.8	10.4	1.0	*	8.0	16.0	33.5	5.0	22.0	5.0	47.2
75–89.9	15.8	31.0	2.0	25.0	20.0	50.0	95.7	10.0	50.0	7.0	203.0
90–100	43.0	46.0	2.5	111.1	110.0	160.0	264.0	20.0	135.0	40.0	728.8
Memo											
Mean value of holdings for families holding asset	27.1	54.9	5.8	547.0	160.3	184.0	121.3	23.1	207.0	39.5	200.7

*Ten or fewer observations.

Note: For questions on income, respondents were asked to base their answers on the calendar year preceding the interview. For questions on saving, respondents were asked to base their answers on the twelve months preceding the interview. Percentage distributions may not sum to 100 because of rounding. Dollars have been converted to 2004 values with the current-methods consumer price index for all urban consumers.

SOURCE: Brian K. Bucks, Arthur B. Kennickell, and Kevin B. Moore, "Table 5B. Family Holdings of Financial Assets, by Selected Characteristics of Families and Type of Asset, 2004 Survey of Consumer Finances," in "Recent Changes in U.S. Family Finances: Evidence from the 2001 and 2004 Survey of Consumer Finances," *Federal Reserve Bulletin*, vol. 92, The Federal Reserve, February 2006, http://www.federalreserve.gov/pubs/oss/oss2/2004/bull0206.pdf (accessed June 20, 2006)

SEC detailing their finances and business dealings. The Securities Exchange Act of 1934 also explicitly outlawed illegal insider trading (described below).

Additional legislation that regulates the securities industry includes:

- Public Utility Holding Company Act. Passed in 1935, this act oversees interstate holding companies that sell or provide electric and gas utilities.

- Trust Indenture Act of 1939. A trust indenture is a formal agreement between a bondholder and an issuer of bonds. The Trust Indenture Act requires this agreement when debt securities such as bonds are offered for public sale.

- Investment Company Act of 1940. This act requires investment and trading companies, such as those that handle mutual funds, to divulge their financial and management information to the public, as well as information about the funds they offer for sale.

- Investment Advisors Act of 1940; amended in 1996. When this act was originally passed, it required most investment advisors to register with the SEC and abide by laws designed to protect investors. In its amended form the act applies only to larger advisors who manage at least $25 million in assets or work with a registered investment company.

- Sarbanes-Oxley Act of 2002. This act is the strongest legislation since the 1940s to impose reforms on the securities industry. Intended to combat fraud and encourage corporate accountability, it also established the Public Company Accounting Oversight Board (PCAOB). Under Sarbanes-Oxley, companies that

trade in the U.S. markets must perform audits of their fraud-prevention and accounting procedures, as well as annual examinations by management of their internal controls. One of the most significant reforms instituted by Sarbanes-Oxley is the provision that bankrupt companies must compensate investors before paying creditors. This provision was largely the result of the WorldCom scandal (described below).

The Commodities Futures Trading Commission

Trading of commodities futures and options in the United States is regulated by the Commodities Futures Trading Commission (CFTC). Established by Congress in 1974, the CFTC is responsible for ensuring integrity in the commodities markets. Like the securities markets, commodities exchanges are not immune to corruption in the forms of fraud, misrepresentation, and price manipulation. The most recent update to the Commodities Exchange Act was the Commodity Futures Modernization Act of 2000.

The sitting U.S. president appoints the five commissioners of the CFTC, who serve staggered five-year terms, as well as a chairman (http://www.cftc.gov/cftc/cftcabout.htm?from=home&page=aboutcftcleft). Under the CFTC chairman's administration are the Office of the Inspector General, which is responsible for internal audits of the CFTC; the Office of International Affairs, which handles the CFTC's involvement in the global markets; and the Office of External Affairs, which serves as the CFTC's media liaison. The CFTC has offices in all U.S. cities that have commodities exchanges: New York, Chicago, Kansas City, and Minneapolis.

WEAKNESSES IN THE MARKET SYSTEM

Even with careful oversight, fraudulent activities can occur in the securities industry. Securities fraud and the ensuing scandals are devastating to investors and to the markets as a whole. There were numerous high-profile instances of accounting scandals and securities fraud in the early twenty-first century.

Illegal Insider Trading

Insider trading is the buying or selling of stock by someone who has information about the company that other stockholders do not have. Most often, it refers to directors, officers, or employees buying or selling their own company's stock. Insider trading by itself is not illegal, but insiders must report their stock transactions to the SEC. Insider trading becomes illegal when it is unreported to the SEC and breaches a fiduciary duty to the corporation; that is, when it violates a duty to act in the corporation's best interests. Most often this happens when someone in the company has confidential information and uses it as the basis for a stock transaction. For example, if a company officer knows that the company is going to file for bankruptcy the next day and sells the company's stock because he or she knows the stock price is going to plummet tomorrow, the trading is illegal. The same goes for someone who gives the information to an outside stockholder so they can act on it.

The best-known case of illegal insider trading in the early twenty-first century involved the company ImClone Systems Inc., media mogul Martha Stewart, and her stock-broker, Peter Bacanovic. The SEC alleged that Bacanovic passed confidential information to Stewart and that she sold her stock in ImClone because of that information. The SEC also accused Stewart and Bacanovic of trying to cover up the matter afterward by lying to federal investigators. The insider trading charge against Stewart was dropped, but she was convicted of lying to investigators and obstruction of justice. Bacanovic was convicted of most of the charges against him. Stewart entered prison to serve a five-month sentence in October 2004 and was released to house arrest in March 2005.

Overvaluing and Accounting Scandals

Overvaluing is the overstatement of income by companies with the assistance of their accountants in order to create an inflated impression of financial success among investors, thereby increasing the value of stock. In the early twenty-first century Wall Street experienced numerous scandals concerning such accounting practices at major corporations. According to Penelope Patsuris of Forbes.com ("The Corporate Scandal Sheet," August 26, 2002, http://www.forbes.com/2002/07/25/accountingtracker.html), inflated figures were reported for such companies as Halliburton, Kmart, Xerox, Merck, Adelphia Communications, Bristol-Meyers Squibb, and AOL Time Warner. The most egregious and notorious breaches of regulations occurred at three companies: Enron, WorldCom, and Tyco. (See Chapter 6.) All three became targets of SEC investigations, with company executives brought up on criminal fraud charges and investors losing billions of dollars.

CHAPTER 8
WEALTH IN AMERICA

All communities divide themselves into the few and the many. The first are the rich and the well-born; the other, the mass of the people.

—Alexander Hamilton, 1787

Wealth is collected assets—cash, commodities, stocks, bonds, businesses, and properties. In the United States a small percentage of people have enormous wealth and the rest of the population has far less wealth. Is this a natural and acceptable result of capitalism or an economic injustice that must be righted for the good of society? This is a debate that has raged since the nation was founded. Some people believe that the accumulation of great wealth is available to anyone in America as the reward for hard work, ingenuity, and wise decision-making. Other people believe that American political, business, and social systems are unfairly structured so as to limit wealth-building by certain segments of the population.

THE COMPONENTS OF WEALTH

The components of wealth can be divided into two broad categories: tangible assets and intangible assets. Tangible assets are things that have value in and of themselves. Examples include gold, land, houses, cars, boats, artwork, jewelry, and all other durable consumer goods with recognizable value in the marketplace. These are material possessions. Intangible assets are financial devices that have worth because they have perceived value. The most obvious examples are stocks and bonds. Other devices often counted as intangible assets include pensions (which are promises of future income), life insurance policies with cash value, and insurance policies on tangible assets, because they protect valuable resources.

The federal government does not measure the overall wealth of individual Americans or the population as a whole. It does compile data on related economic indicators that include wealth assets. These measures are called net worth and personal income.

Net Worth

Net worth is the sum of all assets minus the sum of all liabilities (such as debts). The Federal Reserve (the Fed) computes the aggregate net worth of households and nonprofit organizations on a quarterly and annual basis. These values are published in tabular form in "B.100 Balance Sheet of Households and Nonprofit Organizations" as part of the *Federal Reserve Statistical Release Z.1: Flow of Funds Accounts of the United States*. Table 8.1 shows the net worth data available as of June 2006 for the first quarter of 2006.

ASSETS. Overall, American households and nonprofit organizations (NPOs) had assets of $66 trillion in the first quarter of 2006; of this, $26 trillion was in tangible assets and nearly $40 trillion was in financial assets. Figure 8.1 provides a breakdown of assets by category for 1994 through 2005. Over this period tangible assets increased from roughly one third of total assets to around 40%. The Fed includes only three components in tangible assets: real estate, NPO equipment and software, and consumer durable goods. As shown in Figure 8.2, real estate holdings totaled $22.2 billion, making up nearly 85% of all tangible assets. (See Figure 8.2.)

Financial assets were much more diverse, as shown in Figure 8.3. The largest components were pension fund reserves ($11.1 trillion, or 29% of the total), proprietors' investment (or equity) in unincorporated businesses ($6.8 trillion, or 17% of the total), and deposits ($6.3 trillion, or 16% of the total). Deposits include monies in checking and saving accounts and in money market funds.

LIABILITIES. Assets alone do not provide an indication of the nation's wealth status. Debts and other obligations, known as liabilities, must be subtracted. These liabilities totaled $12 trillion during first-quarter 2006.

TABLE 8.1

Balance sheet of households and nonprofit organizations, first quarter 2006

[Billions of dollars; amounts outstanding end of period, not seasonally adjusted]

	2006 Q1
Assets	**66029.0**
Tangible assets	26222.7
Real estate	22176.9
Households[a, b]	20364.5
Nonprofit organizations	1812.4
Nonprofit organizations[c]	224.2
Consumer durable goods[c]	3821.6
Financial assets	39806.3
Deposits	6251.4
Foreign deposits	66.9
Checkable deposits and currency	338.5
Time and savings deposits	4889.2
Money market fund shares	956.7
Credit market instruments	3215.9
Open market paper	169.3
Treasury securities	464.2
Savings bonds	205.9
Other Treasury	258.2
Agency- and GSE-backed securities	691.3
Municipal securities	860.1
Corporate and foreign bonds	854.2
Mortgages	176.8
Corporate equities[a]	5684.5
Mutual fund shares[d]	4537.4
Security credit	589.5
Life insurance reserves	1096.8
Pension fund reserves	11108.6
Equity in noncorporate business[e]	6786.3
Miscellaneous assets	535.8
Liabilities	**12198.8**
Credit market instruments	11760.5
Home mortgages[f]	8943.6
Consumer credit	2149.6
Municipal securities[g]	212.4
Bank loans n.e.c.	117.9
Other loans and advances	119.5
Commercial mortgages[g]	217.6
Security credit	249.4
Trade payables[g]	166.4
Deferred and unpaid life insurance premiums	22.5
Net worth	**53830.3**
Memo:	
Replacement-cost value of structures:	
Residential	13022.6
Households	12545.2
Farm households	298.1
Nonprofit organizations	179.3
Nonresidential (nonprofits)	1269.7

(See Table 8.1.) Credit market instruments accounted for the vast majority of this total, at $11.8 trillion. Home mortgages ($8.9 trillion) were the single largest credit market instrument, followed by consumer credit ($2.1 trillion).

TRENDS IN NET WORTH. As shown in Table 8.1, the net worth of American households and NPOs totaled nearly $54 trillion in the first quarter of 2006. Figure 8.4 compares this value to net worth values calculated by the Fed for the years 1999 to 2005 and first quarter 2006. Following a downward trend that lasted through 2002, net worth has increased slightly each year through first quarter 2006.

TABLE 8.1

Balance sheet of households and nonprofit organizations, first quarter 2006 [CONTINUED]

[Billions of dollars; amounts outstanding end of period, not seasonally adjusted]

	2006 Q1
Disposable personal income	9301.6
Household net worth as percentage of disposable personal income	578.7
Owners' equity in household real estate[h]	11421.0
Owners' equity as percentage of household real estate[i]	56.1

Note: Sector includes farm households.
[a]At market value.
[b]All types of owner-occupied housing including farm houses and mobile homes, as well as second homes that are not rented, vacant homes for sale, and vacant land.
[c]At replacement (current) cost.
[d]Value based on the market values of equities held and the book value of other assets held by mutual funds.
[e]Net worth of noncorporate business and owners' equity in farm business and unincorporated security brokers and dealers.
[f]Includes loans made under home equity lines of credit and home equity loans secured by junior liens.
[g]Liabilities of nonprofit organizations.
[h]Line 4 less line 32.
[i]Line 49 divided by line 4.

SOURCE: Adapted from "Table B. 100. Balance Sheet of Households and Nonprofit Organizations," in *Federal Reserve Statistical Release Z.1: Flow of Funds Accounts of the United States*, The Federal Reserve, June 8, 2006, http://www.federalreserve.gov/releases/z1/current/z1.pdf (accessed June 26, 2006)

Personal Income

The U.S. Department of Commerce's Bureau of Economic Analysis (BEA) collects data on the personal income of Americans. Figure 8.5 shows the breakdown of personal income by source for 2005, when the total was $10.2 trillion. More than half (56%) of personal income was from wages and salaries. Another 14% was attributed to employer-provided benefits. Interest income and proprietors' income each accounted for 9% of the total. Proprietors' income is income earned by sole proprietorships, partnerships, and tax-exempt cooperatives. The remainder of personal income was from net transfer receipts (6%), dividends (5%), and rental receipts (1%). Net transfer receipts are mostly government social benefits such as old-age, survivors, disability and health insurance; unemployment insurance; veterans benefits; and family assistance funds.

In 2005 compensation (wages, salaries, and employer-provided benefits) amounted to more than $7 trillion and accounted for 70% of total personal income. Figure 8.6 shows the historical annual percentage of personal income comprised of compensation. After rising in the 1960s, the percentage began a gradual decline. As illustrated in Figure 8.7, the percentage of personal income from proprietors' income has also declined since 1960. But the contribution to personal income from receipts on assets—interest and dividends—has increased over this time period.

FIGURE 8.1

Total assets of households and nonprofit organizations, 1994–2005

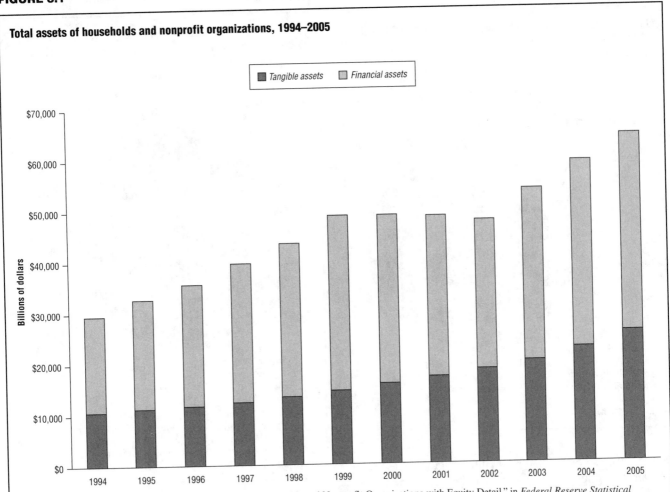

SOURCE: Adapted from "Table B.100.e. Balance Sheet of Households and Nonprofit Organizations with Equity Detail," in *Federal Reserve Statistical Release Z.1: Flow of Funds Accounts of the United States*, The Federal Reserve, June 8, 2006, http://www.federalreserve.gov/releases/z1/current/z1.pdf (accessed June 26, 2006)

DEMOGRAPHICS OF UNEMPLOYMENT. Although the contribution of compensation to personal income has decreased in recent decades, it still accounts for the largest portion of personal income. Thus, employment factors are extremely important to a discussion of wealth and its distribution. Table 8.2 shows the civilian unemployment rate by demographic characteristics for the years 2000 through 2005. In 2005 the overall rate of unemployment for all civilian workers was 5.1%. The average was lower for white workers (4.4%) than for minorities (10%). The lowest unemployment rate for any demographic group was 3.8% among white men age twenty years and older. The highest rate was 36.3% among minority males age sixteen to nineteen years.

POVERTY IN AMERICA

Poverty is defined and measured in different ways by different government entities. At the federal level it is measured using two methods: poverty thresholds and poverty guidelines. Poverty thresholds are set by the U.S. Census Bureau, which also tracks poverty populations in

the United States. The thresholds specify minimum income levels for different sizes and categories of families. For example, in 2005 the poverty threshold for a family of four including two related children in the household was $19,806 per year, according to the Census Bureau.

Poverty guidelines are published by the U.S. Department of Health and Human Services (HHS) for the forty-eight contiguous states, Washington, D.C., Hawaii, and Alaska. According to the HHS, the poverty guidelines are a "simplification" of the poverty thresholds and are used for administrative purposes, such as determining eligibility for specific federal programs. The most recent guidelines were published in the Federal Register on January 24, 2006.

The Poverty Rate

The U.S. Census Bureau calculates the number of people in poverty and the poverty rate using the poverty thresholds. The most recent data were collected during calendar year 2004 as part of the Current Population

FIGURE 8.2

FIGURE 8.3

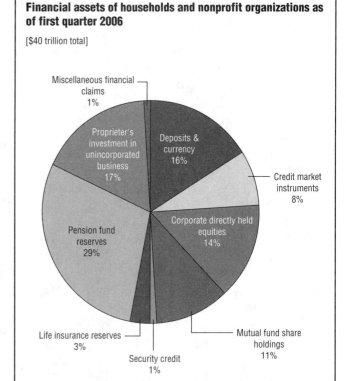

Tangible assets of households and nonprofit organizations as of first quarter 2006

[$26 trillion total]

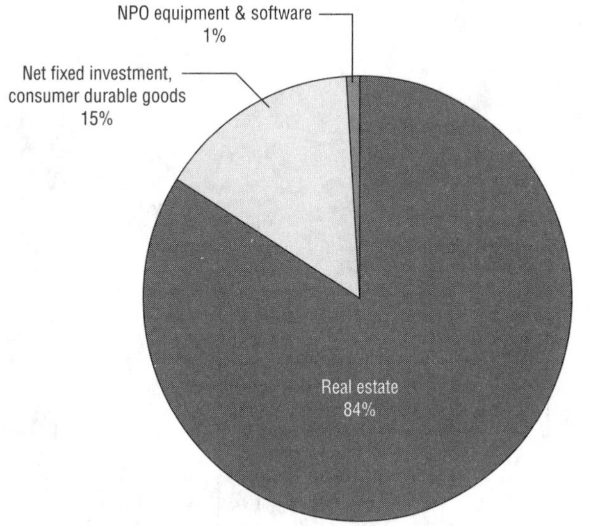

NPO equipment & software 1%

Net fixed investment, consumer durable goods 15%

Real estate 84%

SOURCE: Adapted from "Table B.100. Balance Sheet of Households and Nonprofit Organizations," in *Federal Reserve Statistical Release Z.1: Flow of Funds Accounts of the United States*, The Federal Reserve, June 8, 2006, http://www.federalreserve.gov/releases/z1/current/z1.pdf (accessed June 26, 2006)

Financial assets of households and nonprofit organizations as of first quarter 2006

[$40 trillion total]

Miscellaneous financial claims 1%

Proprietor's investment in unincorporated business 17%

Deposits & currency 16%

Credit market instruments 8%

Corporate directly held equities 14%

Pension fund reserves 29%

Life insurance reserves 3%

Security credit 1%

Mutual fund share holdings 11%

SOURCE: Adapted from "Table B.100. Balance Sheet of Households and Nonprofit Organizations," in *Federal Reserve Statistical Release Z.1: Flow of Funds Accounts of the United States*, The Federal Reserve, June 8, 2006, http://www.federalreserve.gov/releases/z1/current/z1.pdf (accessed June 26, 2006)

Survey, Annual Social and Economic Supplement—a sample survey of approximately one hundred thousand households around the United States. The data were presented and discussed in *Income, Poverty, and Health Insurance Coverage in the United States: 2004* (August 30, 2005, http://www.census.gov/prod/2005pubs/p60-229.pdf).

According to the report, nearly thirty-seven million Americans lived at or below the federal poverty level in 2004. This represents 12.7% of the population. The number of people in poverty has varied widely over the past few decades. In 1960 there were forty million Americans living in poverty. This value dropped to fewer than twenty-five million people in the early 1970s and then began increasing, reaching near the forty million mark during the early 1990s. The number declined to around thirty-one million in 2000 and then rose throughout the early 2000s.

The poverty rate was around 22% in 1960, dropping to around 11% in the early 1970s. The poverty rate topped 15% during the early 1990s and then decreased to around 12% in 2000, before it began to rise again.

There were dramatic demographic differences in the U.S. poverty rate in 2004. The differences by race and ethnicity were as follows:

- Non-Hispanic whites—8.6%
- Asian-Americans—9.8%

- Hispanics—21.9%
- African-Americans—24.7%

The poverty rates for Hispanics and African-Americans were virtually unchanged from 2003. The rate for non-Hispanic whites increased slightly, from 8.2% in 2003. The rate for Asian-Americans decreased from 11.8% in 2003.

Other demographic differences were also significant. The poverty rate in 2004 for those under age eighteen was 17.8%, compared with 11.3% for people ages eighteen to sixty-four, and 9.8% for people age sixty-five and older. Among family types, the highest poverty rate, by far, was experienced by families headed by unmarried females (28.4%). By contrast, the poverty rate for families headed by unmarried males was 13.5%, and for those headed by married couples it was only 5.5%.

The Working Poor

According to the U.S. Bureau of Labor Statistics (BLS) publication *A Profile of the Working Poor, 2004* (May 2006, http://www.bls.gov/cps/cpswp2004.pdf), about 7.8 million people were classified as "working poor"—those people who are in the workforce at least

FIGURE 8.4

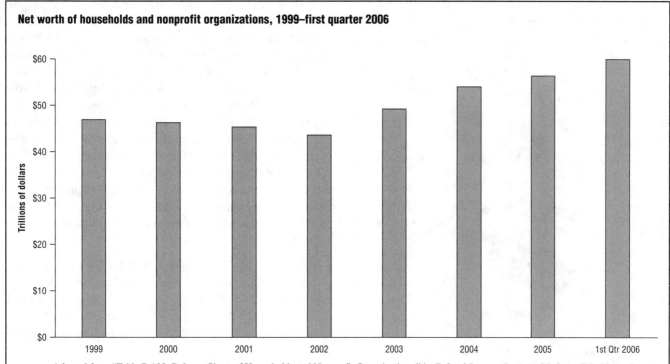

Net worth of households and nonprofit organizations, 1999–first quarter 2006

SOURCE: Adapted from "Table B.100. Balance Sheet of Households and Nonprofit Organizations," in *Federal Reserve Statistical Release Z.1: Flow of Funds Accounts of the United States*, The Federal Reserve, June 8, 2006, http://www.federalreserve.gov/releases/z1/current/z1.pdf (accessed June 29, 2006)

twenty-seven weeks per year but whose income still falls below the poverty level. Just over 6% of American women were among the working poor, compared with 5% of men. Women from all racial and ethnic groups except Asian-Americans were more likely to be among the working poor than men from any racial or ethnic group. African-American women had the highest percentage of working poor (12.5%) of all racial and ethnic groups of either sex.

Although most of the working poor were white (nearly 72%), a greater proportion of African-American and Hispanic workers were among the working poor (10.6% each of African-Americans and Hispanics, versus 4.9% of whites). Just over 10% of all working teenagers ages sixteen to nineteen were among the working poor. The rate was almost double (19.5%) for African-American teens.

Poverty rates varied greatly by educational attainment and occupation. Just over 15% of those in the labor force with less than a high school diploma were among the working poor, compared with only 1.7% of college graduates. In general, management and professional occupations, which tended to require higher levels of education, saw lower amounts of poverty among workers (1.9% were classified as working poor). Occupations in industries such as services and natural resources tended to have more workers living in poverty: 11.2% of service workers were poor in 2004, as were 14.6% of those who

did farming, fishing, or forestry work and 8.3% of workers engaged in construction and extraction occupations.

Analysts consider three continuing problems in the labor market to be responsible for most poverty among working people: low wages, periodic unemployment, and involuntary part-time work. (Involuntary part-time workers are described by the BLS as "persons who, in at least 1 week of the year, worked fewer than 35 hours because of slack work or business conditions, or because they could not find full-time work.") A large majority (80%) of the working poor who typically worked full time experienced at least one of these conditions in 2004.

WEALTH DISTRIBUTION

In January 2006 the Federal Reserve Board issued a report titled "Currents and Undercurrents: Changes in the Distribution of Wealth, 1989–2004" (Arthur B. Kennickell, corrected June 22, 2006, http://www.federalreserve.gov/Pubs/FEDS/2006/200613/200613pap.pdf). The report relies on data collected during the 2004 Survey of Consumer Finances (SCF). The SCF is a survey conducted every three years by the Fed in cooperation with the Internal Revenue Service to collect detailed financial information on American families. The Fed report traces changes in wealth distribution between 1989 and 2004 based on computed net worth values. Table 8.3 shows the distribution of net worth across this time period. All values were computed using

FIGURE 8.5

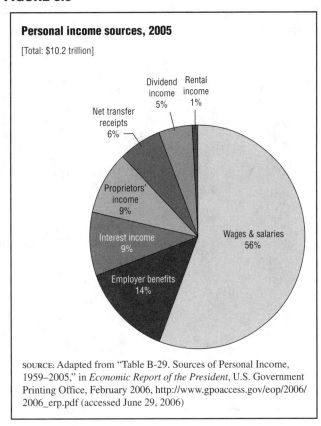

Personal income sources, 2005

[Total: $10.2 trillion]

- Dividend income 5%
- Rental income 1%
- Net transfer receipts 6%
- Proprietors' income 9%
- Interest income 9%
- Employer benefits 14%
- Wages & salaries 56%

SOURCE: Adapted from "Table B-29. Sources of Personal Income, 1959–2005," in *Economic Report of the President*, U.S. Government Printing Office, February 2006, http://www.gpoaccess.gov/eop/2006/2006_erp.pdf (accessed June 29, 2006)

2004 dollars to compensate for the effects of inflation between 1989 and 2004.

In 1989 more than a fourth of families (26.5%) had a net worth of less than $10,000. At the other end of the spectrum, 10.8% had a net worth of at least $500,000. In 2004 the portion of families with a net worth of less than $10,000 was 22.7%, down 3.8 percentage points from 1989. By contrast, the percentage of families in 2004 with a net worth of at least $500,000 had risen by more than half, up 6.9 percentage points to 17.7%.

Gini Coefficients

The Gini coefficient is a mathematically derived value used to describe the inequality in a data distribution. It was developed during the early 1900s by the Italian statistician Corrado Gini (1884–1965). The Fed used the Gini coefficient to measure the extent of the inequality in the distribution of wealth among American families. When used to compute wealth inequality, a value of zero indicates perfect equality, while a value of one indicates that all wealth is held by only one family. The Fed calculated a Gini coefficient of 0.7863 for net worth in 1989 and a value of 0.8047 for net worth in 2004. This indicates that a greater amount of wealth became concentrated in the hands of families at the upper end of the spectrum. In other words, the Gini coefficients suggest that the rich got richer, and the poor got poorer over this time period.

Concentration Ratios

Economists use concentration ratios to show the proportion of wealth held by certain groups within a population. Table 8.4 tabulates the proportion of total net worth and total gross assets held by specific percentile groups as calculated in the Fed report. The ratios shown in the upper table indicate that in 2004 just over one-third (33.4%) of total net worth was held by the wealthiest 1% of families (the families at the 99–100 percentile). The other two-thirds of total net worth was held by the other 99% of families. Another way to look at the data is that the poorest half of the families (those in the 0–50 percentile) held only 2.5% of all net worth in 2004. This value is down from a high of 3.6% in 1995—a decline deemed "significantly different" in the report.

The lower table in Table 8.4 shows the concentration ratios for total gross assets. In 2004 the wealthiest 1% of families held 29.5% of total gross assets. The poorest 50% of families held only 5.8% of total gross assets. This marked a decline from the assets they held in 1992, 1995, and 1998.

WEALTH DEMOGRAPHICS

In February 2006 the Fed released another report on wealth titled "Recent Changes in U.S. Family Finances: Evidence from the 2001 and 2004 Survey of Consumer Finances" (*Federal Reserve Bulletin*, http://www.federalreserve.gov/pubs/bulletin/2006/financesurvey.pdf). The report examines changes in family income and net worth between the SCFs conducted in 2001 and 2004. Overall it found that average pretax family income decreased by 2.3% between 2001 and 2004. (Income values were adjusted for the effects of inflation.) The Fed also analyzed the median pretax family income. The median is the value at which half of the values are greater than the median and the other half are less than the median. Between 2001 and 2004 the median pretax family income increased by 1.6%.

Table 8.5 shows family net worth by demographic characteristics for the 1995, 1998, 2001, and 2004 SCFs. Between 2001 and 2004 the median net worth of all families grew from $91,700 to $93,100, an increase of 1.5%. The mean (average) net worth grew from $421,500 to $448,200, an increase of 6.3%. The Fed notes that the wealth increase was most pronounced for families in the middle-income range.

A variety of factors are cited for overall changes in wealth between 2001 and 2004; most notable are:

- An increase in homeownership combined with strong growth in real estate appreciation (increase in value over time)

- A decrease in wages

FIGURE 8.6

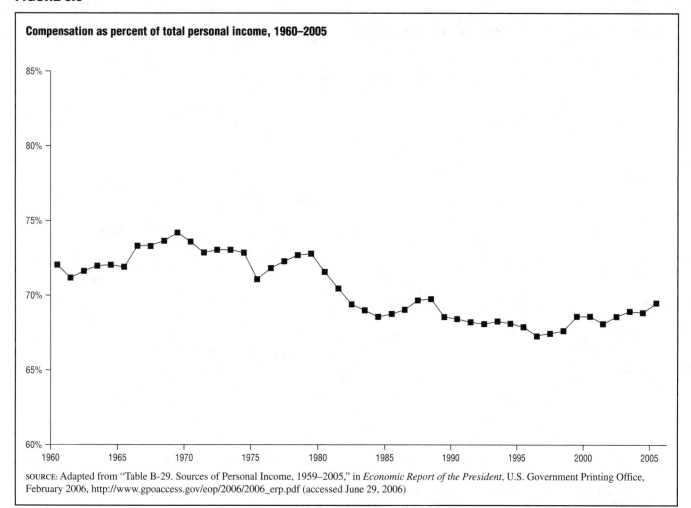

Compensation as percent of total personal income, 1960–2005

SOURCE: Adapted from "Table B-29. Sources of Personal Income, 1959–2005," in *Economic Report of the President*, U.S. Government Printing Office, February 2006, http://www.gpoaccess.gov/eop/2006/2006_erp.pdf (accessed June 29, 2006)

- A decrease in stock ownership and investment income
- An increase in the amount of debt held relative to total assets

The report notes that average wages declined by 3.6% between 2001 and 2004. The median wage also decreased, by 6.2%. The Fed concludes that wealth growth over this time period was weak compared with strong growth experienced between 1992 and 1995 and between 1995 and 1998. Also, the wealth growth between 2001 and 2004 was not consistent across most demographic groups as it had been in the earlier periods.

Race

As shown in Table 8.5, the mean net worth of white families in 2004 was $561,800, while for minority families it was $153,100. The median net worth of white families was $140,700, while for minority families it was $24,800.

Wealth grew for both white and minority families between 2001 and 2004; in fact, the growth for all minorities grouped together outpaced the growth for white families. The average and median net worth of white families increased by 8.3% and 8.6%, respectively. The average and median net worth of minority families increased by 23.7% and 29.8%, respectively.

However, the report notes that African-American families lagged behind other minorities in wealth growth. The median net worth of African-American families grew from $20,300 in 2001 to $20,400 in 2004, an increase of around 0.5%. The average net worth increased from $80,700 to $110,600 over this period, an increase of 37%. This suggests that only a very small number of African-American families improved their net worth, and those families were at the top of the wealth class. By contrast, median and average net worth both increased by more than 8% for white families. This indicates that a greater number of white families improved their financial condition and the gains were more evenly distributed among the wealth classes.

Other Demographics

The data in Table 8.5 indicate that families with the highest average net worth in 2004 had the following characteristics:

FIGURE 8.7

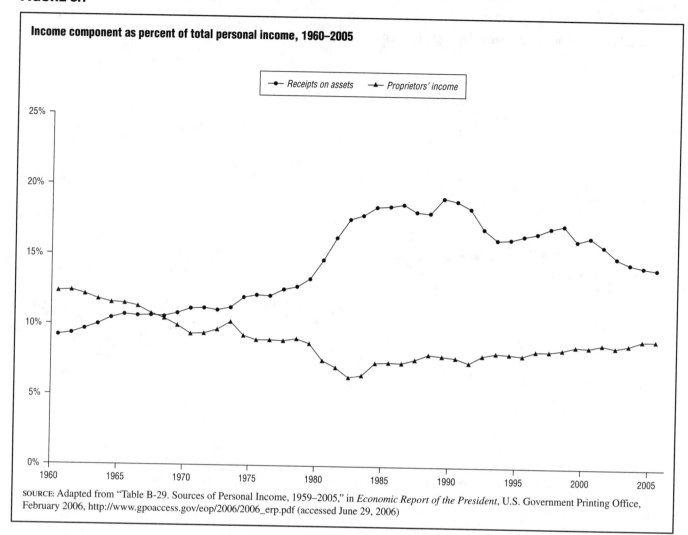

Income component as percent of total personal income, 1960–2005

● Receipts on assets ▲ Proprietors' income

SOURCE: Adapted from "Table B-29. Sources of Personal Income, 1959–2005," in *Economic Report of the President*, U.S. Government Printing Office, February 2006, http://www.gpoaccess.gov/eop/2006/2006_erp.pdf (accessed June 29, 2006)

- A head of household between age fifty-five and sixty-four years old
- A head of household with a college degree
- A self-employed head of household
- Living in the Northeast
- Owning a home

Comparison of data from 1995 and 2004 shows that all demographic groups improved their average net worth over this time period. However, there are variations in median changes. For example, the mean/average net worth of families with a head of household younger than thirty-five increased from $53,200 in 1995 to $73,500 in 2004. Their median net worth, however, decreased from $14,800 to $14,200. The same trend is evident for families headed by a person with no high school diploma and for nonhomeowners. In each case, mean/average net worth increased, but median net worth decreased. The Fed acknowledges that the reasons for this disparity in the growth of

mean and median net worth are complex but attributes it to distributional changes within the demographic groups.

Nonfinancial Assets

Nonfinancial assets are large material items such as real estate, business-related machinery, and automobiles, as well as ownership in businesses. Table 8.6 shows that 92.5% of American families held nonfinancial assets in 2004. The highest percentage of families (86.3%) owned at least one vehicle. A majority (69.1%) owned their primary residence. Smaller percentages owned other residential property (12.5%), had business equity (11.5%), held equity in a nonresidential property (8.3%), or held some other nonfinancial asset (7.8%). As expected, families with higher incomes were more likely to have nonfinancial assets.

Families in the lowest twentieth percentile of income, nonhomeowners, and families in which the head of household was not working were least likely to hold

TABLE 8.2

Civilian unemployment rate by demographic characteristics, 2000–05

[Percent, monthly data seasonally adjusted]

Year or month	All Civilian workers	White* Total	White Males Total	White Males 16–19 years	White Males 20 years and over	White Females Total	White Females 16–19 years	White Females 20 years and over	Black and other or black or African American* Total	Black Males Total	Black Males 16–19 years	Black Males 20 years and over	Black Females Total	Black Females 16–19 years	Black Females 20 years and over
2000	4.0	3.5	3.4	12.3	2.8	3.6	10.4	3.1	7.6	8.0	26.2	6.9	7.1	22.8	6.2
2001	4.7	4.2	4.2	13.9	3.7	4.1	11.4	3.6	8.6	9.3	30.4	8.0	8.1	27.5	7.0
2002	5.8	5.1	5.3	15.9	4.7	4.9	13.1	4.4	10.2	10.7	31.3	9.5	9.8	28.3	8.8
2003	6.0	5.2	5.6	17.1	5.0	4.8	13.3	4.4	10.8	11.6	36.0	10.3	10.2	30.3	9.2
2004	5.5	4.8	5.0	16.3	4.4	4.7	13.6	4.2	10.4	11.1	35.6	9.9	9.8	28.2	8.9
2005	5.1	4.4	4.4	16.1	3.8	4.4	12.3	3.9	10.0	10.5	36.3	9.2	9.5	30.3	8.5
2004:															
Jan	5.7	5.0	5.0	14.4	4.6	5.0	15.0	4.4	10.3	10.9	43.7	9.4	9.8	26.2	9.0
Feb	5.6	4.9	5.0	15.2	4.6	4.8	14.9	4.2	9.6	9.9	30.0	9.1	9.4	22.5	8.8
Mar	5.7	5.1	5.2	16.2	4.7	4.9	13.4	4.5	10.2	10.6	36.7	9.4	9.9	23.8	9.3
Apr	5.5	5.2	5.2	17.5	4.6	4.7	13.2	4.2	9.8	10.2	30.3	9.4	9.3	25.5	8.6
May	5.6	4.9	5.3	18.1	4.7	4.5	12.5	4.0	10.0	10.3	30.6	9.5	9.7	31.9	8.6
June	5.6	5.0	5.1	16.3	4.5	4.9	13.3	4.4	10.2	10.6	34.0	9.5	9.9	32.1	8.8
July	5.5	4.8	4.8	15.7	4.3	4.7	14.5	4.2	11.1	11.9	36.9	10.6	10.5	37.2	9.1
Aug	5.4	4.9	4.9	16.0	4.3	4.5	14.5	4.0	10.5	11.6	34.0	10.5	9.5	23.8	8.8
Sept	5.4	4.8	4.8	15.9	4.2	4.5	13.7	4.0	10.4	11.4	36.3	10.1	9.5	20.8	9.0
Oct	5.4	4.7	4.7	17.5	4.2	4.4	12.3	3.9	10.8	11.7	37.2	10.3	10.0	32.1	8.9
Nov	5.4	4.6	4.6	15.4	4.2	4.5	13.2	4.1	10.7	11.8	37.3	10.3	9.8	26.8	9.0
Dec	5.4	4.6	4.8	18.2	4.1	4.4	13.2	3.9	10.8	12.0	39.4	10.6	9.7	25.8	9.0
2005:															
Jan	5.2	4.5	4.6	16.4	4.0	4.3	11.9	3.9	10.5	11.2	29.8	10.3	9.9	31.5	8.8
Feb	5.4	4.6	4.7	18.1	4.1	4.4	12.8	4.0	10.8	11.8	35.0	10.6	9.9	28.9	9.1
Mar	5.1	4.4	4.6	17.7	3.9	4.1	10.9	3.8	10.3	10.8	36.1	9.3	9.9	29.7	9.0
Apr	5.1	4.4	4.4	17.5	3.8	4.4	12.8	4.0	10.3	10.9	38.5	9.2	9.8	32.9	8.7
May	5.1	4.4	4.4	17.4	3.8	4.4	12.9	3.9	10.0	10.6	36.8	9.1	9.6	35.0	8.3
June	5.0	4.3	4.2	15.8	3.7	4.4	12.3	3.9	10.3	11.1	37.5	9.7	9.6	26.9	8.8
July	5.0	4.3	4.2	15.5	3.7	4.4	11.7	4.0	9.4	9.7	38.9	8.3	9.1	27.4	8.2
Aug	4.9	4.2	4.3	15.3	3.7	4.2	12.4	3.7	9.7	10.0	39.5	8.6	9.3	32.6	8.2
Sept	5.1	4.5	4.5	15.3	4.0	4.4	11.4	4.0	9.5	9.8	33.7	8.7	9.2	32.5	8.1
Oct	4.9	4.4	4.4	15.1	3.8	4.5	13.3	4.0	9.1	9.7	35.0	8.5	8.6	30.3	7.5
Nov	5.0	4.2	4.2	15.1	3.6	4.3	12.6	3.9	10.6	11.3	44.9	9.4	10.0	31.5	9.0
Dec	4.9	4.3	4.3	13.8	3.8	4.3	12.9	3.8	9.3	9.3	23.6	8.6	9.3	25.2	8.5

Note: Unemployed as percent of civilian labor force in group specified. Data relate to persons 16 years of age and over.
*Beginning in 2003, persons who selected this race group only. Prior to 2003, persons who selected more than one race were included in the group they identified as the main race. Data for black or African American were for black prior to 2003. Data discontinued for black and other series.

SOURCE: Adapted from "Table B-43. Civilian Unemployment Rate by Demographic Characteristics,1965–2005," in *Economic Report of the President,* U.S. Government Printing Office, February 2006, http://www .gpoaccess.gov/eop/2006/2006_erp.pdf (accessed June 26, 2006)

TABLE 8.3

Percent distribution of net worth in 2004 dollars, selected years 1989–2004

	1989	1992	1995	1998	2001	2004
<0	7.2	7.2	7.1	8.0	6.9	7.1
=0	3.9	3.2	2.6	2.5	2.6	1.7
1–999	4.0	3.0	2.4	3.2	2.7	2.3
1K–2.49K	3.1	3.6	2.5	2.4	2.3	3.2
2.5K–4.9K	4.3	3.4	3.4	3.2	3.3	4.0
5K–9.9K	4.0	4.9	5.5	4.7	4.6	4.4
10K–24.9K	8.0	9.2	9.2	7.9	7.9	7.8
25K–49.9K	9.3	10.5	10.0	9.4	9.0	8.8
50K–99.9K	13.3	14.2	15.8	12.5	12.2	11.9
100K–249.9K	20.8	21.5	22.2	21.9	19.1	18.6
250K–499.9K	11.3	10.0	9.9	12.5	13.5	12.4
500K–999.9K	5.6	5.2	5.5	6.5	8.4	9.6
>=1M	5.2	4.2	3.8	5.3	7.5	8.1

SOURCE: Adapted from Arthur B. Kennickell, "Table 2. Percent Distribution of New Worth in 2004 Dollars, 1989–2004," in *Currents and Undercurrents: Changes in the Distribution of Wealth, 1989–2004*, Federal Reserve Board, January 30, 2006 (corrected June 22, 2006), http://www.federalreserve.gov/pubs/oss/oss2/papers/concentration.2004.4.pdf (accessed June 30, 2006)

TABLE 8.4

Proportions of total net worth and of gross assets held by various percentile groups, selected years 1989–2004

	Net worth percentile group				
	0–50	50–90	90–95	95–99	99–100
	Proportion of total net worth held by group				
1989	3.0	29.9	13.0	24.1	30.1
1992	3.3	29.6	12.5	24.4	30.2
1995	3.6	28.6	11.9	21.3	34.6
1998	3.0	28.4	11.4	23.3	33.9
2001	2.8	27.4	12.1	25.0	32.7
2004	2.5	27.9	12.0	24.1	33.4
	Proportion of total gross assets held by group				
1989	5.4	32.5	12.6	22.3	27.1
1992	6.6	32.1	12.0	22.6	26.7
1995	7.5	31.2	11.4	19.5	30.4
1998	6.7	30.8	10.9	21.7	29.9
2001	5.6	29.9	11.7	23.4	29.5
2004	5.8	31.0	11.4	22.2	29.5

SOURCE: Adapted from Arthur B. Kennickell, "Table 5. Proportions of Total Net Worth and of Gross Assets Held by Various Percentile Groups, 1989–2004," in *Currents and Undercurrents: Changes in the Distribution of Wealth, 1989–2004*, Federal Reserve Board, January 30, 2006 (corrected June 22, 2006), http://www.federalreserve.gov/pubs/oss/oss2/papers/concentration.2004.4.pdf (accessed June 30, 2006)

nonfinancial assets. There was a notable difference among races: 95.8% of white families held nonfinancial assets in 2004 compared with 84% of minority families.

Financial Assets

Table 7.3 in Chapter 7 shows the percentage of families holding financial assets in 2004 by demographic characteristics. The data indicate that 93.8% of all families held some type of financial asset. Most common were transaction accounts (checking, savings, money market deposit accounts, money market mutual funds, and call accounts at brokerages)—91.3% of families held these accounts. Nearly half of families (49.7%) had retirement accounts. Note that this category does not include Social Security benefits and certain employer-sponsored defined benefit plans. Nearly a quarter of families (24.2%) had cash value life insurance policies. Smaller percentages held stocks (20.7%), savings bonds (17.6%), pooled investment funds (15%), certificates of deposit (12.7%), and bonds (1.8%). Ten percent of families held financial assets of other types.

Overall, families most likely to hold financial assets were those in the highest income brackets, those with a head of household age seventy-five or older, those with a self-employed head of household, and homeowners. Comparison among races indicates that 97.2% of white families held financial assets in 2004, compared with 85% of minority families. The largest difference lies in retirement accounts. More than half (56.1%) of white families had retirement accounts, compared with only 32.9% of minority families. Stock ownership also showed disparities. More than one quarter (25.5%) of white families owned stocks in 2004, compared with only 8% of minority families.

WEALTH INEQUALITY—IS IT A PROBLEM?

Although the data are clear that wealth inequality exists in America, there is contentious debate about whether or not this condition poses a problem to the economy and to society. A certain amount of inequality is built into a capitalist economy by its very nature. But with immense wealth growing rapidly among the already richest 1% of Americans, and a correspondingly shrinking middle class, many economists worry that the perceived economic success of the 2000s may be just an illusion.

Wealth Inequality Seen as Harmful

The debate over wealth inequality has always been a politically partisan issue, with those on the "right" arguing that the market should be allowed to adjust itself with regard to wages and income and those on the "left" maintaining that widespread financial inequality causes numerous social and economic problems. This latter viewpoint was explained at length in an opinion piece published in the *New York Times* on October 20, 2002. In "For Richer" commentator Paul Krugman asserts that wealth inequality has severe economic, political, and social consequences for the nation.

Krugman asserts that wage controls and other measures taken by the government during the Great Depression and World War II created a broad and stable middle class in the United States. An abundance of high-paying unionized manufacturing jobs ensured that less-educated working class people could maintain a standard of living

TABLE 8.5

Family net worth, selected years 1995–2004

[Thousands of 2004 dollars]

Family characteristic	1995 Median	1995 Mean	1998 Median	1998 Mean	2001 Median	2001 Mean	2004 Median	2004 Mean
All families	**70.8**	**260.8**	**83.1**	**327.5**	**91.7**	**421.5**	**93.1**	**448.2**
	(2.4)	(6.4)	(3.2)	(10.7)	(3.3)	(7.1)	(4.3)	(9.7)
Percentile of income								
Less than 20	7.4	54.7	6.8	55.4	8.4	56.1	7.5	72.6
20–39.9	41.3	97.4	38.4	111.5	39.6	121.8	34.3	122.0
40–59.9	57.1	126.0	61.9	146.6	66.5	171.4	71.6	193.8
60–79.9	93.6	198.5	130.2	238.3	150.7	311.3	160.0	342.8
80–89.9	157.7	316.8	218.5	377.1	280.3	486.6	311.1	485.0
90–100	436.9	1,338.0	524.4	1,793.9	887.9	2,406.7	924.1	2,534.4
Age of head (years)								
Less than 35	14.8	53.2	10.6	74.0	12.3	96.6	14.2	73.5
35–44	64.2	176.8	73.5	227.6	82.6	276.4	69.4	299.2
45–54	116.8	364.8	122.3	420.2	141.6	517.6	144.7	542.7
55–64	141.9	471.1	148.2	617.0	193.3	775.4	248.7	843.8
65–74	136.6	429.3	169.8	541.1	187.8	717.9	190.1	690.9
75 or more	114.5	317.9	145.6	360.3	161.2	496.2	163.1	528.1
Education of head								
No high school diploma	27.9	103.7	24.5	91.4	27.2	109.7	20.6	136.5
High school diploma	63.9	163.7	62.7	182.9	61.8	192.5	68.7	196.8
Some college	57.6	232.3	85.6	275.5	76.3	303.8	69.3	308.6
College degree	128.6	473.7	169.7	612.3	227.2	845.7	226.1	851.3
Race or ethnicity of respondent								
White non-Hispanic	94.3	308.7	111.0	391.1	129.6	518.7	140.7	561.8
Nonwhite or Hispanic	19.5	94.9	19.3	116.5	19.1	123.8	24.8	153.1
Current work status of head								
Working for someone else	60.3	168.4	61.2	194.8	69.3	240.1	67.2	268.5
Self-employed	191.8	862.8	288.0	1,071.3	375.2	1,340.6	335.6	1,423.2
Retired	99.9	277.2	131.0	356.5	120.4	479.2	139.8	469.0
Other not working	4.5	70.1	4.1	85.8	9.5	191.7	11.8	162.3
Region								
Northeast	102.0	308.9	109.3	351.3	98.3	480.0	161.7	569.1
Midwest	80.8	244.7	93.1	288.5	111.3	361.6	115.0	436.1
South	54.2	229.5	71.0	309.6	78.6	400.4	63.8	348.0
West	67.4	286.1	71.1	379.1	93.3	468.8	94.8	523.7
Housing status								
Owner	128.1	373.7	153.2	468.7	182.9	594.8	184.4	624.9
Renter or other	6.0	53.8	4.9	50.4	5.1	58.5	4.0	54.1
Percentile of net worth								
Less than 25	1.2	−.2	.6	−2.1	1.2	†	1.7	−1.4
25–49.9	34.7	37.6	37.9	41.6	43.4	47.0	43.6	47.1
50–74.9	117.1	122.6	139.7	149.1	166.8	176.6	170.7	185.4
75–89.9	272.3	293.6	357.7	372.6	458.2	478.6	506.8	526.7
90–100	836.7	1,766.7	1,039.1	2,244.2	1,386.6	2,936.1	1,430.1	3,114.2

†Less than 0.05 ($50).

Note: For questions on income, respondents were asked to base their answers on the calendar year preceding the interview. For questions on saving, respondents were asked to base their answers on the twelve months preceding the interview. Percentage distributions may not sum to 100 because of rounding. Dollars have been converted to 2004 values with the current-methods consumer price index for all urban consumers.

SOURCE: Brian K. Bucks, Arthur B. Kennickell, and Kevin B. Moore, "Table 3. Family Net Worth, by Selected Characteristics of Families, 1995–2004 Surveys," in "Recent Changes in U.S. Family Finances: Evidence from the 2001 and 2004 Survey of Consumer Finances," *Federal Reserve Bulletin*, vol. 92, The Federal Reserve, February 2006, http://www.federalreserve.gov/pubs/oss/oss2/2004/bull0206.pdf (accessed June 20, 2006)

---

similar to that of highly educated professionals. Krugman believes that changing social attitudes—a "new permissiveness"—have permitted wealth inequality to grow unchecked since the 1970s. Krugman uses as an example the enormous growth in the salaries of chief executive officers (CEOs) of major corporations. He claims that ideas about corporate responsibility and financial prudence kept CEO salaries in check until the 1970s and 1980s, when a new societal attitude emerged that Krugman describes as "greed is good." Krugman notes that in 1970 the top one-tenth of 1% of American taxpayers had average earnings that were seventy times as much as the average American. By 1998 the same segment had incomes that were three hundred times that of the average American. Yet there has not been an uproar among the middle and lower classes about wealth inequality.

TABLE 8.6

Family holdings of nonfinancial assets, 2004

Family characteristic	Vehicles	Primary residence	Other residential property	Equity in nonresidential property	Business equity	Other	Any nonfinancial asset	Any asset
				Percentage of families holding asset				
All families	**86.3**	**69.1**	**12.5**	**8.3**	**11.5**	**7.8**	**92.5**	**97.9**
Percentile of income								
Less than 20	65.0	40.3	3.6	2.7	3.7	3.9	76.4	92.2
20–39.9	85.3	57.0	6.9	3.8	6.7	4.4	92.0	97.8
40–59.9	91.6	71.5	10.0	7.6	9.5	7.5	96.7	99.8
60–79.9	95.3	83.1	14.0	10.6	12.0	10.4	98.4	100.0
80–89.9	95.9	91.8	19.3	12.8	16.0	8.3	99.1	99.8
90–100	93.1	94.7	37.2	20.8	34.7	16.7	99.3	100.0
Age of head (years)								
Less than 35	82.9	41.6	5.1	3.3	6.9	5.5	88.6	96.5
35–44	89.4	68.3	9.4	6.4	13.9	6.0	93.0	97.7
45–54	88.8	77.3	16.3	11.4	15.7	9.7	94.7	98.3
55–64	88.6	79.1	19.5	12.8	15.8	9.2	92.6	97.5
65–74	89.1	81.3	19.9	10.6	8.0	9.0	95.6	99.5
75 or more	76.9	85.2	9.7	7.7	5.3	8.5	92.5	99.6
Race or ethnicity of respondent								
White non-Hispanic	90.3	76.1	14.0	9.2	13.6	9.3	95.8	99.3
Nonwhite or Hispanic	76.1	50.8	8.9	5.8	5.9	3.8	84.0	94.4
Current work status of head								
Working for someone else	89.7	66.5	10.4	6.8	5.8	7.1	93.8	98.4
Self-employed	91.2	79.1	25.8	18.7	58.1	12.9	97.5	99.1
Retired	79.0	75.8	12.8	7.9	3.5	7.1	89.8	97.7
Other not working	66.9	40.0	5.4	*	6.9	6.4	76.3	89.6
Housing status								
Owner	92.3	100.0	15.7	11.0	14.7	9.2	100.0	100.0
Renter or other	73.0	—	5.4	2.4	4.3	4.6	75.9	93.3
Percentile of net worth								
Less than 25	69.8	15.2	*	*	*	2.9	73.7	91.7
25–49.9	89.2	71.2	4.9	4.1	5.6	5.4	97.5	100.0
50–74.9	92.0	93.4	12.7	8.3	11.2	7.8	99.0	100.0
75–89.9	95.2	96.2	23.1	15.1	19.9	12.3	99.8	100.0
90–100	93.1	96.9	45.6	28.8	40.8	18.8	99.9	100.0
				Median value of holdings for families holding asset (thousands of 2004 dollars)				
All families	**14.2**	**160.0**	**100.0**	**60.0**	**100.0**	**15.0**	**147.8**	**172.9**
Percentile of income								
Less than 20	4.5	70.0	33.0	11.0	30.0	4.5	22.4	17.0
20–39.9	7.9	100.0	65.0	30.0	30.0	7.5	71.1	78.3
40–59.9	13.1	135.0	55.0	36.0	62.5	10.0	131.2	154.4
60–79.9	19.8	175.0	100.0	47.0	150.0	10.0	197.2	289.4
80–89.9	25.8	225.0	98.0	60.0	100.0	17.5	281.8	458.5
90–100	33.0	450.0	268.3	189.0	350.0	50.0	651.2	1,157.7
Age of head (years)								
Less than 35	11.3	135.0	82.5	55.0	50.0	5.0	32.3	39.2
35–44	15.6	160.0	80.0	42.2	100.0	10.0	151.3	173.4
45–54	18.8	170.0	90.0	43.0	144.0	20.0	184.5	234.9
55–64	18.6	200.0	135.0	75.0	190.9	25.0	226.3	351.2
65–74	12.4	150.0	80.0	78.0	100.0	30.0	161.1	233.2
75 or more	8.4	125.0	150.0	85.8	80.3	11.0	137.1	185.2
Race or ethnicity of respondent								
White non-Hispanic	15.7	165.0	105.0	66.0	135.0	16.5	164.8	224.5
Nonwhite or Hispanic	9.8	130.0	80.0	30.0	66.7	10.0	64.1	59.6
Current work status of head								
Working for someone else	14.9	160.0	88.0	40.0	50.0	10.0	141.9	161.2
Self-employed	21.9	248.0	141.5	125.0	174.0	30.0	335.4	468.3
Retired	10.1	130.0	100.0	60.0	120.0	25.0	131.7	165.6
Other not working	10.7	130.0	86.0	*	25.0	20.0	60.0	30.3
Housing status								
Owner	17.5	160.0	100.0	62.0	122.8	17.5	201.6	289.9
Renter or other	7.2	—	80.0	56.0	50.0	8.0	8.4	12.2

TABLE 8.6

Family holdings of nonfinancial assets, 2004 [CONTINUED]

Family characteristic	Vehicles	Primary residence	Other residential property	Equity in nonresidential property	Business equity	Other	Any nonfinancial asset	Any asset
			Median value of holdings for families holding asset (thousands of 2004 dollars)					
Percentile of net worth								
Less than 25	5.6	65.0	*	*	*	3.0	7.4	7.7
25–49.9	11.9	85.0	25.6	14.9	17.5	6.0	72.4	84.5
50–74.9	17.4	159.3	65.0	25.0	55.0	10.0	188.1	257.3
75–89.9	22.6	250.0	100.0	73.9	150.0	25.0	360.8	600.2
90–100	30.6	450.0	325.0	250.0	527.4	80.0	907.7	1,572.6
Memo								
Mean value of holdings for families holding asset	20.1	246.8	267.3	298.1	765.5	66.6	366.3	538.4

*Ten or fewer observations.
—Not applicable.
Notes: For questions on income, respondents were asked to base their answers on the calendar year preceding the interview. For questions on saving, respondents were asked to base their answers on the twelve months preceding the interview.
Percentage distributions may not sum to 100 because of rounding. Dollars have been converted to 2004 values with the current-methods consumer price index for all urban consumers. The definition of vehicles is a broad one that includes cars, vans, sport-utility vehicles, trucks, motor homes, recreational vehicles, motorcycles, boats, airplanes, and helicopters. Of families owning any type of vehicle in 2004, 99.8 percent had a car, van, sport-utility vehicle, motorcycle, or truck. The remaining types of vehicle were held by 13.3 percent of families.

SOURCE: Brian K. Bucks, Arthur B. Kennickell, and Kevin B. Moore, "Table 8B. Family Holdings of Nonfinancial Assets and of Any Asset, by Selected Characteristics of Families and Type of Asset, 2004 Survey of Consumer Finances," in "Recent Changes in U.S. Family Finances: Evidence from the 2001 and 2004 Survey of Consumer Finances," *Federal Reserve Bulletin*, Vol. 92, The Federal Reserve, February 2006, http://www.federalreserve.gov/pubs/oss/oss2/2004/bull0206.pdf (accessed June 20, 2006)

Krugman believes that policy makers perpetuate wealth inequality in America and that the United States is becoming a plutocracy—a system in which the wealthy control the power of government. He points to the estate tax as an example. This is a federal tax assessed against a person's wealth when that person dies. There are numerous deductions and loopholes that prevent the tax from being assessed against the entire value of an estate. (As discussed in Chapter 9, as of 2005 the first $1.5 million of an individual's estate or the first $3 million of a married couple's estate was exempt from the estate tax.) Krugman writes that in 1999 only the top 2% of estates in the United States paid any estate tax at all. Possible elimination of the estate tax is an ongoing topic of political discussion, despite the very limited number of people that would be affected. Krugman maintains that this move toward estate tax elimination is driven by wealthy, politically conservative, policy makers (and media outlets that are friendly to them) who seek to convince the public that the estate tax threatens the economic security of middle-class Americans.

Krugman concludes: "as the gap between the rich and the rest of the population grows, economic policy increasingly caters to the interests of the elite, while public services for the population at large—above all, public education—are starved of resources. As policy increasingly favors the interest of the rich and neglects the interest of the general population, income disparities grow even wider."

In August 2006 journalists Steve Greenhouse and David Leonhardt wrote in their *New York Times* article,

"Real Wages Fail to Match a Rise in Productivity" (August 28, 2006, http://www.nytimes.com/2006/08/28/business/28wages.html?ex=1158984000&en=c9d8a39c0a1dbcbe&ei=5070): "With the economy beginning to slow, the current expansion has a chance to become the first sustained period of economic growth since World War II that fails to offer a prolonged increase in real wages for most workers." What this means for the larger economy, according to Greenhouse and Leonhardt, is that a greater share of money goes back into companies rather to workers' paychecks: "In the first quarter of 2006, wages and salaries represented 45 percent of gross domestic product, down from almost 50 percent in the first quarter of 2001 and a record 53.6 percent in the first quarter of 1970, according to the Commerce Department." Ultimately, this means that less money is available to average workers to spend as consumers. By contrast, Greenhouse and Leonhardt cite an analysis by economists Emmanuel Saez and Thomas Piketty, who note that "in 2004, the top 1 percent of earners—a group that includes many chief executives—received 11.2 percent of all wage income, up from 8.7 percent a decade earlier and less than 6 percent three decades ago."

Wealth Inequality Seen as Not Harmful

On the other side of this issue are those who believe that wealth inequality does not pose a problem to the American economy or social system. This viewpoint is generally associated with conservative political thinking, which holds that market forces must be allowed to adjust themselves without government interference. One idea that is regularly expressed by politicians in this camp is that what's good for the rich is good for the rest of us. This philosophy was espoused by President Ronald Reagan, who championed "trickle down" economic policy—economic actions (such as tax cuts beneficial to the wealthy) that encourage greater investment in business growth, thus increasing employment, wages, and other benefits to those in the middle and lower classes.

An article in the June 2003 edition of the conservative journal *National Review* argues that income inequality is not harmful to America. In "Rich Man, Poor Man: How to Think about Income Inequality—Hint: It's Not as Bad as You May Think," commentator Kevin A. Hassett rebuts many of the criticisms leveled against income inequality. In fact, Hassett asserts that evidence shows that income inequality in very poor undeveloped countries probably limits economic growth, but not so in wealthy developed countries, where economies and income inequality grow together.

Hassett believes that unease over wealth inequality is driven by social views on the "basic justice" of society, but he argues that there are similarly compelling arguments against taking from the rich to benefit the poor. Hassett says, "In the real world, differences emerge between citizens because of both luck and choices. Virtually every circumstance is a mixture of these two cases. This distinction is important, because it makes it difficult, if not impossible, to conceive of scenarios where justice clearly supports forceful redistribution." Also, Hassett notes that taking resources from the rich limits their ability and incentive to start and grow businesses, which will ultimately hurt American workers even more. He concludes that on a global scale, nations emphasizing free-market capitalism (such as the United States) have done a better job of raising the standard of living of their poor than nations in which socialist views have encouraged more equitable distribution of wealth.

CHAPTER 9
THE ROLE OF THE GOVERNMENT

In general, the art of government consists in taking as much money as possible from one party of the citizens to give to the other.

—Voltaire, 1764

OVERVIEW

The government has many roles in the U.S. economy. Like other businesses, the government spends and makes money, consumes goods and services, and employs people. Federal, state, and local governments raise funds directly through taxes and fees. They often borrow money from the public by selling securities, such as bonds. A bond is an investment in which people loan money to the government for a specified time and interest rate. Governments also disburse money via contracts with businesses or through social programs that benefit the public.

Finally, the federal government is a manipulator of the U.S. economy. It influences macroeconomic factors, such as inflation and unemployment, through fiscal policy and monetary policy. Fiscal policy revolves around spending and taxation. Monetary policy is concerned with the amount of money in circulation and operation of the nation's central banking system.

FUNDING GOVERNMENT SERVICES

Governments are responsible for providing services that individuals cannot effectively provide for themselves, such as military defense, fire and police departments, roads, education, social services, and environmental protection. Some government entities also provide public utilities, such as water, sewage treatment, or electricity. To generate the revenue necessary to provide services, governments collect taxes and fees and charge for many services they provide to the public. If these revenues are not sufficient to fund desired programs, governments borrow money.

Taxation

Even before the United States became an independent nation, taxes were a significant issue for Americans. The Stamp Act of 1765 was the first tax imposed specifically on the American colonies by the British Parliament and was strongly resisted by the colonists, who maintained that only representative legislatures in each colony possessed the right to impose taxes. This view, that "taxation without representation" was tyranny, contributed to the opposition to British rule that led to the Revolutionary War (1775–83). Of course, it was necessary for the newly independent colonies to establish taxes of their own. As Benjamin Franklin wrote, "In this world nothing can be said to be certain, except death and taxes" (November 13, 1789), and over the next two centuries a complex taxation code was developed at the federal, state, and local levels.

The most common taxes levied by federal, state, and local governments are:

- Income taxes—charged on wages, salaries, and tips

- Payroll taxes—Social Security insurance and unemployment compensation, which are paid by employers and withdrawn from payroll checks

- Property taxes—levied on the value of property owned, usually real estate

- Capital gains taxes—charged on the profit from the sale of an asset such as stock or real estate

- Corporate taxes—levied on the profits of a corporation

- Estate taxes—charged against the assets of a deceased person

- Excise taxes—collected at the time something is sold or when a good is imported

- Wealth taxes—levied on the value of assets rather than on the income they produce

TABLE 9.1

Number of governmental units by type, selected years 1952–2002

Type of government	1952*	1962	1967	1972	1977	1982	1987	1992	1997	2002
Total units*	16,807	91,237	81,299	78,269	79,913	81,831	83,237	85,006	87,504	87,576
U.S. government	*	*	*	*	*	*	*	*	*	
State government	50	50	50	50	50	50	50	50	50	50
Local governments*	16,756	91,186	81,248	78,218	79,862	81,780	83,186	84,955	87,453	87,525
County	3,052	3,043	3,049	3,044	3,042	3,041	3,042	3,043	3,043	3,034
Municipal	16,807	18,000	18,048	18,517	18,862	19,076	19,200	19,279	19,372	19,429
Township and town	17,202	17,142	17,105	16,991	16,822	16,734	16,691	16,656	16,629	16,504
School district	67,355	34,678	21,782	15,781	15,174	14,851	14,721	14,422	13,726	13,506
Special district	12,340	18,323	21,264	23,885	25,962	28,078	29,532	31,555	34,683	35,052

*Adjusted to include units in Alaska and Hawaii which adopted statehood in 1959.

SOURCE: Adapted from "Table 415. Number of Governmental Units by Type: 1952 to 2002," in *Statistical Abstract of the United States: 2006*, U.S. Census Bureau, 2005, http://www.census.gov/prod/2005pubs/06statab/stlocgov.pdf (accessed June 16, 2006)

Taxes are broadly defined as being either direct or indirect. Direct taxes (such as income taxes) are paid by the entity on whom the tax is being levied. Indirect taxes are passed on from the responsible party to someone else. Examples of indirect taxes include business property taxes, gasoline taxes, and sales taxes, which are levied on businesses but passed on to consumers via increased prices.

When individuals with higher incomes pay a higher percentage of a tax, it is called a "progressive" tax; when those with lower incomes pay a larger percentage of their income, a tax is considered "regressive." The federal income tax is an example of a progressive tax, because individuals with higher incomes are subject to higher tax rates. Sales and excise taxes are regressive, because the same tax applies to all consumers regardless of income, so less prosperous individuals pay a higher percentage of their incomes.

Borrowing against the Future

Like many members of the public, government entities sometimes spend more than they make. When cash revenues from taxes, fees, and other sources are not sufficient to cover spending, money must be borrowed. One method used by government to borrow money is the selling of securities, such as bonds, to the public. A bond is basically an IOU that a government body writes to a buyer. The buyer pays money up front in exchange for the IOU, which is redeemable at some point in the future (the maturity date) for the amount of the original loan plus interest. In addition, the federal government has the ability to write itself IOUs—to spend money now that it expects to make in the future.

U.S. government bodies borrow money because they are optimistic that future revenues will cover the IOUs they have written. This optimism is based in part on the power that governments have to tax their citizens and control the cost of provided government services.

Although tax increases and cuts in services can be enacted to raise money, these actions have political and economic repercussions. Politicians who wish to remain in office are reluctant to displease their constituents. Furthermore, the more citizens pay in taxes, the less money they will have to spend in the marketplace or invest in private business, hurting the overall economy. As a result, governments must weigh their need to borrow against the future likely consequences of paying back the loan.

LOCAL GOVERNMENTS

The U.S. Census performs a comprehensive *Census of Government* every five years; the most recent was completed in 2002. In between the censuses, annual surveys are conducted to collect certain data on government finances and employment. Information from both sources is included in the 2006 *Statistical Abstract of the United States*.

The 2002 Census found 87,525 local government units in operation, as shown in Table 9.1. These units are comprised of counties, municipalities, townships, school districts, and special districts. Special district governments usually perform a single function, such as flood control or water supply. For example, Florida is divided into five Water Management Districts, each of which is responsible for managing and protecting water resources and balancing the water needs of other government units within its jurisdiction.

Local Revenues

The latest survey data for local government revenues were compiled over 2002–03 and are shown in Figure 9.1. Local governments took in just over $1.1 trillion that year. More than three-fourths of the money came from only three sources: intergovernmental transfers (37%), property taxes (25%), and charges for services (14%). Intergovernmental transfers are funds supplied by the

FIGURE 9.1

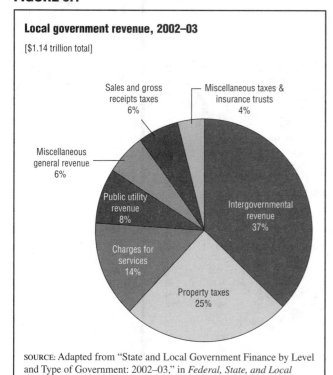

Local government revenue, 2002–03

[$1.14 trillion total]

- Sales and gross receipts taxes 6%
- Miscellaneous taxes & insurance trusts 4%
- Miscellaneous general revenue 6%
- Public utility revenue 8%
- Charges for services 14%
- Intergovernmental revenue 37%
- Property taxes 25%

SOURCE: Adapted from "State and Local Government Finance by Level and Type of Government: 2002–03," in *Federal, State, and Local Governments: State and Local Government Finances: 2002–03*, U.S. Census Bureau, April 8, 2005, http://ftp2.census.gov/govs/estimate/03stl001.xls (accessed May 25, 2006)

employees to pay for worker programs, such as retirement benefits.

PROPERTY TAXES. A property tax is tax levied on the value of land, buildings, businesses, or personal property, including business equipment and automobiles. According to the U.S. Department of the Treasury, property taxes in the United States date back to the Massachusetts Bay Colony in 1646, and the separate states began imposing property taxes soon after declaring independence from Britain. A property tax is an example of an *ad valorem* tax. *Ad valorem* is a Latin phrase meaning "according to the value."

Property taxes are generally levied annually and calculated by multiplying the property value by an assessment ratio to obtain a taxable value. Assessment ratios can vary from less than 0.1 (less than 10%) to in excess of 1.0 (greater than 100%). The calculated taxable value is multiplied by a tax rate typically expressed in tax dollars per hundred or thousand dollars of value. For example, a home valued at $150,000 in an area with an assessment ratio of 0.5 (50%) would have a taxable value of $75,000. Assuming a tax rate of $3 per $1,000 of value, the property tax would be 3 times $75, or $225. Tax rates based on $1,000 of value are also known as millage rates.

Government entities at the local and sometimes state level determine the tax rate and the assessment ratio for their area. If permitted by their constituents, governments may choose to increase these values to raise additional revenue. Because real estate generally increases in value over time, property taxes can increase each year even if the tax rate and the assessment ratio remain constant.

AMERICA'S LARGEST CITIES. Table 9.2 shows a detailed breakdown of revenues collected by America's twenty largest cities (by population) during 2002. New York City had, by far, the largest revenue, taking in more than $55 billion. This included $22.2 billion from taxes and $22.5 billion in intergovernmental loans. New York City's tax revenue is highly dependent on property taxes, which totaled nearly $8.9 billion in 2002. This contrasts with other cities, such as Los Angeles and Chicago, where taxes on sales and gross receipts garnered more money than property taxes.

federal and state governments. State funds accounted for the vast majority of intergovernmental transfers during 2002–03.

Taxes, particularly property taxes, are an important source of revenue for many local governments. Property taxes accounted for a fourth of all revenue during 2002–03 and were the largest single source of self-generated money. Consumption taxes were also collected on sales and gross receipts. This includes selective taxes levied against particular goods, such as motor fuels, alcoholic beverages, and tobacco products. Miscellaneous taxes include personal and corporate income taxes, motor vehicle license taxes, and a wide variety of other taxes.

The revenue included in "charges for services" comes from many local sources, including hospitals, sewage treatment facilities, solid waste management, parks and recreation areas, airports, and educational facilities (for example, the sale of school lunches).

Other revenue sources for local governments are public utilities, miscellaneous general revenue, and insurance trusts. Public utilities primarily supply electricity, water, natural gas, and public transportation (such as buses and trains). Miscellaneous general revenue comes from a variety of sources, including interest payments and the sale of public property. Insurance trusts are monies collected from the paychecks of local government

Local Expenditures

Local governments spent $1.2 trillion on annual expenses during 2002–03. A breakdown by expense is shown in Figure 9.2. Education was the largest single component, accounting for $450 billion and comprising nearly 40% of the total. Spending on public health, welfare, and hospitals; utilities; environmental and housing concerns; and public safety (police, fire, etc.) each accounted for roughly 10% of the total.

TABLE 9.2

Revenue for the twenty largest U.S. cities, 2002

[In millions of dollars; 55,349 represents $55,349,000,000]

Cities ranked by 2000 population	Total revenue[a]	General revenue — Total	Intergovernmental — Total	Intergovernmental — From federal government	Intergovernmental — From state/local government	Intergovernmental — From local government	General revenue from own sources — Total	Taxes — Total	Taxes — Property	Sales and gross receipts — Total	Sales and gross receipts — General sales	Sales and gross receipts — Public utilities	Current charges — Total	Current charges — Parks and recreation	Current charges — Sewerage[b]	Miscellaneous — Total	Miscellaneous — Interest earnings	Utility revenue[c]	Employee retirement revenue[c]
New York, NY	55,349	52,718	22,536	3,246	19,178	112	30,182	22,235	8,897	4,480	3,373	436	5,369	54	1,003	2,578	708	2,908	—
Los Angeles, CA	7,903	6,019	1,011	407	482	122	5,007	2,421	850	983	351	531	1,727	81	467	860	438	2,811	—
Chicago, IL	4,955	4,887	1,298	410	887	—	3,589	2,042	641	1,165	196	504	925	—	144	621	275	312	—
Houston, TX	2,531	2,290	212	153	41	18	2,078	1,212	615	561	342	175	586	23	277	280	153	291	—
Philadelphia, PA[d]	5,322	4,757	2,033	451	1,434	148	2,724	2,043	374	189	108	95	544	15	202	137	84	837	—
Phoenix, AZ	2,335	2,125	749	310	412	27	1,376	751	189	512	369	51	473	26	166	152	119	233	132
San Diego, CA	2,245	1,903	433	178	139	115	1,470	745	262	390	217	110	354	47	194	372	135	210	—
Dallas, TX	1,618	1,744	83	51	31	—	1,661	798	424	357	211	20	646	29	194	217	149	194	—
San Antonio, TX	2,249	1,079	176	41	127	—	903	445	210	219	151	52	283	29	203	176	127	1,303	256
Detroit, MI	4,364	3,876	2,404	355	2,017	32	1,472	912	414	152	—	101	344	13	170	217	59	232	—
San Jose, CA	1,421	1,463	257	75	104	78	1,206	667	276	256	138	49	316	20	266	223	100	18	—
Honolulu, HI[d]	1,134	1,000	172	111	60	—	829	534	382	95	—	—	217	15	154	77	33	133	—
Indianapolis, IN[d]	2,181	1,643	518	77	429	13	1,125	629	495	41	—	83	363	24	186	134	66	534	—
San Francisco, CA[d]	4,787	4,844	1,726	378	1,344	—	3,117	1,699	747	551	341	83	1,135	35	68	283	194	319	71
Jacksonville, FL[d]	2,264	1,252	173	51	122	9	1,079	590	357	219	125	—	247	—	147	242	209	941	—
Columbus, OH	1,212	1,064	206	61	135	—	858	516	36	16	—	31	253	23	129	89	53	148	—
Austin, TX	1,806	971	82	45	33	—	889	407	195	184	123	24	309	—	143	174	117	921	—
Baltimore, MD[d]	2,373	2,419	1,381	89	1,220	72	1,037	806	495	63	—	19	129	11	72	102	40	78	—
Memphis, TN	2,967	1,602	1,031	24	506	501	571	364	303	49	—	—	140	48	60	67	31	1,268	98
Milwaukee, WI	878	884	439	78	317	44	444	208	197	—	—	—	163	—	84	74	33	55	—

—Represents or rounds to zero.

[a]Includes revenue sources not shown separately.

[b]Includes solid waste management.

[c]Includes water, electric, and transit.

[d]Represents, in effect, city-county consolidated government.

SOURCE: Adapted from "Table 447. City Government—Revenue for Largest Cities: 2002," in *Statistical Abstract of the United States: 2006, Section 8, State and Local Government Finances and Employment*, U.S. Department of Commerce, Census Bureau, 2005, http://www.census.gov/prod/2005pubs/06statab/stlocgov.pdf (accessed June 16, 2006)

FIGURE 9.2

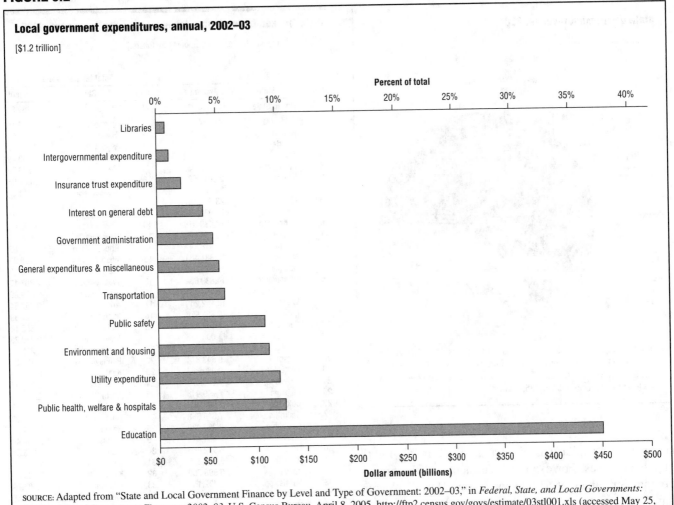

Local government expenditures, annual, 2002–03

[$1.2 trillion]

SOURCE: Adapted from "State and Local Government Finance by Level and Type of Government: 2002–03," in *Federal, State, and Local Governments: State and Local Government Finances: 2002–03*, U.S. Census Bureau, April 8, 2005, http://ftp2.census.gov/govs/estimate/03stl001.xls (accessed May 25, 2006)

According to the 2002–03 survey, salaries and wages for local government employees amounted to $464 billion or 39% of the total expenditures for the year.

In March 2005 the U.S. Census Bureau estimated that local governments employed the equivalent of 11.7 million full-time employees. The payroll for that month was $42 billion. Education positions were the single-largest component, accounting for 6.8 million employees and $23 billion in payroll (more than half of employee numbers and payroll). The second-largest component was comprised of police, fire, and corrections officers. More than 1.3 million of them were employed by local governments in March 2005 and accounted for nearly $6 billion of monthly payroll (http://ftp2.census.gov/govs/apes/05locus.txt).

STATE GOVERNMENTS

In January 2006 the U.S. Census Bureau published comprehensive financial data for 2004 for the fifty state governments. These data are available at http://www.census.gov/govs/www/state.html.

State Revenues

According to the U.S. Census Bureau, state governments had revenues of nearly $1.6 trillion in 2004. Figure 9.3 provides a breakdown of revenue by source. Intergovernmental revenue (funds from the federal government) accounted for one-fourth of the total. Insurance trusts were the largest source of self-generated revenue for states, comprising 24% of the total. Other major sources of revenue included sales taxes (18%) and individual income taxes (12%). Charges for services, miscellaneous general revenue, and miscellaneous taxes (such as property taxes) each accounted for 7% or less of the total.

In May 2006 the U.S. Census Bureau released detailed data on state tax collections for 2005. Each of the fifty states is ranked in Table 9.3 by total tax collected and tax per capita. In general, the largest and most populous states collected the most taxes. Four states—California, New York, Florida, and Texas—accounted for nearly one-third of all taxes collected in 2005. Tax

FIGURE 9.3

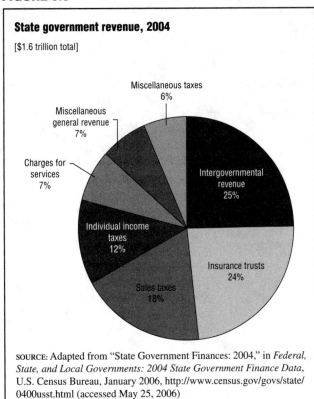

State government revenue, 2004

[$1.6 trillion total]

- Miscellaneous taxes 6%
- Miscellaneous general revenue 7%
- Charges for services 7%
- Intergovernmental revenue 25%
- Individual income taxes 12%
- Insurance trusts 24%
- Sales taxes 18%

SOURCE: Adapted from "State Government Finances: 2004," in *Federal, State, and Local Governments: 2004 State Government Finance Data*, U.S. Census Bureau, January 2006, http://www.census.gov/govs/state/0400usst.html (accessed May 25, 2006)

TABLE 9.3

States ranked by total state taxes and per capita amount, 2005

[Amounts in thousands. Per capita amounts in dollars.]

	Total tax			Total tax per capita	
Rank	State	Amount	Rank	State	Amount
	United States	647,886,410		United States	2,189.84
1	California	98,434,685	1	Vermont	3,600.16
2	New York	50,190,396	2	Hawaii	3,477.93
3	Florida	33,894,971	3	Wyoming	3,417.77
4	Texas	32,784,942	4	Connecticut	3,300.49
5	Pennsylvania	27,262,969	5	Delaware	3,228.79
6	Illinois	26,411,689	6	Minnesota	3,093.93
7	Ohio	24,006,560	7	Massachusetts	2,815.23
8	Michigan	23,525,187	8	Alaska	2,798.66
9	New Jersey	22,933,999	9	California	2,724.31
10	North Carolina	18,639,618	10	New Jersey	2,630.65
11	Massachusetts	18,014,681	11	New York	2,606.62
12	Virginia	15,918,847	12	Rhode Island	2,443.07
13	Minnesota	15,881,131	13	Wisconsin	2,429.96
14	Georgia	15,675,655	14	Maryland	2,410.23
15	Washington	14,839,634	15	West Virginia	2,367.17
16	Maryland	13,497,281	16	Washington	2,359.99
17	Wisconsin	13,452,250	17	Arkansas	2,357.84
18	Indiana	12,853,976	18	Michigan	2,324.39
19	Connecticut	11,584,728	19	Maine	2,323.12
20	Arizona	11,008,428	20	New Mexico	2,319.23
21	Tennessee	10,007,292	21	North Dakota	2,202.97
22	Missouri	9,543,814	22	Pennsylvania	2,193.32
23	Kentucky	9,090,882	23	Kentucky	2,178.50
24	Louisiana	8,638,674	24	Nebraska	2,158.36
25	Alabama	7,799,948	25	North Carolina	2,146.68
26	Colorado	7,648,456	26	Virginia	2,103.72
27	South Carolina	7,318,388	27	Ohio	2,094.08
28	Oklahoma	6,859,030	28	Nevada	2,074.72
29	Arkansas	6,552,449	29	Illinois	2,069.40
30	Oregon	6,522,665	30	Idaho	2,053.51
31	Iowa	5,750,629	31	Indiana	2,049.42
32	Kansas	5,598,700	32	Kansas	2,039.60
33	Mississippi	5,432,152	33	Montana	2,003.79
34	Nevada	5,010,443	34	Iowa	1,938.85
35	Utah	4,686,381	35	Oklahoma	1,933.21
36	New Mexico	4,471,477	36	Louisiana	1,909.52
37	Hawaii	4,434,356	37	Florida	1,905.28
38	West Virginia	4,301,156	38	Utah	1,897.32
39	Nebraska	3,796,551	39	Mississippi	1,859.69
40	Maine	3,071,161	40	Arizona	1,853.58
41	Idaho	2,934,459	41	Oregon	1,791.45
42	Delaware	2,725,095	42	Georgia	1,727.73
43	Rhode Island	2,628,747	43	South Carolina	1,719.95
44	Vermont	2,242,902	44	Alabama	1,711.27
45	New Hampshire	2,022,146	45	Tennessee	1,678.23
46	Montana	1,875,545	46	Missouri	1,645.49
47	Alaska	1,858,311	47	Colorado	1,639.54
48	Wyoming	1,739,646	48	New Hampshire	1,543.62
49	North Dakota	1,403,293	49	Texas	1,434.16
50	South Dakota	1,110,035	50	South Dakota	1,430.46

SOURCE: "States Ranked by Total State Taxes and Per Capita Amount: 2005," in *Federal, State, and Local Governments: 2005 State Government Tax Collections*, U.S. Department of Commerce, U.S. Census Bureau, May 22, 2006, www.census.gov/govs/statetax/05staxrank.html (accessed July 3, 2006)

collected per capita was highest in small and/or lightly populated states. For example, Vermont had the highest tax rate per capita, at $3,600 per person. Hawaii, Wyoming, Connecticut, and Delaware were also in the top five.

STATE SALES TAXES. As shown in Figure 9.3, sales taxes are a major source of revenue for state governments. The Federation of Tax Administrators (FTA) is a nonprofit organization that provides research services for the tax administrators of all fifty states. According to the FTA, forty-five states and the District of Columbia assessed sales taxes as of January 1, 2006. The five states without a sales tax were Alaska, Delaware, Montana, New Hampshire, and Oregon. The state sales tax rates ranged from a low of 2.9% in Colorado to values of 7% and greater in California, Mississippi, and Tennessee. Nearly all states exempted prescription drugs and food from sales taxes. The FTA data are available at http://www.taxadmin.org/fta/rate/sales.html.

STATE INCOME TAXES. The FTA also compiles information on state income tax rates at http://www.taxadmin.org/fta/rate/ind_inc.html. As of January 1, 2006, forty-three states and the District of Columbia imposed income taxes. The states that did not tax income were Alaska, Florida, Nevada, South Dakota, Texas, Washington, and Wyoming. Two additional states, Tennessee and New Hampshire, taxed only personal income derived from dividends and interest.

According to the FTA, several states imposed a single rate for all income levels, including Colorado (4.6%), Illinois (3%), Indiana (3.4%), Massachusetts (5.3%), Michigan (3.9%), Pennsylvania (3.1%), and Rhode Island (25% of federal tax liability). Many states have devised tax codes based on multiple income brackets. Overall, tax rates varied from a low of 0.4% in Iowa to a high of 9.5% in Vermont.

FIGURE 9.4

State government expenditures, 2004

[Total: $1.4 trillion]

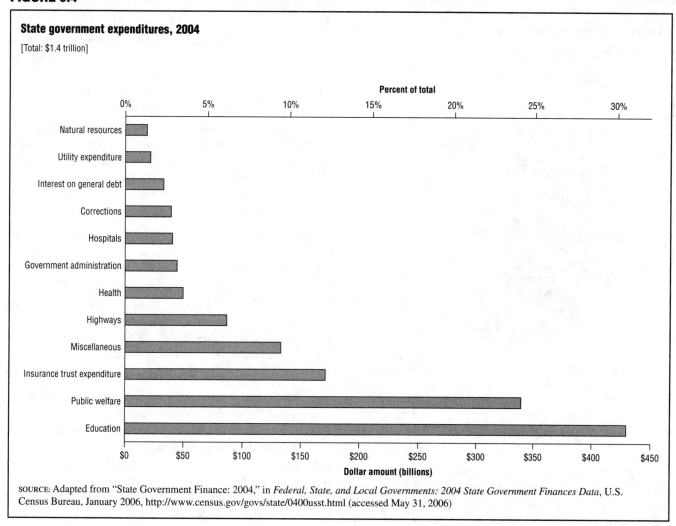

SOURCE: Adapted from "State Government Finance: 2004," in *Federal, State, and Local Governments: 2004 State Government Finances Data*, U.S. Census Bureau, January 2006, http://www.census.gov/govs/state/0400usst.html (accessed May 31, 2006)

State Expenditures

The U.S. Census Bureau reports that state governments had expenditures in excess of $1.4 trillion during 2004. More than one-fourth of this total (28%) was in the form of transfers to other governments, such as local governments within the state. The remainder was devoted to spending priorities at the state level. A breakdown of all expenditures is shown in Figure 9.4. Education was the single-largest expense, at $429 billion, accounting for just over 30% of all money expended. State spending on education is primarily for higher education, such as colleges and universities.

The states spent $339 billion on public welfare during 2004. This expense accounted for nearly one-fourth of all state government expenditures. Payments from insurance trusts amounted to 12% of state spending. All other expenditures each accounted for less than 10% of state spending.

In March 2005 the U.S. Census Bureau estimated that state governments employed the equivalent of 4.2 million full-time employees. The payroll for that month was $16 billion. Education positions were, by far, the single-largest component, accounting for 3.2 million employees and $13 billion in payroll (more than three-fourths of employee numbers and payroll). The second-largest contingent was comprised of corrections officers. Nearly half a million of them were employed by state governments in March 2005, accounting for $1.6 billion of monthly payroll (http://ftp2.census.gov/govs/apes/05stus.txt).

FEDERAL GOVERNMENT

For accounting purposes the federal government operates on a fiscal year (FY) that begins in October and runs through the end of September. Thus, fiscal year 2007 covers the time period of October 1, 2006, through September 30, 2007. Each year by the first Monday in February the U.S. president must present a proposed budget to the U.S. House of Representatives. This is the amount of money that the president estimates will be required to operate the federal government during the next fiscal year.

FIGURE 9.5

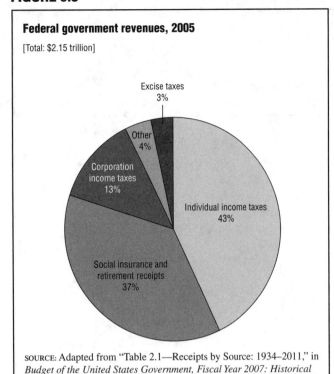

Federal government revenues, 2005

[Total: $2.15 trillion]

- Excise taxes 3%
- Other 4%
- Corporation income taxes 13%
- Individual income taxes 43%
- Social insurance and retirement receipts 37%

SOURCE: Adapted from "Table 2.1—Receipts by Source: 1934–2011," in *Budget of the United States Government, Fiscal Year 2007: Historical Tables*, U.S. Government Printing Office, 2006, http://www.whitehouse.gov/omb/budget/fy2007/sheets/hist02z1.xls (accessed May 31, 2006)

It can take several months for the House to debate, negotiate, and approve a final budget. Then the budget must also be approved by the U.S. Senate. This entire process can take many months, and sometimes longer than a year. This means that the federal government can be well into (or beyond) a fiscal year before knowing the exact amount of its budget for that year.

Detailed data on the finances of the federal government are maintained by the Office of Management and Budget (OMB), an executive office of the U.S. president. The OMB assists the president in preparing the federal budget and supervises budget administration. Information on the FY 2007 budget is available at http://www.whitehouse.gov/omb/budget/fy2007/. Budget documents include historical tables providing annual data on federal government receipts, outlays, debt, and employment dating back to 1940 or earlier. The FY 2007 budget includes final values for years through 2005 and estimates for 2006 through 2011.

Federal Revenues

The Federal government had revenues (receipts) of nearly $2.2 trillion in 2005. A breakdown by category is provided in Figure 9.5. Individual income taxes were the largest single component, amounting to $927 billion, or 43%, of the total. The second-largest source of revenue was social insurance and retirement receipts, at $794 billion, or 37%, of the total. Corporation income taxes

accounted for another 13%, followed by other revenue at 4% and excise taxes at 3%.

TAXES ON INCOME. The federal income tax was authorized in 1913 with ratification of the Sixteenth Amendment to the Constitution: "The Congress shall have power to lay and collect taxes on incomes, from whatever source derived, without apportionment among the several states, and without regard to any census or enumeration." In the United States tax rates are approved by Congress and signed into law by the president; the Internal Revenue Service (IRS), a bureau of the Department of the Treasury, enforces the tax codes and collects tax payments, which are due each year on April 15.

The percentage of an individual's income that he or she pays in federal tax is based on his or her income level, which determines the individual's "tax bracket." Tax brackets change as Congress modifies the tax codes, but individuals with higher incomes are always taxed at a higher rate than individuals with lower incomes. Through a variety of tax credits and deductions, individuals can lower the amount of income on which taxes are calculated, thereby lowering the amount of tax they pay.

The federal tax on corporate income has been in effect since 1909. Because corporations are owned, and individuals derive income from them, the potential exists for "double taxation," that is, the same income taxed twice, once as corporate income and, when the profits have been distributed to shareholders, again as individual income. To reduce the effects of double taxation, various credits and deductions have been enacted throughout the years to allow income to pass through a corporation without being taxed until it reaches the individual. Credits and depreciation schedules reduce the amount of revenue subject to tax.

SOCIAL INSURANCE AND RETIREMENT RECEIPTS. Social insurance and retirement receipts are collected to fund specific programs for people who are retired, disabled, unemployed, or poor. The primary programs are Social Security and Medicare. Social Security provides funds to most workers who retire or become disabled. It also pays money to the survivors of workers who die. Medicare is a health insurance program for poor people.

As of 2006 the federal government collects money to pay for these two programs as follows:

- Social Security—a tax of 12.4% on earned annual income up to $94,200. In other words, people who earn more than the annual limit pay the tax on $94,200, no matter how much they earn.

- Medicare—a tax of 2.9% on earned annual income. No income limit.

These taxes are known as "payroll taxes," because they are assessed based on the amounts that businesses pay their workers. Half of the tax (6.2% for Social Security plus 1.45% for Medicare) is paid by wage earners and is deducted from their paychecks; the other half is paid directly by employers. Self-employed people pay the entire tax bill but can deduct half of it as a business expense when they file income taxes.

Unemployment insurance is a joint federal-state program almost entirely funded by employers. Employers that meet certain criteria (regarding number of employees and amount of payroll) pay both state and federal unemployment taxes.

EXCISE TAXES AND OTHER RECEIPTS. Sales and excise taxes are considered taxes on consumption. Although there is no federal sales tax, the federal government does levy excise taxes on such items as airplane tickets, gasoline, alcoholic beverages, firearms, and cigarettes. Excise taxes on certain commodities are often hypothecated, meaning they are used to pay for a related government service. For example, fuel taxes are typically used to pay for road and bridge construction or public transportation, or a cigarette excise may go to cover government-supported health care programs. Excise taxes can be intended to generate revenue or to discourage use of the taxed product (as in high cigarette taxes that raise the per-pack cost in an attempt to discourage smoking).

The category "other receipts" in Figure 9.5 includes estate and gift taxes and customs duties and fees. Estate and gift taxes are taxes on wealth. Estate taxes are levied against a person's estate after that person dies; gift taxes are levied against the giver while the giver is alive. Estate and gift taxes only apply to amounts over specified limits. For example, in 2005 the first $1.5 million of an individual's estate or the first $3 million of a married couple's estate was exempt from the estate tax.

Customs duties are taxes charged on goods imported into the United States. The taxes vary by product and by exporting nation.

Federal Spending

According to the OMB, the federal government spent nearly $2.5 trillion during fiscal year 2005. The OMB breaks down expenditures into broad categories called superfunctions and narrower categories called functions. Table 9.4 shows spending by superfunction and function. Overall, human resources are the largest expenditure for the federal government, accounting for nearly two-thirds of spending during 2005. The largest single component of federal spending is for the Social Security program, which accounted for 21% of expenditures. Social Security was followed by national defense (20%), income security (14%), Medicare (12%), and health (10%). Together these five categories accounted for almost three-fourths of federal spending.

TABLE 9.4

Federal government outlays, 2005

[Billions of dollars]

	Amount	% of net total by superfunction	% of net total by superfunction or function
National defense	495	20%	20%
Human resources	1,586	63%	
Education, training, employment, and social services	98		4%
Health	251		10%
Medicare	299		12%
Income security	346		14%
Social Security	523		21%
Veterans benefits and services	70		3%
Physical resources	130	5%	
Energy	0.4		0.02%
Natural resources and environment	28		1%
Commerce and housing credit	8		0.3%
Transportation	68		3%
Community and regional development	26		1%
Net interest	184	7%	7%
Other functions	142	6%	
International affairs	35		1%
General science, space and technology	24		1%
Agriculture	27		1%
Administration of justice	40		2%
General government	17		1%
Allowances	—		
Undistributed offsetting receipts	−65		
Total, federal outlays	2,472	100%	100%

SOURCE: Adapted from "Table 3.1—Outlays by Superfunction and Function: 1940–2011," in *Budget of the United States Government, Fiscal Year 2007: Historical Tables*, U.S. Government Printing Office, 2006, http://www.whitehouse.gov/omb/budget/fy2007/sheets/hist03z1.xls (accessed May 31, 2006)

According to the U.S. Census Bureau, the federal government employed more than 2.7 million civilian (nonmilitary) employees as of December 2005. The civilian payroll for that month was $13.5 billion. The largest contingent of workers (nearly 800,000 people) worked for the U.S. Postal Service. It accounted for more than a quarter of civilian employees and payroll. The next two largest workforces were employed in national defense/international relations and natural resources (http://ftp2.census.gov/govs/apes/05fedfun.pdf).

The Department of Defense (DoD) reports that it employed nearly 1.4 million military personnel on full-time active duty at the end of fiscal year 2005. The DoD had outlays of $127 billion for all military personnel (active- and reserve-duty) for that year (http://www.dod.mil/comptroller/defbudget/fy2007/fy2007_summary_tables_whole.pdf).

Federal Deficits and Surpluses

If the government spends less money than it takes in during a fiscal year, the difference is known as a "budget

FIGURE 9.6

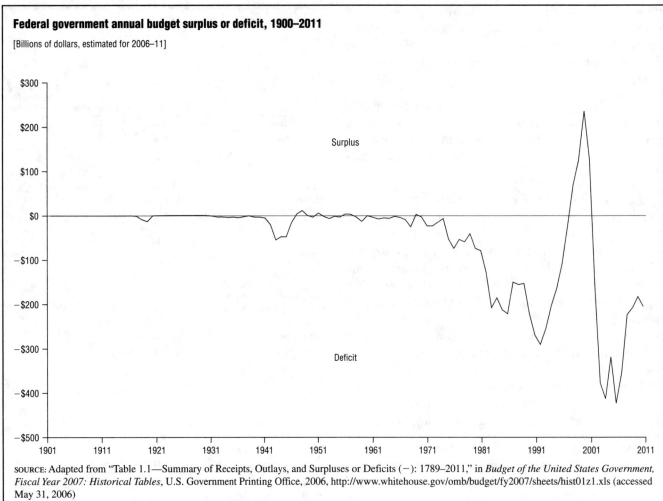

Federal government annual budget surplus or deficit, 1900–2011

[Billions of dollars, estimated for 2006–11]

SOURCE: Adapted from "Table 1.1—Summary of Receipts, Outlays, and Surpluses or Deficits (−): 1789–2011," in *Budget of the United States Government, Fiscal Year 2007: Historical Tables*, U.S. Government Printing Office, 2006, http://www.whitehouse.gov/omb/budget/fy2007/sheets/hist01z1.xls (accessed May 31, 2006)

surplus." Likewise, if spending is higher than revenues, the difference is called a budget deficit. A balanced budget occurs when spending and revenue are the same.

Figure 9.6 shows the annual surplus or deficit for the years 1900 through 2011 as reported in the OMB's FY 2007 budget (years 2006–11 are estimated). In general, the federal government had a balanced budget for more than half of the twentieth century, excluding slight deficits that occurred around World War I and II. Beginning in 1970 the United States had an annual deficit for nearly three decades. The years 1998 through 2002 had budget surpluses. In 2000 the surplus reached a record $236 billion. Budget deficits returned in 2003, 2004, and 2005 and are forecast by the OMB for 2006 through 2011. In 2005 the federal deficit was $318 billion.

National Debt

Whenever the federal government has a budget deficit, the U.S. Department of the Treasury must borrow money to cover the difference. The total amount of money that the Treasury has borrowed over the years is known as the federal debt, or more commonly, the "national debt." Budget surpluses cause the debt to go down, while deficits increase the debt.

As shown in Figure 9.7, the national debt was very low until the early 1940s, when it jogged upward in response to World War II government spending. Over the next three decades the debt increased at a slow pace. During the late 1970s the national debt began a steep climb that has continued into the 2000s. The budget surpluses from 1998 through 2002 had a slight dampening effect on the growth of the debt but did not actually decrease the amount of debt. The budget deficits of the following years sent the debt into another rapid incline. By the end of fiscal year 2005, the national debt stood at $7.93 trillion.

BORROWED MONEY AND IOUS. The national debt has two components: money that the federal government has borrowed from the public and money that the federal government has loaned itself. The public loans money to the federal government by buying federal bonds and other securities. The government borrows the money with a promise to pay it back with interest after a set term. Some of the most common federal securities sold to the public are

126 The Role of the Government

The American Economy

FIGURE 9.7

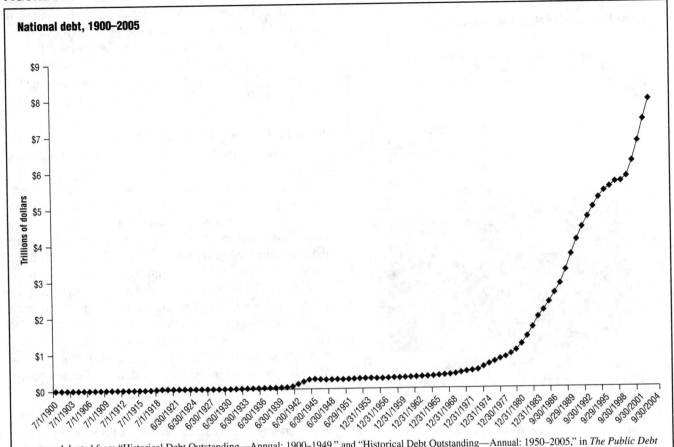

National debt, 1900–2005

SOURCE: Adapted from "Historical Debt Outstanding—Annual: 1900–1949," and "Historical Debt Outstanding—Annual: 1950–2005," in *The Public Debt Online*, U.S. Department of the Treasury, Bureau of the Public Debt, October 6, 2004 and October 13, 2005, http://publicdebt.treas.gov/opd/opdhisto3.htm and http://www.publicdebt.treas.gov/opd/opdhisto4.htm (accessed June 2, 2006)

Treasury bills, Treasury notes, Treasury bonds, and savings bonds. These vary in value, interest paid, and set terms. Public investors include individuals and businesses (both domestic and foreign) and state and local governments.

The federal government also borrows from itself. This is debt owed by one Treasury account to another. Most of the so-called internal debt involves federal trust funds. For example, if a trust fund takes in more revenue in a year than is paid out, it loans the extra money to another federal account. In exchange, the loaning trust fund receives an interest-bearing security (basically an IOU) that is redeemable in the future from the Treasury. This accounting procedure is explained in simple terms in a 2003 publication from the Congressional Budget Office (CBO) titled *Federal Debt and the Commitments of Federal Trust Funds* available at http://www.cbo.gov/ftpdocs/39xx/doc3948/10-25-LongRangeBrief4.pdf. The report sums up the situation as follows: "What is in the trust funds is simply the government's promise to pay itself back at some time in the future."

As of June 1, 2006, the Treasury Department reported the national debt as $8.3 trillion, broken down as follows:

- Owed to the public—$4.8 trillion or 58% of the total
- Intragovernmental—$3.5 trillion or 42% of the total

The portion of the national debt that the government owes to itself has grown substantially since the 1990s. In 1997 intragovernmental debt comprised 30% of the total debt. As shown in Figure 9.8, the CBO projects that this portion of the debt will continue to increase and by 2012 will far exceed the debt owed to the public.

AS A PERCENTAGE OF GDP. Economists often discuss the national debt in terms of its percentage of gross domestic product (GDP; the total value of all goods and services produced by an economy), because a debt amount by itself does not provide a complete picture of the effect of that debt on the one who owes it. Figure 9.9 shows the national debt as a percentage of GDP for fiscal years 1960 through 2003. Comparison of this graphic with Figure 9.7 indicates that even though the numerical amount of the debt was increasing over this time period, its annual share of the GDP did not always follow suit. From 1960 through 1980 the debt-to-GDP ratio decreased. It increased over the next decade and a half and then dipped again in the late 1990s and early 2000s—a period

FIGURE 9.8

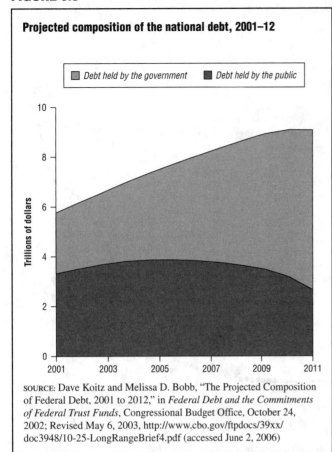

Projected composition of the national debt, 2001–12

Debt held by the government ■ Debt held by the public

SOURCE: Dave Koitz and Melissa D. Bobb, "The Projected Composition of Federal Debt, 2001 to 2012," in *Federal Debt and the Commitments of Federal Trust Funds*, Congressional Budget Office, October 24, 2002; Revised May 6, 2003, http://www.cbo.gov/ftpdocs/39xx/doc3948/10-25-LongRangeBrief4.pdf (accessed June 2, 2006)

coinciding with budget surpluses. At the end of fiscal year 2003 the national debt equaled approximately 60% of the nation's GDP.

THE BURDEN ON THE ECONOMY. The national debt represents a twofold burden on the U.S. economy. The debt owed to the public imposes a current burden. The federal government pays out interest to investors, and these interest payments are funded by current taxpayers. The debt that the federal government owes to itself is a future burden. At some point in the future the securities issued for intragovernmental debt must be redeemed for cash. The government will have to raise these funds by raising taxes, reducing spending, and/or borrowing more money from the public.

INTERNATIONAL COMPARISON. In 2004 the Government Accountability Office (GAO) compared the national debts of seven industrialized nations: Canada, France, Germany, Italy, Japan, the United Kingdom, and the United States. This comparison was based on the total government debt held by each nation (that is, the sum of national, state or regional, and local debt). For each nation the GAO calculated the total government debt as a percentage of national GDP. It found that the debt-to-GDP ratio of the United States was approximately forty-four. This was greater than the ratios of the United Kingdom, Canada,

and France, but less than the ratios of Germany, Japan, and Italy. All of the nations except Japan and Italy had ratios between thirty and fifty. Japan's ratio was nearly seventy-two and Italy's ratio exceeded ninety-four (*Federal Debt: Answers to Frequently Asked Questions—An Update*, August 2004, http://www.gao.gov/new.items/d04485sp.pdf).

PUBLIC INVESTMENT AND TAXES

In order to fund itself, the federal government uses the money of its constituents. The buying of federal securities, such as bonds, represents a voluntary investment in government by the public. Federal securities are considered a safe low-risk investment because they are backed by an entity that has been in business for more than two hundred years and has a proven track record of fiscal soundness. However, money invested in government securities is not available for private investment. In general, private investments are seen as more stimulating for the economy because they provide direct funds for growth, such as the building of new factories and hiring new workers. Public (government) investment may or may not have a stimulating effect on the economy, depending on how the funds are spent.

Taxes represent an involuntary investment by the public in government. The impact of taxes on the economy is a source of never-ending debate in U.S. politics. Taxing personal income decreases the spending power of the individual; people have less money to invest in private enterprise or to use to consume goods and services. Limited taxation is favored by those who believe that workers and companies with more available money to spend will participate to a greater extent in the economy. This, they say, will lead to economic growth. But others observe that cutting taxes without severely reducing government spending quickly leads to large budget deficits and undermines the government programs that provide a social safety net to the disadvantaged.

The Bush Tax Cuts

Historically, the U.S. Republican party has advocated smaller government and lower taxes. The Economic Growth and Tax Relief and Reconciliation Act of 2001 (EGTRRA) was initiated by the administration of George W. Bush and is commonly referred to as the "Bush tax cuts." The EGTRRA instituted a series of tax rate reductions and incentive measures to be phased in over several years. Included in the law were increases in income tax credits for families with children and reductions in estate, gift, and generation-skipping transfer taxes (GST; a special tax on property transfers from grandparents to their grandchildren) but did not address business taxes. It also called for reductions in the tax brackets. EGTRRA was designed to "sunset" (expire) in 2011 unless additional measures are passed to extend its provisions.

FIGURE 9.9

National debt as a percentage of gross domestic product (GDP), 1960–2003

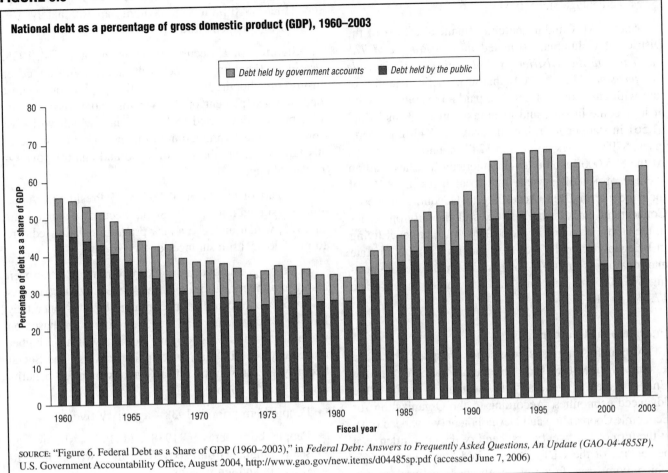

SOURCE: "Figure 6. Federal Debt as a Share of GDP (1960–2003)," in *Federal Debt: Answers to Frequently Asked Questions, An Update (GAO-04-485SP)*, U.S. Government Accountability Office, August 2004, http://www.gao.gov/new.items/d04485sp.pdf (accessed June 7, 2006)

The Jobs and Growth Tax Relief Reconciliation Act of 2003 (JGTRRA) accelerated implementation of EGTRRA, reduced taxes on capital gains and dividends, and increased deductions for property depreciation.

Following implementation of the tax cuts, total income tax receipts from individual and corporate taxpayers were at the lowest level as a share of GDP since 1942, and federal receipts from personal income taxes were at the lowest level since 1966, according to Isaac Shapiro in "Federal Income Taxes, as a Share of GDP, Drop to Lowest Level Since 1942, According to Final Budget Data" (Center on Budget and Policy Priorities, October 21, 2003).

President Bush was reelected in 2004 and has indicated that he favors making the provisions of EGTRRA permanent as a way to stimulate the U.S. economy. The president asserts that his policies will reduce poverty by lowering taxes for low- and lower-middle income families. In addition, the administration asserts that tax breaks benefit families by helping them reduce their debt.

Critics of the president's tax policy point out that changes in the tax structure unfairly shift the burden from corporations and wealthy individuals to low- and middle-class wage earners, that tax cuts already instituted have erased the federal surplus built up in the late 1990s, and that further tax cuts will lead to unacceptable increases in government debt. In a letter to the President's Advisory Panel for Tax Reform (March 18, 2005), Cassandra Q. Butts and John S. Irons of the Center for American Progress concluded, "Overall, the federal tax system has become increasingly reliant on the regressive payroll tax, has shifted the burden of tax payment from the wealthy to the middle class, and has allowed corporations to avoid paying their fair share of taxes. The president's stated future goals for the tax system . . . will only exacerbate the degree to which the system has become unfair."

Tax Burden

The amount of tax an individual or family pays to the government, including their income, payroll, excise, and other taxes, is known as their tax burden. According to Isaac Shapiro in "Overall Federal Tax Burden on Most Families—Including Middle-Income Families—at Lowest Levels in More Than Two Decades" (Center on Budget and Policy Priorities, April 10, 2002), the median four-person family with two dependents paid 6.8% of its income in federal income tax in 2001, which was the lowest percentage since 1957.

Natwar M. Gandhi, the chief financial officer of the District of Columbia, estimated in *Tax Rates and Tax Burdens: In the District of Columbia—A Nationwide Comparison* (August 2004) that an American family of four with an income of $50,000 paid an average of 8.3% of its income in state and local taxes in 2003, including $1,561 in state or local income taxes, $1,843 in property taxes, $797 in sales taxes, and $247 in automobile taxes. At the $75,000 income level, American families paid an average of $6,832 in state and local taxes, or 9.1% of their income in 2003. According to Gandhi, Bridgeport, Connecticut, had the highest taxes of the fifty-one cities in the study. Families at the $50,000 income level living in Bridgeport paid 13% of their income ($7,501) in state and local taxes in 2003. For families in Bridgeport earning $75,000, the state and local tax burden increased to 17.7%, or $13,272.

International Comparisons

Although Americans commonly complain about the amount of taxes they pay, the overall tax burden in the United States is generally lower than it is in other advanced economies. According to the Organization for Economic Cooperation and Development (www.oecd.org), at the turn of the twenty-first century the tax burden as a percentage of the GDP in the United States was 29.6%, which compared favorably with such nations as the United Kingdom (37.4%), Canada (35.8%), France (45.3%), Germany (37.9%), and Sweden (54.2%), but was higher than Korea (26.1%) and Japan (27.1%).

According to "How Competitive Is the U.S. Tax System?," a study issued by the Joint Economic Committee of the U.S. Congress in April 2004, the United States imposed the lowest taxes on the personal income of wealthy individuals during 2003 among eight leading industrial nations and was the only country without a national sales tax. (See Table 9.5.) However, when comparing tax rates in the United States with those in Australia, Canada, France, Germany, Italy, Japan, Spain, and the United Kingdom, the study reported that the U.S. corporate tax rate, which is 35% at its maximum, was among the highest, and the United States was the only country to tax corporate profits at both the corporate and the individual levels—that is, the corporation pays corporate taxes on its profits, and when the profits are distributed to shareholders as dividends, the shareholders also pay taxes on that income.

THE FUTURE OF SOCIAL SECURITY AND MEDICARE

As shown in Table 9.4, Social Security and Medicare are two of the most expensive programs operated by the federal government. Together in 2005 they accounted for more than $800 billion of spending, approximately one-third of total expenditures.

Signing Social Security into law on August 14, 1935, President Franklin D. Roosevelt said, "We can never insure one hundred percent of the population against one hundred percent of the hazards and vicissitudes of life, but we have tried to frame a law which will give some measure of protection to the average citizen and to his family against the loss of a job and against poverty-ridden old age."

As part of his "War of Poverty," President Lyndon Johnson signed into law the Social Security Amendments of 1965, which included a new program called Medicare to provide health insurance for the elderly.

The program conditions and requirements have been changed numerous times over the succeeding decades. As of 2006, people qualify for retirement benefits once they have worked for ten years. Benefit amounts are based on wage history; thus, higher paid workers will have higher retirement benefits than lower-paid workers. The Social Security Administration sets an age at which full benefits can be paid as follows:

• People born prior to 1938—age sixty-five

• People born between 1938 and 1959—sliding age scale ranging from sixty-five and two months to sixty-six and ten months

• People born in 1960 and later—age sixty-seven

People who have worked for at least ten years are eligible for permanently reduced retirement benefits starting at age sixty-two. Benefits for widows, widowers, and family members have varying age requirements and other conditions that must be met. Medicare coverage begins at age sixty-five for everyone except certain disabled people who can qualify earlier.

Since their inception, the Social Security and Medicare programs have been a source of partisan contention and debate. Much of the debate has centered on how the programs should be funded and the role of government in social welfare. In recent years attention has turned to concerns about how the nation can afford these programs in the future as the population ages and there are fewer wage earners contributing to the plans.

Fewer Contributors, More Beneficiaries

Figure 9.10 shows the percentage of the U.S. population age sixty-five or older for 1950 through 2004 and projected through 2080. A huge increase in the aged population is expected to take place during the 2010s and 2020s due to the baby boom that followed World War II. But as these workers retire, there will be fewer workers contributing to the plan, because succeeding

TABLE 9.5

Tax rates in large advanced economies, 2003

[2003 unless otherwise indicated]

Type of tax	Australia	Canada	France	Germany	Italy	Japan	Spain	UK	USA 2003	USA 2000
Corporate Standard rate	30%	24.6–38.6% fed.+prov.	34.33%, territorial	27.9575%	34%	30%	35%	30%	35% fed.+ 0–12% state	35% fed.+ 0–9.99% state
Capital gains	Standard rate	Standard rate, 50% excluded	Standard rate	0%	Standard rate	Standard rate	Standard rate	Standard rate	Standard rate	Standard rate
Dividend tax	Standard rate	0%	0%	0%	Standard rate, 56.25% cred.	Standard rate, 50% ex.	Effectively 0%	0%	Standard rate	Standard rate
Personal Income tax, top rate	47% from A$60,000	39–48.2% fed.+prov. fr. C$103,000	49.58% from €47,131	47% from €52,293	45% from €70,000	50% natl.+ local from ¥18 mn.	35.1–45% natl.+local from €45,000	40% from £30,500	35% fed.+ 0–11% state fr US$311,950	39.6% fed.+ 0–9.3% state fr. $288,350
Payroll tax on employee	1.5%	4.95%, max. C$1,802 fed.	10%	13.65%, max. €7,610	9.89% to €80,391	0.7% no max.+13.46%, ¥1.2mn. max.	6.35–6.4% to €31,824	11% to £30,420, then 1%	fed. 1.45% no max.+6.2% to US $87,000	fed. 1.45% no max.+6.2% to US $76,200
Payroll tax on employer	0% federal, ~6% state	7.05%, max. C$2,621 fed.	4.25–13.6%	13.65%, max. €7,610	23.81% to €80,391	1.6% no max.+13.46%, ¥1.2mn. max.	30.6–32.3% to €31,824	12.8%	fed. 1.45% no max.+6.2% to US$87,000	fed. 1.45% no max.+6.2% to US$76,200
Sales or value added tax	10%	7% fed.+ 0–10% prov.	19.6%	16%	20% natl.+ 4.5% local	5%	16%	17.5%	0% federal+ 0–7.25% state	0% federal+ 0–7% state
Interest tax	Income rate	Income rate	17.6%, €15,000 ex.	Income rate, €1,550 ex.	12.5%	20%	Income rate	Up to 40%	Income rate	Income rate
Dividend tax	Income rate	Income rate	Income rate	Income rate, 50% excluded	12.5%	Income rate	Income rate	10%, 32.5% fr. £30,500	5–15%; double taxed 5–15%	Income rate; double taxed 10–20%
Long term capital gains	Income rate, 50% ex.	Income rate, 50% excluded	17.6%, €15,000 ex.	0%	12.5%	10%	15%	Income rate, £7,900 ex.	Income rate	Income rate
Short term capital gains	Income rate	Income rate, 50% ex.	17.6%, €15,000 ex.	Income rate, 50% ex.	27%	20%	Income rate	Income rate, £7,900 ex.	Income rate	Income rate
Retirement savings tax	15% to A$109,924*, then 30%	0%	0%	Income rate, 70% average excluded	12.5% on capital gains	0%	0%	0%	0%	0%
—limit on contribution	A$87,141	C$13,500	€24,000	€918	€5,165	¥180,000	€8,000–24,250	UK£3,600–36,720	US$3,000–3,500 (IRAs)	US$2,000 (IRAs)
Tax on retirement income	15% first A$1.12mn. lifetime, then income rate	Income rate	Income rate	Income rate, sliding ex. (73% for 65-year old) 17–50%	Income rate, 40% excluded	Favorable rates, up to ¥3.49mn ex.	Income rate on interest	Income rate, 25% excluded	Income rate	Income rate
Inheritance tax, top rates	0%	0%	5–60%, €1,500 ex.	17–50%, €1,100 ex.	0%, but other taxes, €150,000 ex.	20–50%, ¥25mn. excluded	7.65–81.6%	40%, £242,000 excluded	18–49% fed., US$1.1mn. ex., + state	18–55% fed., US$675,000. ex., + state
Wealth tax	0%	0%	0.55–1.8%, €720,000 ex.	0%	0%	0%	0.2–2.5%, €108,182 + house ex.	0%	0% federal+ 0–0.15% state	0% federal+ 0–0.15% state
Forbes index	41.57%	38.07%	40.75%	50.47%	41.95%	24.9	36.67%	33.03%	28.93%	33.6%
Govt./GDP	36.4%	40.1%	54.4%	49.4%	48.5%	38.3%	39.3%	42.8%	35.9%	
Growth 00–03	1.8%	1.6%	1.2%	0.7%	1.3%	1.4%	1.7%	1.9%	1.4%	1.4%

Notes: *In taxable income. All the countries listed tax personal income on a worldwide basis. "Income rate" means that the rates of the income tax apply. Rates are for single filers and apply only to national taxes unless indicated. Abbreviations: cred.=credit; ex.=excluded; fed.=federal; fr.=from; max.=maximum; min.=minimum; mn.=million; natl.=national; prov.=provincial. Currency symbols: A$=Australian dollar; C$=Canadian dollar; €=euro; £=British pound; ¥=Japanese yen.

SOURCE: "Table 1. Tax Rates in Large Advanced Economies (2003)," in *How Competitive Is the U.S. Tax System?* Joint Economic Committee, United States Congress, April 2004, http://www.house.gov/jec/tax/04-20-04.pdf (accessed July 3, 2006)

FIGURE 9.10

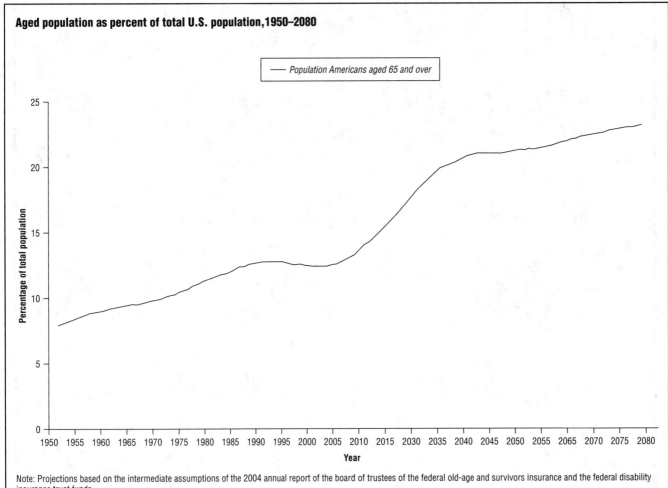

Aged population as percent of total U.S. population,1950–2080

— Population Americans aged 65 and over

Percentage of total population

Year

Note: Projections based on the intermediate assumptions of the 2004 annual report of the board of trustees of the federal old-age and survivors insurance and the federal disability insurance trust funds.

SOURCE: "Figure 12. Changes in Aged Population as a Share of Total U.S. Population (1950–2080)," in *Federal Debt: Answers to Frequently Asked Questions, An Update (GAO-04-485SP)*, U.S. Government Accountability Office, August 2004, http://www.gao.gov/new.items/d04485sp.pdf (accessed June 7, 2006)

generations have been smaller due to declining birth rates. At the same time, life expectancies have been increasing, meaning that elderly people are living longer past retirement age and collecting benefits for more years.

Figure 9.11 is an estimate from the Social Security Administration (SSA) of the number of workers contributing to Social Security per beneficiary. In 1960 there were approximately five workers per beneficiary. By 2000 this number had dropped close to 3.5 workers. The SSA estimates that by 2060 there will be only about two workers contributing for each beneficiary. This is expected to put unprecedented stresses on the Social Security system.

Funding Social Security

On May 1, 2006, the Social Security Board of Trustees published its annual report on the status of the Social Security trust funds—OASI (Old-Age and Survivors

Insurance) and DI (Disability Insurance). The report is titled *The 2006 Annual Report of the Board of Trustees of the Federal Old-Age and Survivors Insurance and Federal Disability Insurance Trust Funds* (http://www.ssa.gov/OACT/TR/TR06/tr06.pdf). The report notes that approximately 159 million people had earnings covered by Social Security during 2005. Together the OASI and DI trust funds had revenues of $702 billion, of which 85% came from payroll taxes. The remaining 15% was from interest earnings and taxes assessed on benefits. More than $520 billion was paid in benefits to forty-eight million people as follows:

- Thirty-three million retirees and their dependents

- Eight million disabled workers and their dependents

- Seven million survivors of deceased workers

The trustees project that tax revenues will be less than program costs beginning in 2017. At that point the trust funds will be used to pay the shortfall so that payments to

FIGURE 9.11

Number of workers contributing to Social Security system per beneficiary, 1960–2080

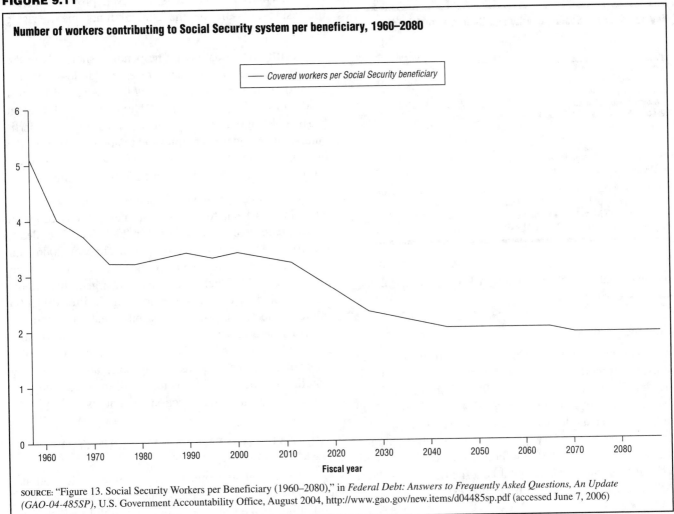

SOURCE: "Figure 13. Social Security Workers per Beneficiary (1960–2080)," in *Federal Debt: Answers to Frequently Asked Questions, An Update (GAO-04-485SP)*, U.S. Government Accountability Office, August 2004, http://www.gao.gov/new.items/d04485sp.pdf (accessed June 7, 2006)

beneficiaries can continue at expected levels. The trust funds will be exhausted in 2040, and over the following four decades the program's annual income will fund 70–74% of the benefits currently available to beneficiaries. Accessing the trust funds will put pressure on the federal budget, as the federal government has often borrowed money from the trust funds to pay for other programs but will no longer be able to do so.

In total, the trustees estimate that the Social Security program will be short by $4.6 trillion over a seventy-five-year period.

FIXING THE PROBLEM. How best to prepare for future shortfalls in Social Security is a fiercely debated issue in American government. During early 2005 President George W. Bush campaigned for significant reform of the Social Security program, including allowing younger workers to opt out of the Social Security plan and establish their own retirement savings accounts. This came to be known as "privatization" of Social Security.

Democrats in Congress did not accept that a radical reform of the program was necessary to recover the shortfall, as the actual deficit over a seventy-five-year period, according to the Social Security Board of Trustees' 2006 report, was expected to be only 2.02%. In other words, the payroll tax for Social Security would need to be increased by 2.02% to make up the difference. Democrats have suggested that such a sum could also be recouped by removing the cap on income subject to FICA taxes (those mandated by the Federal Insurance Contribution Act), for instance, but President Bush has adamantly dismissed any alternatives that could be construed as a tax increase.

In addition, the president's plan to privatize Social Security has been opposed by influential seniors groups, including AARP (formerly the American Association of Retired Persons), a special interest group for people over age fifty. The AARP advocates increasing the income limit subject to Social Security withholding. As of 2006, the limit was $94,200; it has been raised many times over the years. The AARP also encourages the federal government to invest trust fund assets differently so as to reap higher rates of return (http://www.aarp.org/

TABLE 9.6

Key dates for the Social Security and Medicare trust funds

	OASI	DI	OASDI	HI
First year outgo exceeds income excluding interest	2018	2005	2017	2006
First year outgo exceeds income including interest	2028	2013	2027	2010
Year trust fund assets are exhausted	2042	2025	2040	2018

OASI = Old-Age and Survivors Insurance
DI = Disability Insurance
OASDI = combined Old-Age and Survivors and Disability Insurance
HI = Hospital Insurance (Medicare)

SOURCE: "Key Dates for the Trust Funds," in *A Summary of the 2006 Annual Social Security and Medicare Trust Fund Reports*, Social Security Administration, May 22, 2006, http://www.ssa.gov/OACT/TRSUM/trsummary.html (accessed June 6, 2006)

money/social_security/frequently_asked_questions_about_social_security.html).

Funding Medicare

According to the 2006 Social Security Board of Trustees' report, the largest Medicare trust fund, HI (Hospital Insurance), took in $199 billion during 2005. The vast majority of this money (86%) was from payroll taxes. The remainder came from interest earnings, taxes on benefits, beneficiary premiums, and other sources, including a transfer of $0.5 billion from the general fund. The HI trust fund pays hospital benefits (known as "Part A" under Medicare) to all beneficiaries.

The trustees note that the Medicare HI trust fund faces a shortfall much sooner than the OASI and DI funds. As shown in Table 9.6, benefits to be paid out will exceed income (including interest) as early as 2010. The HI trust fund is expected to be exhausted by 2018. Immediately after exhaustion, tax revenues will be sufficient to pay only 80% of HI costs. That number will drop to 29% by 2080. The HI trust fund faces extreme funding problems in future decades because technological advances are expected to dramatically increase health care costs in the United States.

The Medicare Supplementary Medical Insurance (SMI) trust fund had revenues of $158 billion during 2005. SMI covers the costs of physician services (Part B) and prescription drugs (Part D). Coverage under Parts B and D is optional and requires payment of monthly premiums. These are subtracted from the beneficiaries' Social Security checks. Part D coverage is relatively new, having been added to the Medicare program in late 2003. In 2005 the SMI trust fund was financed largely by revenues from the general fund and supplemented with beneficiary premiums and interest earnings. Because SMI is not dependent on payroll taxes, it is not expected to experience the same kind of shortfalls facing the OASI,

DI, and HI trust funds. It is, however, projected to put increasing pressure on the general fund due to rising health care costs.

FIXING THE PROBLEM. The pending shortfalls in the Medicare HI trust fund have received far less national attention than the problems facing the OASI and DI trust funds. In his 2006 State of the Union address President Bush spoke about the need for health care reform, particularly in Medicare. The president called Medicare "the binding commitment of a caring society." Concrete reform measures, however, have not been forthcoming.

Some analysts maintain that the administration's attention has been focused on the new Part D program of Medicare, which was enacted in 2003. The final deadline for signing up for the program was in May 2006, and much attention was paid to encouraging enrollment among seniors. Other critics have charged that Medicare's problems were being ignored until after the 2006 midterm elections. All congressional seats and about a third of senatorial seats were up for reelection in November 2006. Medicare reform is likely to require politically unpopular actions, such as raising taxes and/or reducing benefits. Politicians are reluctant to discuss such unpleasant topics during their election campaigns.

FEDERAL GOVERNMENT MANIPULATION OF MACROECONOMICS

The federal government plays a role in the national economy as a tax collector, spender, and employer. Federal policy makers also engage in purposeful manipulation of the U.S. economy at the macroeconomic level—for example, influencing supply and demand factors. This was not always the case. Prior to the 1930s the government mostly maintained a hands-off approach to macroeconomic affairs—a tradition dating back to the founding of the nation. The ravages of the Great Depression brought a level of desperation (the unemployment rate, for example, was as high as 25%) that encouraged leaders to attempt to influence macroeconomic factors. Although these efforts were largely futile at soothing deep economic depression, they accustomed a generation of Americans to the idea of government interference in economic affairs.

When immense federal spending during World War II helped end the Great Depression, policy makers believed they had discovered a new solution, a government solution, for economic downturns. Government efforts to manage macroeconomic factors became a routine matter over the following decades. These manipulations are commonly divided into two categories, known as fiscal policy and monetary policy.

Fiscal Policy

The word "fiscal" is derived from the Latin term *fiscalis*, meaning "treasury." It is believed that a fiscalis was originally a woven basket in which money was kept. In modern English the word "fiscal" has become synonymous with the word "financial." The federal government's fiscal policy is concerned with the collection and spending of public money so as to influence macroeconomic affairs. Examples of fiscal policy include:

- Increasing government spending to spur businesses to produce more and hire more, lowering the unemployment rate

- Increasing taxes to pull money out of the hands of consumers; this can lower excessive demand that is driving high inflation rates

- Decreasing taxes to put more money in the hands of consumers to increase demand and consequently increase supply (production)

These examples illustrate optimistic outcomes. In reality, the actions of fiscal policy can have complicated (and unforeseen) effects on the U.S. economy. The situation described in the first example can backfire if production does not grow fast enough to satisfy consumer demand. The result will be rising prices and high inflation rates. Likewise, tax increases and decreases can have unexpected and undesirable consequences. The relationships between the major macroeconomic factors—unemployment, inflation, and supply and demand—are complex and difficult to keep in balance.

Fiscal policy is strongly associated with the economist John Maynard Keynes and is a cornerstone of Keynesian economics.

Monetary Policy

Monetary policy is concerned with influencing the supply of money and credit and the demand for them to achieve specific economic goals. The actions of monetary policy are not as direct and obvious as the tax and spend activities associated with fiscal policy. Monetary changes are achieved indirectly through the nation's banking system. Some results of monetary policy changes are as follows:

- An increase in the amount of money that banks can loan to the public. This leads to greater borrowing, which puts more money into the hands of consumers, increasing demand for goods and services.

- A decrease in the amount of money that banks can loan to the public. This leads to less borrowing, which slows the growth of the money supply and dampens demand, which can reduce high inflation rates.

- Lower interest rates on loans. This encourages borrowing, which increases the money supply and consumer demand.

- Higher interest rates on loans. This discourages people from borrowing more money, which slows the growth of the money supply and can reduce high inflation rates.

Just as in fiscal policy, it is difficult to achieve the exact results desired. Oversupply of money and credit will aggravate price inflation if production cannot meet increased consumer demand. Likewise, undersupply can lower consumer demand too much and stifle economic growth. The challenge for the government is deciding when, and by how much, money supply and credit availability should be changed to maintain a healthy economy. These decisions and manipulations are made by the nation's central bank, the Federal Reserve.

THE FEDERAL RESERVE SYSTEM. In 1913 the U.S. Congress passed the Federal Reserve Act to form the nation's central bank. The Federal Reserve System (or the Fed, as it is commonly called) was granted power to manipulate the money supply—the total amount of coins and paper currency in circulation, along with all holdings at banks, credit unions, and other financial institutions.

The Fed includes a seven-member board of governors headquartered in Washington, D.C., and twelve Reserve Banks located in major cities around the country—Boston, New York City, Philadelphia, Cleveland, Richmond, Atlanta, Chicago, St. Louis, Minneapolis, Kansas City, Dallas, and San Francisco.

The Fed uses three techniques to indirectly achieve its stated goals of "maximum employment, stable prices, and moderate long-term interest rates":

- Open market operations—The Fed buys and sells government securities on the financial markets. The resulting money transfers ultimately lower or raise the amount of money that banks have available to loan to the public and the associated interest rates.

- Discount rate adjustments—The Fed raises or lowers the discount rate. This is the rate that it charges banks for short-term loans. In response, the banks adjust the federal funds rate, the rate they charge each other for loans. Then the banks adjust the prime rate, the interest rate they charge their best customers (typically large corporations). In the end, these adjustments affect the interest rates paid by the general public on mortgages, car loans, credit cards, etc.

- Reserve requirement adjustments—The Fed raises or lowers the reserve requirement, the amount of readily available money that banks must have to operate. Each bank's reserve requirement is based on a percentage of the total amount of money that customers have deposited at that bank. Money above the reserve requirement can be loaned out by the banks. Changes in the reserve requirement influence bank decisions about loans to the public.

CHAPTER 10
INTERNATIONAL TRADE AND AMERICA'S PLACE IN THE GLOBAL ECONOMY

Those who have money go abroad in the world.

— Chinese proverb

Technology has made it easier to go abroad in the world. American companies can sell their goods and services on a global market. Likewise, American consumers can purchase merchandise made around the world—and they do so in large numbers. Global trade is driven by the same forces that control the U.S. market: supply and demand. But there is the added complication of numerous, very different national governments trying to exert influence over trade and market factors in their favor. The U.S. economy is preeminent in the global economy when it comes to national production. But the United States buys far more from foreign lands than it sells to them. Economists disagree about whether this trade imbalance is a good or bad thing for America.

AMERICA'S PLACE IN THE GLOBAL ECONOMY

According to the Central Intelligence Agency's *World Factbook*, the international gross domestic product (GDP) was $60.7 trillion during 2005. (See Table 10.1.) The United States had the largest economy of any single nation ($12.4 trillion), followed by China ($8.9 trillion), Japan ($4 trillion), and India ($3.6 trillion). The combined nations of the European Union (EU) had a GDP of $12.2 trillion, putting the EU in a position just below the U.S. in terms of economic strength. The GDP values in Table 10.1 were calculated based on purchasing power parity. This is an accounting method useful for comparing very different economies. The CIA explains that each non-U.S. GDP listed in Table 10.1 was calculated by valuing that economy's goods and services at the prices prevailing in the United States.

In 2005 the United States accounted for 20% of the world's GDP, but it was home to less than 5% of the world's population.

How the U.S. Compares

America's rise as the global economic leader has resulted from a combination of many factors—geographical, political, social, and financial. The United States has also been fortunate, in that it escaped the ravages of two world wars that severely damaged the industrial infrastructure of other nations. In general, America's dominance is attributed to its wealth in natural resources, a motivated and educated labor force, numerous technological innovations, and a sociopolitical climate conducive to economic growth.

NATURAL RESOURCES. Natural resources are commodities that can be taken from the environment and either used in the manufacture of other products or sold in their original form. Forestry, fishing, and mining are classified as natural resources industries. Natural resources are considered either renewable or nonrenewable. Renewable resources are those that can be replanted or restocked (such as trees and fish), while nonrenewable resources, such as minerals, cannot be replaced once they become depleted. A country's natural resources can affect the overall health of its economy. As the fourth-largest country in the world, at 3.7 million square miles, the United States has direct access to two oceans; numerous rivers and waterways; coal, oil, and mineral deposits; fertile soil for farming; and many heavily forested areas, all of which make it one of the richest geographical regions on the planet.

LABOR. The highly skilled and well-trained U.S. labor force is one of the most important elements of America's economic success. As of the first quarter of 2006, the labor force consisted of more than 150 million employees. The U.S. Department of Labor's Bureau of Labor Statistics (BLS) measures the productivity of American workers using the ratio of output of goods and services to labor hours devoted to producing that output. According to the BLS, productivity of the

TABLE 10.1

Gross domestic product (purchasing power parity), 25 wealthiest countries, 2005

Rank	Country	GDP (purchasing power parity)	Date of Information
1	World	$60,710,000,000,000	2005 est.
2	United States	$12,360,000,000,000	2005 est.
3	European Union	$12,180,000,000,000	2005 est.
4	China	$8,859,000,000,000	2005 est.
5	Japan	$4,018,000,000,000	2005 est.
6	India	$3,611,000,000,000	2005 est.
7	Germany	$2,504,000,000,000	2005 est.
8	United Kingdom	$1,830,000,000,000	2005 est.
9	France	$1,816,000,000,000	2005 est.
10	Italy	$1,698,000,000,000	2005 est.
11	Russia	$1,589,000,000,000	2005 est.
12	Brazil	$1,556,000,000,000	2005 est.
13	Canada	$1,114,000,000,000	2005 est.
14	Mexico	$1,067,000,000,000	2005 est.
15	Spain	$1,029,000,000,000	2005 est.
16	Korea, South	$965,300,000,000	2005 est.
17	Indonesia	$865,600,000,000	2005 est.
18	Australia	$640,100,000,000	2005 est.
19	Taiwan	$631,200,000,000	2005 est.
20	Turkey	$572,000,000,000	2005 est.
21	Iran	$561,600,000,000	2005 est.
22	Thailand	$560,700,000,000	2005 est.
23	South Africa	$533,200,000,000	2005 est.
24	Argentina	$518,100,000,000	2005 est.
25	Poland	$514,000,000,000	2005 est.

SOURCE: Adapted from "Rank Order—GDP (Purchasing Power Parity)," in *The World Factbook*, Central Intelligence Agency, June 13, 2006, http://www.cia.gov/cia/publications/factbook/rankorder/2001rank.html (accessed June 29, 2006)

FIGURE 10.1

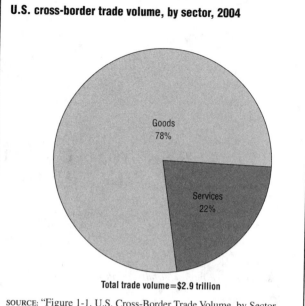

U.S. cross-border trade volume, by sector, 2004

Goods 78%

Services 22%

Total trade volume=$2.9 trillion

SOURCE: "Figure 1-1. U.S. Cross-Border Trade Volume, by Sector, 2004," in *Recent Trends in U.S. Services Trade: 2006 Annual Report*, U.S. International Trade Commission, June 2006, http://hotdocs.usitc.gov/docs/pubs/332/pub3857.pdf (accessed June 28, 2006)

nonfarm business sector increased by 3.7% in the first quarter of 2006 and has experienced annual increases in excess of 2% each year since 1998.

Technology

American companies have long been at the forefront of technological innovation, pioneering such developments over the years as electricity, factory assembly lines, and computer software. These new technologies have increased both worker productivity and business efficiency, which, in turn, allows companies to deliver goods and services at lower costs to consumers, stimulating spending and boosting the economy. At the same time, advances in technology can affect the job market. At times new technologies lead to more jobs as workers are needed to design, manufacture, and service them. On the other hand, such advances can also cause job losses as increased efficiency streamlines processes so that fewer employees are needed.

SOCIOPOLITICAL ENVIRONMENT. The sociopolitical environment of the United States has played a major role in the nation's rise to dominance in the global economy. Although people argue about the proper role of government in the nation's economic affairs, the relatively free-market-based system that has developed in the United States has proved to be conducive to economic growth.

GLOBAL AND U.S. TRADE

World trade totaled $11 trillion in 2004 according to *International Trade Statistics 2005*, a publication of the World Trade Organization (WTO; http://www.wto.org/english/res_e/statis_e/its2005_e/its05_toc_e.htm). The value of merchandise trade was $8.9 trillion, while trade in commercial services was $2.1 trillion. Manufactured products accounted for nearly three-fourths of the value of trade in merchandise. The two single-largest sectors in commercial services were travel and transportation, each accounting for around one-fourth of the total value of that category. Overall, the WTO reports that the value of worldwide trade increased by 9% between 2000 and 2004.

According to the U.S. Department of Commerce's International Trade Administration, the United States had $2.9 trillion in trade during 2004. This is just over a quarter of all global trade reported by the WTO for that year. As shown in Figure 10.1, more than three-quarters of U.S. trade volume during 2004 was in goods. Services comprised only 22% of the total by volume.

U.S. Trade in Goods

Table 10.2 provides a breakdown of goods imported and exported by the United States in 2003, 2004, and 2005. Two different totals are given—a total using a balance of payments (BOP) basis and a total using a Census basis. These values represent different accounting methods used by the Bureau of Economic Analysis (BEA) and the U.S. Census Bureau, respectively, to track international trade of goods.

TABLE 10.2

Imports and exports of goods by principal end-use category, 2003–05

[In millions of dollars. Seasonally adjusted.]

Period	Total balance of payments basis	Net adjustments	Total census basis[a]	End-use commodity category					
				Foods, feeds, beverages	Industrial supplies[b]	Capital goods	Automotive vehicles, etc.	Consumer goods	Other goods
Exports									
2003	713,415	−11,356	724,771	55,026	173,043	293,673	80,633	89,908	32,487
2004	807,516	−11,259	818,775	56,570	203,960	331,555	89,213	103,075	34,404
2005	894,631	−11,347	905,978	58,955	233,079	362,686	98,578	115,715	36,964
Imports									
2003	1,260,717	3,596	1,257,121	55,831	313,818	295,867	210,139	333,878	47,587
2004	1,472,926	3,221	1,469,704	62,143	412,827	343,491	228,195	372,943	50,106
2005	1,677,371	3,916	1,673,455	68,094	523,881	379,227	239,512	407,168	55,572

[a]Detailed data are presented on a census basis. The information needed to convert to a BOP basis is not available.
[b]Includes petroleum and petroleum products.
Note: Details may not equal totals due to seasonal adjustment and rounding.

SOURCE: Adapted from "Exhibit 5. Exports of Goods by Principal End-Use Category," and "Exhibit 5a. Imports of Goods by Principal End-Use Category," in *U.S. International Trade in Goods and Services, Annual Revision for 2005*, U.S. Department of Commerce, Bureau of Economic Analysis, 2006, http://www.bea.gov/bea/newsrelarchive/2006/trad1306.xls (accessed June 29, 2006)

IMPORTED GOODS. As shown in Table 10.2, nearly $1.7 trillion in goods was imported into the United States in 2005. The industrial supplies category had the most imports, accounting for $524 billion of the total. According to the BEA, petroleum and petroleum products comprised nearly half of the industrial supplies shipped into the country during 2005. Consumer goods accounted for more than $400 billion of total imports. This category includes a wide variety of household, sporting, and personal use items. The largest value components were pharmaceutical preparations, apparel, and household goods, including televisions. The U.S. imported $379 billion in capital goods in 2005. Capital goods are items such as machinery, equipment, apparatuses, engines, machine parts, aircraft, tractors, telecommunication devices, computers and computer accessories, and similar goods (excluding automotive vehicles and parts). Computer and telecommunication devices were the largest value components of this category. Nearly $240 billion in automotive vehicles, parts, and engines were imported in 2005. Foods, feeds, and beverages accounted for $68 billion in imports, with fish and seafood comprising the largest percentage by value. Other goods imported into the U.S. during 2005 had a value of nearly $56 billion.

The U.S. Census Bureau tracks total imports and exports of goods to and from the United States on a monthly and yearly basis. For calendar year 2005 America's top ten trading partners and the value of goods traded with them were as follows:

- Canada—$499 billion
- Mexico—$290 billion
- China—$285 billion
- Japan—$194 billion
- Germany—$119 billion
- United Kingdom—$90 billion
- South Korea—$71 billion
- Taiwan—$57 billion
- France—$56 billion
- Malaysia—$44 billion

Together these ten countries accounted for just over two-thirds of all U.S. trade value during 2005 (http://www.census.gov/foreign-trade/statistics/highlights/top/top0512.html).

EXPORTED GOODS. The United States exported around $900 billion worth of goods in 2005, as shown in Table 10.2. The largest category of exports was capital goods, totaling nearly $363 billion. Computers and computer equipment (particularly semiconductors) and civilian aircraft were major exports for the United States. Just over $233 billion in industrial supplies were exported. Chemicals and plastic materials were the largest single components of this category. The value of exported consumer goods was nearly $116 billion in 2005. Pharmaceutical preparations were, by far, the largest component. Exports of automotive vehicles, engines, and parts totaled nearly $99 billion. The sum for exported foods, feeds, and beverages was approximately $59 billion. Soybeans, grains, and meat products accounted for the largest percentage by value. Other goods exported during 2005 totaled nearly $37 billion.

U.S. Trade in Services

U.S. trade in services during 2004 is broken down by import and export categories in Figure 10.2. American

FIGURE 10.2

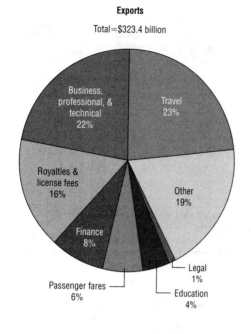

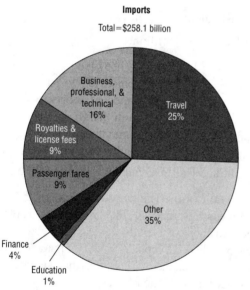

U.S. cross-border services exports and imports, by industry, 2004

Exports

Total = $323.4 billion

Business, professional, & technical 22%

Travel 23%

Royalties & license fees 16%

Other 19%

Finance 8%

Legal 1%

Passenger fares 6%

Education 4%

Imports

Total = $258.1 billion

Business, professional, & technical 16%

Travel 25%

Royalties & license fees 9%

Passenger fares 9%

Other 35%

Finance 4%

Education 1%

Notes: Trade data exclude public-sector transactions. Totals may not equal 100 percent due to rounding.

SOURCE: "Figure 2-3. U.S. Cross-Border Services Exports and Imports, by Industry, 2004," in *Recent Trends in U.S. Services Trade: 2006 Annual Report*, U.S. International Trade Commission, June 2006, http://hotdocs.usitc.gov/docs/pubs/332/pub3857.pdf (accessed June 28, 2006)

The service export values do not completely show America's business presence in foreign lands. Increasingly, U.S. companies operate affiliate offices abroad, and their sales of services have become an important factor in American trade. This growth is shown in Figure 10.3, which tracks the value of U.S. exports of services and the sales of services by U.S.-owned foreign affiliates from 1994 through 2003. In 2003 the latter sector had $477 billion in sales, up from less than $200 billion in 1994. According to the U.S. International Trade Commission, the industries accounting for the largest shares of foreign affiliate sales of services during 2003 were insurance (17%), finance (9%), and broadcasting and telecommunications (7%). The major locations of these affiliates were in the United Kingdom (which accounted for nearly a fourth of all foreign locations), Japan, Canada, and various European countries. Taken as a whole, Europe accounted for more than half of all foreign locations for U.S.-owned affiliates.

U.S. TRADE BALANCE

The difference between exports and imports over a specific time period is known as the balance of trade (balance of trade = exports - imports). A positive balance of trade is called a surplus. This is a situation in which the value of exports is greater than the value of imports. A negative balance of trade is called a deficit. This occurs when the value of imports exceeds the value of exports.

As shown in Figure 10.4, the United States has had a trade deficit for goods every year since 1976, with record levels reached in the 2000s. The values in Figure 10.4 were calculated using the balance of payments basis. In 2004 there was a trade surplus of $48.5 billion for services. This was more than offset by an enormous trade deficit of $666.2 billion for goods. Obviously, the United States imported far more in goods during 2004 than it exported. Likewise, the numbers shown in Table 10.2 for 2005 trade of goods indicate that an even larger trade deficit in goods (more than $780 billion) occurred during that year.

The historical trade balance in services has been quite different. It grew from mildly negative numbers during the 1960s to a peak of $91 billion in the late 1990s. But the surplus has been shrinking since that time. This is illustrated in Figure 10.5, which shows that growth in service exports was not as strong as the growth in service imports during the early 2000s.

The Trade Deficit and the Dollar

The trade deficit is directly linked to the value of the U.S. dollar on foreign exchange markets. A dollar can be exchanged for equivalent amounts of any other foreign currency. The exchange rate for any given foreign currency at any given time depends on many complex

businesses sold more than $323 billion worth of services that year. American consumers paid for just over $258 billion in foreign-provided services. Travel services were the primary component of both imports and exports. Other major categories included business, professional, and technical services and royalties and license fees.

FIGURE 10.3

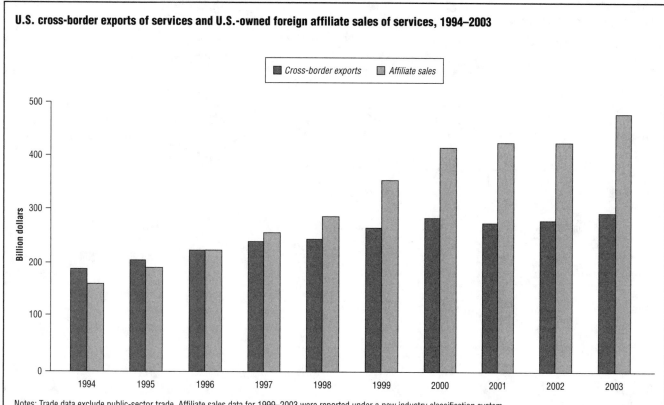

U.S. cross-border exports of services and U.S.-owned foreign affiliate sales of services, 1994–2003

Notes: Trade data exclude public-sector trade. Affiliate sales data for 1999–2003 were reported under a new industry classification system.

SOURCE: "Figure 2-1. U.S. Cross-Border Exports of Services and U.S.-Owned Foreign Affiliate Sales of Services, 1994–2003," in *Recent Trends in U.S. Services Trade: 2006 Annual Report*, U.S. International Trade Commission, June 2006, http://hotdocs.usitc.gov/docs/pubs/332/pub3857.pdf (accessed June 28, 2006)

economic factors, and exchange rates can vary widely over time.

When the dollar weakens compared with a foreign currency, it means that each dollar "buys" less of the foreign currency than it did before. Consequently, each dollar buys less goods from that nation. On the other hand, each unit of the foreign currency is now worth more in American dollars and has more purchasing power of American goods. For example, when the dollar weakens compared with the Japanese yen, Japanese goods cost more to Americans, but American goods become cheaper for Japanese consumers. As a result, imports from Japan to the United States are likely to decrease, while exports from the U.S. to Japan will probably increase.

Likewise, when the dollar strengthens, it buys more foreign currency (and more foreign goods) than it did before. Thus, a stronger dollar is associated with higher imports into the United States, and fewer exports to foreign lands. According to the Federal Reserve, the dollar appreciated by 5.8% compared with the Euro and by 4.8% against the yen on an average annual basis during the late 1990s (August 2001, "To What Extent Does Productivity

Drive the Dollar?," http://www.ny.frb.org/research/current_issues/ci7-8/ci7-8.html). The relatively strong dollar made foreign goods cheaper for Americans and American goods more expensive for other countries, and unsurprisingly this period coincided with ballooning growth in the U.S. trade deficit, as shown in Figure 10.4.

Many economists believe that the reduced U.S. trade deficit in goods during the late 1980s and early 1990s was associated with a rapid weakening of the dollar that occurred at the same time. The trade deficit reduction is evidenced as an upward spike in the bottom line in Figure 10.4 during this period. The trade deficit grew increasingly larger each year between 1980 and 1987 and then suddenly reversed its path for several years. During this time Americans were importing fewer foreign goods than before, because foreign goods suddenly cost more.

The Trade Deficit and the Flow of Capital

When Americans buy more foreign goods, more dollars flow into the foreign exchange markets. This provides greater opportunities for foreigners to invest in U.S. financial instruments, such as stock, bonds, and T-bills. These purchases are tracked by the federal government in what is called the capital account. As shown

FIGURE 10.4

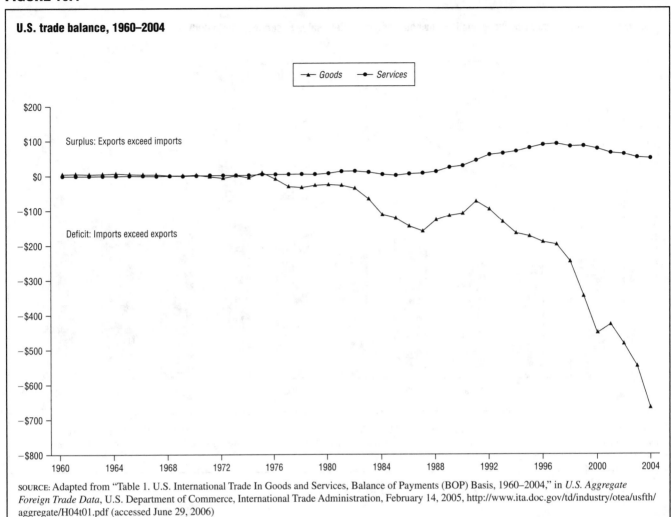

U.S. trade balance, 1960–2004

Legend: ▲ Goods   ● Services

Surplus: Exports exceed imports

Deficit: Imports exceed exports

SOURCE: Adapted from "Table 1. U.S. International Trade In Goods and Services, Balance of Payments (BOP) Basis, 1960–2004," in *U.S. Aggregate Foreign Trade Data*, U.S. Department of Commerce, International Trade Administration, February 14, 2005, http://www.ita.doc.gov/td/industry/otea/usfth/aggregate/H04t01.pdf (accessed June 29, 2006)

in Figure 10.6, net capital inflows to the United States increased dramatically beginning in the late 1990s. This represented a large capital account surplus, meaning that foreign investors purchased much more in U.S. assets than American investors purchased in foreign assets. These assets include financial instruments, loans, and foreign direct investments. Capital inflows have grown to become a significant factor in the U.S. economy. In 2004 they accounted for nearly 6% of the nation's GDP.

Is the Trade Deficit Good or Bad?

America's enormous trade deficit is a subject of great debate among economists and politicians. Some believe that the deficit is bad for the economy and that steps should be taken by the government to correct the imbalance. Others contend that the deficit is a natural consequence of a strong U.S. economy and should not be an issue of concern.

THE TRADE DEFICIT—THE NEGATIVE VIEWPOINT. The Economic Policy Institute (EPI) is a nonprofit, non-

partisan think tank located in Washington, D.C., that prides itself on analyzing economic issues so as to represent the interests of low- and middle-income Americans. In 1999 an EPI economist, Robert E. Scott, testified before a Congressional committee on international trade issues. The written testimony is titled "The U.S. Trade Deficit: Are We Trading Away Our Future?" (July 22, 1999, http://www.epinet.org/content.cfm/webfeatures_viewpoints_tradetestimony) and is considered representative of the viewpoints of those who believe that the U.S. trade deficit has negative consequences for America.

In his testimony Scott asserts that a growing trade deficit has been extremely harmful to the United States and is associated with the elimination of American jobs (particularly high-paying jobs for skilled workers in manufacturing and other goods-producing industries) and a reduction in the wages of noncollege-educated workers. Scott blames "unbalanced trading relationships" that the U.S. has developed with other countries and a "pattern of neglect" on behalf of the federal government toward American industry.

FIGURE 10.5

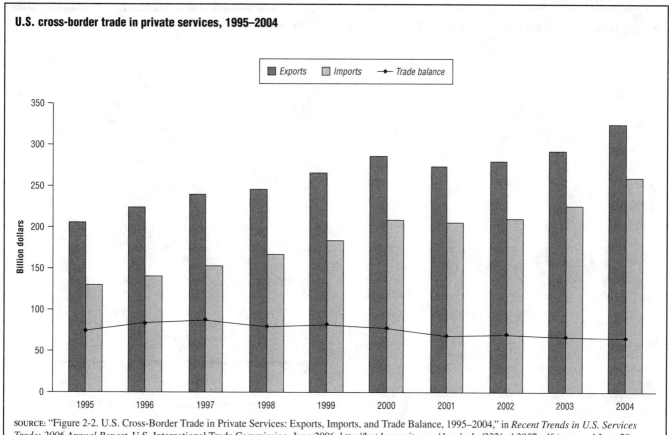

U.S. cross-border trade in private services, 1995–2004

SOURCE: "Figure 2-2. U.S. Cross-Border Trade in Private Services: Exports, Imports, and Trade Balance, 1995–2004," in *Recent Trends in U.S. Services Trade: 2006 Annual Report*, U.S. International Trade Commission, June 2006, http://hotdocs.usitc.gov/docs/pubs/332/pub3857.pdf (accessed June 28, 2006)

THE TRADE DEFICIT—THE POSITIVE VIEWPOINT. The Cato Institute is an independent policy research organization located in Washington, D.C. Its Center for Trade Policy Studies is a noted advocate of free (unfettered) global trade. On its Web site (http://www.freetrade.org/pubs/pas/tpa-002.html) the organization includes an article written by Daniel T. Griswold titled "America's Maligned and Misunderstood Trade Deficit" (April 20, 1998). The article covers many of the arguments commonly expressed by those who believe that the ballooning trade deficit is not a bad phenomenon.

Griswold notes that negative attitudes about a trade deficit have deep historical roots and probably stem from the days when precious metals, such as gold and silver, were used to pay for imports. Because nations wanted to increase their hoards of gold and silver, it was desirable to export more goods than were imported. Griswold believes that now people misinterpret a growing trade deficit as a sign that America's industrial competitiveness is weakening and that foreign nations are using unfair trade policies against the United States. He disputes both these claims and asserts that the trade deficit simply reflects macroeconomic factors, such as national tendencies to spend, save, or invest money. Griswold concludes: "Trade deficits may even be good news for the economy,

because they signal global investor confidence in the United States and rising purchasing power among domestic consumers."

TRADE AGREEMENTS

The U.S. government has long been part of free trade agreements with other individual countries (known as "bilateral" agreements) and with groups of countries (known as trading "blocs"). U.S. bilateral free trade agreements in effect as of May 2006 are listed in Table 10.3. They apply to Australia, Bahrain, Chile, Colombia, Costa Rica, Dominican Republic, El Salvador, Guatemala, Honduras, Israel, Jordan, Morocco, Nicaragua, Oman, Peru, and Singapore.

In this context free trade means the ability to buy and sell goods across international borders with a minimum of tariffs or other interferences. Tariffs (or import taxes) are fees charged by a country to import goods into that country. Figure 10.7 shows the average U.S. tariff as a percent charged on imported goods from 1930 through 2005. U.S. tariffs were relatively high during the early 1930s but decreased dramatically over the following decades. Table 10.4 lists important milestones in American trade history that have affected U.S. tariffs.

FIGURE 10.6

Net capital inflows to the United States, 1995–2004

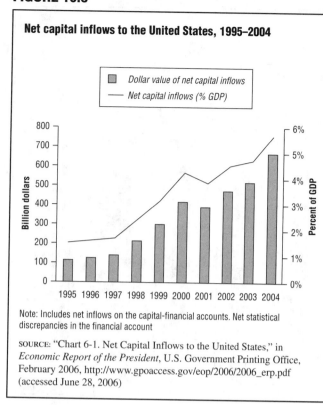

Note: Includes net inflows on the capital-financial accounts. Net statistical discrepancies in the financial account

SOURCE: "Chart 6-1. Net Capital Inflows to the United States," in *Economic Report of the President*, U.S. Government Printing Office, February 2006, http://www.gpoaccess.gov/eop/2006/2006_erp.pdf (accessed June 28, 2006)

TABLE 10.3

U.S. bilateral trade agreements

Free trade agreement	Signed	Entered into force
Australia	May 2004	January 2005
Bahrain	September 2004	January 2006
Central America-Dominican Republic (CAFTA-DR)	August 2004	a
Chile	June 2003	January 2004
Colombia[b]	c	
Israel	April 1985	September 1985
Jordan	October 2000	December 2001
Morocco	June 2004	January 2006
Oman	January 2006	d
Peru[b]	April 2006	d
Singapore	May 2003	January 2004

[a]Ratified by the United States, the Dominican Republic, El Salvador, Guatemala, Honduras, and Nicaragua. Pending ratification by Costa Rica.
[b]Trade Promotion Agreement (TPA).
[c]Negotiations were concluded February 2006.
[d]Pending ratification by parties.
Note: Negotiations are planned or pending with Korea, Malaysia, Panama, the Southern African Customs Union (SACU), Thailand, and the United Arab Emirates.

SOURCE: "Table 2-1. U.S. Bilateral Agreements," in *Recent Trends in U.S. Services Trade: 2006 Annual Report*, U.S. International Trade Commission, June 2006, http://hotdocs.usitc.gov/docs/pubs/332/pub3857.pdf (accessed June 28, 2006)

Opponents to trading blocs argue that when countries with strong economies—like the United States, Japan, and the countries of the EU—negotiate agreements, smaller nations with developing economies are left at an unfair disadvantage because they are excluded from the favorable terms of the agreement ("The Pros and Cons of Pursuing Free-Trade Agreements," Economic and Budget Issue Brief, Congressional Budget Office, July 31, 2003, http://www.cbo.gov/showdoc.cfm?index=4458&sequence=0).

Priorities regarding trade policy have shifted over the years according to the state of the economy. During the recession of the late 1970s, American producers called for the government to institute measures—such as high tariffs—to protect them from international competition. During the growth period of the 1980s, however, the focus of companies turned to their own international expansion, and by the 1990s a push for free trade had gained increased momentum.

NAFTA

The United States, Canada, and Mexico implemented the North American Free Trade Agreement (NAFTA) on January 1, 1994. A primary objective of NAFTA has been the complete elimination of barriers to trade among the three signing countries. Many tariffs were dropped immediately; others have been or are being phased out. Agricultural products were an integral part of NAFTA.

All agricultural provisions are to be implemented by 2008.

NAFTA has had a positive effect on the marketability of goods among the participating nations. Efficient production of goods that are exported from one country to another keeps pricing fair and competitive as nations produce and export the goods for which they already have the natural resources and the best pools of employee talent.

But there has been concern that importing goods from other countries could cause the loss of jobs in the United States. In "The High Price of 'Free' Trade" (November 17, 2003, http://www.epinet.org/content.cfm/briefingpapers_bp147), Robert E. Scott of the Economic Policy Institute estimated that by 2002 approximately 879,000 U.S. jobs—mostly high-paying manufacturing industry positions—were displaced as a result of NAFTA's removal of trade barriers.

Until 2002 workers displaced due to NAFTA were eligible for the NAFTA-Transitional Adjustment Assistance program, administered by the U.S. Department of Labor Employment and Training Administration (ETA) division, which offered "rapid and early response to the threat of unemployment and the opportunity to receive reemployment assistance, including job search assistance, retraining and income support while in training, to enhance and ease the transition to a new job." The ETA estimates that more than five hundred thousand workers received help through the program (http://www.doleta.gov/tradeact/nafta_certs.cfm). Because of the

FIGURE 10.7

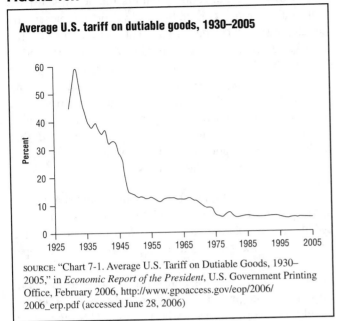

Average U.S. tariff on dutiable goods, 1930–2005

SOURCE: "Chart 7-1. Average U.S. Tariff on Dutiable Goods, 1930–2005," in *Economic Report of the President*, U.S. Government Printing Office, February 2006, http://www.gpoaccess.gov/eop/2006/2006_erp.pdf (accessed June 28, 2006).

TABLE 10.4

Important milestones in U.S. trade history

Milestone (years of negotiation)	Year signed into U.S. law	Administrations involved
Reciprocal Trade Agreements Act of 1934	1934	Roosevelt
Kennedy Round (1962–1967)	1962	Kennedy, Johnson
Tokyo Round (1973–1979)	1979	Nixon, Ford, Carter
Uruguay Round Agreements Act (1986–1994)	1994	Reagan, G.H.W. Bush, Clinton
North American Free Trade Agreement (1990–1993)	1994	G.H.W. Bush, Clinton
Trade Act of 2002 and Renewal of Trade Promotion Authority (2001–2002)	2002	G.W. Bush

SOURCE: "Table 7-1. Important Milestones in American Trade History," in *Economic Report of the President*, U.S. Government Printing Office, February 2006, http://www.gpoaccess.gov/eop/2006/2006_erp.pdf (accessed June 28, 2006)

impact on U.S. employment, free trade agreements such as NAFTA remain controversial.

The European Union

In 1957 six European countries signed the Treaty of Rome, establishing the European Economic Community (EEC). In 1992 the Maastricht Treaty was signed, officially establishing the EU. After centuries of war, leaders of European countries hoped that by engaging in commerce they could create long-term stability and enforce the rule of law in cooperative democratic societies. The EU, one of the most important trading partners of the United States, expanded in 2004 from fifteen nations to twenty-five, creating the largest trading bloc in history.

As of May 2006, the EU included Austria, Belgium, Cyprus, Czech Republic, Denmark, Estonia, Finland, France, Germany, Greece, Hungary, Ireland, Italy, Latvia, Lithuania, Luxembourg, Malta, Poland, Portugal, Slovakia, Slovenia, Spain, Sweden, The Netherlands, and United Kingdom. Candidate countries for admission to the EU in the future included Bulgaria, Croatia, Romania, and Turkey.

GATT and the World Trade Organization

One of the most important trade agreements is the General Agreement on Tariffs and Trade (GATT), which was first signed by the United States and twenty-two other countries in 1947. This agreement dealt primarily with industrial products and marked a trend toward the increasing globalization of the world economy. The agreement reduced tariffs, removed other obstacles to international trade, and clarified rules surrounding barriers to free trade. Agriculture was for the most part kept

out of the initial negotiations. By the end of the 1980s more than one hundred countries had ratified the GATT.

A series of GATT negotiations that concluded in 1994 created the World Trade Organization (WTO), which replaced GATT and now functions as the principal international body charged with administering rules for trade among member countries. The new agreements covered a range of topics, including agriculture, food safety, animal and plant health regulations, technical standards (testing and certification), import licensing procedures, trade in services, intellectual property rights (including trade in counterfeit goods), as well as rules and procedures for settling disputes. As of December 2005, the WTO consisted of 149 member countries.

THE INTERNATIONAL MONETARY FUND

At the United Nations Monetary and Financial Conference—more commonly known as the Bretton Woods conference because it took place in Bretton Woods, New Hampshire—in July 1944, the forty-five countries fighting on the side of the Allied forces in World War II negotiated the creation of the International Monetary Fund (IMF), a global financial system. The IMF extends short-term loans to members experiencing economic instability. As a condition of receiving its credit assistance, the IMF requires the debtor country to enact significant reform of its economic structure, and often of its political structure as well, eliminating corruption and establishing effective institutions such as courts. The conditions for being granted a loan can include drastic cuts in government spending; privatizing government-owned enterprises, such as railroads and utilities; establishing higher interest rates; increasing taxes; and eliminating subsidies on such necessities as food and fuel.

Critics have maintained that the austerity demanded by the IMF can have devastating social consequences, including severe unemployment, crippling price increases in the cost of basic goods, and political instability resulting from widespread dissatisfaction. As of July 2006 the IMF included 184 member countries.

THE WORLD BANK

At the same conference that created the International Monetary Fund in July 1944, the International Bank for Reconstruction and Development (IBRD) was established. The IBRD and the International Development Association (IDA) are commonly known as the World Bank. The World Bank is not a bank in the traditional sense of the word but an agency of the United Nations. The World Bank works to combat world poverty by providing low-interest loans, interest-free credit, and grants to developing countries. As of July 2006 the IBRD and IDA included 184 and 165 member countries, respectively.

In its early days the World Bank often participated in such large projects as dam building. Today it supports the efforts of governments in developing countries to build schools and health centers, provide water and electricity, fight disease, and protect the environment. The World Bank is one of the world's largest sources of development assistance. According to *The World Bank Annual Report 2005*, the organization provided $22 billion in loans during 2005 to developing countries worldwide.

GLOBALIZATION AND THE ANTIGLOBALIZATION MOVEMENT

The move toward global free trade, or "globalization," has generated intense controversy. Proponents maintain that globalization has the potential to improve living standards throughout the world. Their arguments include the following:

- Countries and regions will become more productive by concentrating on industries in which they have a natural advantage and trading with other nations for goods in which they do not have an advantage.

- Multinational corporations will be able to realize economies of scale—that is, operate more economically because they are buying in bulk, selling to a much larger market, and utilizing a much larger labor pool. This will increase productivity and lead to greater prosperity.

- Free trade will lead to faster growth in developing countries.

- Increased incomes and the development of job-related skills among the citizens of poorer nations will foster the spread of information, education, and, ultimately, democracy.

Critics of globalization point out the negative effects that multinational corporations have on people in the developing world. They argue that most of the profits from free trade flow to the United States and other industrialized countries; that local industries can be destroyed by competition from wealthier nations, causing widespread unemployment and social disruption; that centuries of cultural tradition can be quickly obliterated by the influence of international companies; and that multinational corporations often impinge on national sovereignty to protect their profits.

Critics also note that the free trade policies are often applied unfairly, as the United States insists that other countries open their markets to American goods at the same time that it protects its own producers from competition. For example, the U.S. government has established numerous tariffs and regulations that raise the prices of imported food products, denying poor farmers in the developing world access to the lucrative U.S. market. In addition, opponents of globalization point out that the spread of multinational corporations can be detrimental to workers in industrialized nations by exporting high-paying jobs to countries with lower labor costs, and that international competition in the labor market could actually lead to lower living standards in the industrialized world.

The "antiglobalization movement" is not an organized group but rather an umbrella term for many independent organizations who oppose the pursuit of corporate profits at the expense of social justice in the developing world. These groups often protest the actions of such organizations as the WTO, the IMF, and the World Bank for their perceived bias toward corporations and wealthy nations. In 1999 a WTO conference in Seattle, Washington, became a lightning rod for the movement, drawing more than forty thousand protestors in a massive demonstration that generated intense media attention and completely overshadowed the meeting itself.

SANCTIONS

The United States has used trade sanctions (stopping some or all forms of trade with a country) as a political tool against countries that are thought to violate human rights, tolerate drug trafficking, support terrorism, and, most recently, with nations that are suspected of producing or storing weapons of mass destruction. In recent decades the U.S. has imposed trade embargoes on countries including Iraq, Cuba, and North Korea. The United States has also restricted trade with Burma, Iran, Libya, Sudan, and Syria. As of August 2006, more specific sanctions against Iran were being considered because of that country's burgeoning nuclear weapons industry.

Because of the immense size of the U.S. economy, the effect of sanctions can be crippling.

The Trade Act of 1974 allowed the United States to impose sanctions on countries with unfair trade policies. The Jackson-Vanik amendment to this legislation barred the president from granting favorable trade status to countries that limited emigration, and required annual certification for communist countries, including China. This amendment was repealed in 2000, marking a major step in the restoration of relations between China and the United States. The Chinese market presents an enormous opportunity for U.S. exports, but it has remained difficult to penetrate by U.S. exporters. On December 11, 2001, China was admitted as a member of the WTO.

THE CHANGING FACE OF FREE TRADE

Trade Promotion Authority

President George W. Bush signed the Trade Act of 2002 (HR 3009) on August 6, 2002. The act gives the U.S. president Trade Promotion Authority (TPA), under which future international trade agreements will be subject to an up-or-down vote, but not amendment, in Congress. TPA is designed to promote freer trade by giving other countries confidence that the agreements they negotiate with the U.S. diplomats will not be subject to attempts and changes and renegotiation when they are submitted to Congress for ratification.

Parity in Labor Standards and Environmental Laws

Discrepancies in labor and environmental regulations among trading nations have formed another barrier to free trade. The administration of President Bill Clinton pushed to impose the same labor and environmental standards on trading nations that the United States imposes on itself. The move was designed to discourage trading partners from exploiting workers and abusing the environment in order to keep capital costs lower and prices down, thus making their goods and services more competitive than U.S. goods in the global market. Before NAFTA was signed, the United States insisted on assurances from Canada and Mexico that they would enforce labor and environmental laws before it would ratify the agreement.

Intellectual Property

Technological advancements have posed new challenges to world trade. As private-sector investment in information technology continues, world economies are becoming even more interconnected. Proponents of free trade, including the United States, have pushed for more protection of intellectual property rights, abuse of which poses a major barrier to world trade. As defined by the UN in the *Convention Establishing the World Intellectual Property Organization* (July 14, 1967; amended September 28, 1979), intellectual property includes:

- Literary, artistic, and scientific works
- Performances of performing artists, phonograms, and broadcasts
- Inventions in all fields of human endeavor
- Scientific discoveries
- Industrial designs
- Trademarks, service marks, and commercial names and designations
- Protection against unfair competition and all other rights resulting from intellectual activity in the industrial, scientific, literary or artistic fields

Challenges for the international community include establishing minimum standards for protecting intellectual property rights and procedures for enforcement and dispute resolution. These challenges are not new. As early as 1883, with the fourteen-member Paris Union for the Protection of Industrial Property, states recognized the special nature of creative works, including inventions, trademarks, and industrial designs. Soon afterward, in 1886, the Berne Union for the Protection of Literary and Artistic Works extended the model of international protection to such copyrighted works as novels, short stories, poems, plays, songs, operas, musicals, sonatas, drawings, paintings, sculptures, and architectural works.

WORLD INTELLECTUAL PROPERTY ORGANIZATION. In 1893 the Paris Union and the Berne Union combined to form the United International Bureaus for the Protection of Intellectual Property, which maintained its headquarters in Berne, Switzerland. This organization evolved eventually into the World Intellectual Property Organization (WIPO), located in Geneva, Switzerland, which carries out a program designed to:

- Harmonize national intellectual property legislation and procedures
- Provide services for international applications for industrial property rights
- Exchange intellectual property information
- Provide legal and technical assistance to developing and other countries
- Facilitate the resolution of private intellectual property disputes
- Marshal information technology as a tool for storing, accessing, and using valuable intellectual property information

As of 2006, WIPO included 183 member nations, including the United States.

FEDERAL INITIATIVES—FOCUS ON KNOCKOFFS. Knockoffs (or counterfeit goods) are copies of legitimate goods sold in the marketplace. In the past knockoffs were primarily imitations of select items with upscale brand names, such as designer purses or watches. They appealed to some consumers who wanted to pay low prices for inferior-quality merchandise that could masquerade as expensive brand-name items. Purchases were usually conducted by street or back-alley vendors in large cities. In recent years the knockoff industry has greatly matured, spreading its scope to include many different consumer goods that can be purchased (knowingly or unknowingly) in a wide variety of markets.

During the early 2000s the U.S. government stepped up its campaign against the manufacture, distribution, and sale of knockoffs. In March 2004 Attorney General John Ashcroft established an Intellectual Property Task Force within the U.S. Department of Justice. The task force published recommendations calling for greater focus on criminal prosecution both at home and abroad, additional regulatory measures, and enhanced public education about the negative impact of intellectual property crime on the American economy. Later that year the U.S. Department of Commerce launched the Strategy Targeting Organized Piracy (STOP) initiative to link together numerous agencies engaged in the protection of intellectual property rights.

In March 2006 President Bush signed the Stop Counterfeiting in Manufactured Goods Act to strengthen federal laws and expand the tools available to law enforcement agencies to combat goods counterfeiting. The action was driven by growing evidence that knockoffs pose a serious problem to the U.S. and global economies, public safety, and even national security. In 2005 law enforcement officials testified before a U.S. Senate subcommittee that international terrorist groups were involved in knockoff trade in the United States to raise money for their organizations ("Hezbollah Pushes Prada?" March 26, 2005, http://money.cnn.com/2005/05/26/news/terror_knockoffs/index.htm).

Officials note that knockoffs have moved out of back allies and into mainstream American markets. A position paper published by the U.S. Chamber of Commerce in 2005 warns that "fakes are infiltrating the supply chain and making their way into legitimate retail outlets" (http://www.uschamber.com/ncf/initiatives/counterfeiting.htm). The Chamber cites a number of events in which consumers were harmed by defective knockoffs, including counterfeit batteries sold at retail stores. According to the *Seattle Post Intelligencer*, several upscale companies, such as Gucci, have hired legal firms to search the Internet looking for Web sites selling knockoffs of brand-name goods ("Lawyers Fighting Online Knockoffs,"

March 29, 2006, http://seattlepi.nwsource.com/business/264694_fakes29.html). According to the article, the exclusive jeweler Tiffany & Co. has filed a lawsuit against the online auction service eBay alleging that eBay participated in trademark fraud by facilitating the sale of Tiffany knockoffs during 2004. The case was expected to go to trial in late 2006.

The U.S. Chamber of Commerce's 2005 paper *What Are Counterfeiting and Piracy Costing the American Economy?* reports that knockoffs cost U.S. businesses $200 to $250 billion in lost sales in 2004. Global losses were estimated at around $500 billion.

Foreign Ownership of U.S. Assets.

The huge growth in the U.S. trade deficit is associated with like growth in foreign ownership of U.S. stocks, bonds, and other financial instruments. In addition, the overall strength of the American economy has encouraged foreign businesses to enter or expand their participation in U.S. industries. This trend is of major concern to some analysts and politicians, who fear that America has become too dependent on foreign money. The danger to the U.S. economy as a whole lies in the possibility that foreigners might suddenly decide to pull out of American financial assets. This could destabilize the stock market and result in higher interest rates, which would dampen U.S. economic growth.

In February 2005 a committee of the U.S. Treasury reported on the issue with respect to foreign ownership of government securities (http://www.ustreas.gov/press/releases/js2221.htm). At that time just over 50% of U.S. Treasury securities were held by foreigners, including private and government sectors. The committee concluded that this situation did not pose a threat to the overall health of the U.S. economy. In fact, it was noted that having a broad global pool of investors was more desirable from a stability standpoint than relying on a more narrow pool of only domestic investors. The Treasury committee also believes that if foreign investment were to slow or cease, domestic investors would "fill the void." The report notes that "high foreign ownership of U.S. Treasuries—and of U.S. financial assets in general—should pose little risk to the economy. It is a reflection of the globalization of financial markets as well as the particular attraction of U.S. assets that foreign ownership of virtually all U.S. financial assets has risen sharply."

Foreign participation in U.S.-based industries has garnered a lot of public attention during the 2000s. In February 2006 DP World, a company owned by the Middle Eastern nation the United Arab Emirates (UAE), announced its intention to purchase Peninsular and Oriental (P&O) Steam Navigation Company, a British company that manages operations at numerous U.S. ports. DP World is based in the city of Dubai in the UAE. The Dubai ports deal (as it came to be known) set off a firestorm of controversy in the United States. Although the deal was staunchly supported by President Bush, critics noted that some of the hijackers of U.S. airplanes on September 11, 2001, were from the United Arab Emirates. They also pointed out the national security implications of putting ports management into the hands of a foreign-owned company, particularly one based in the Middle East.

The deal received widespread media attention and garnered intense opposition from the public and many Republican and Democratic leaders in the House and the Senate. In March 2006 DP World announced its intention to finalize its deal with P&O but divest itself of U.S. port operations. According to Fox News, the U.S. port operations were to be fully transferred to a U.S.-based company on the condition that DP World "will not suffer economic loss" ("Bush Faces Rancor over Port Deal," March 10, 2006, http://www.foxnews.com/story/0,2933, 187431,00.html).

IMPORTANT NAMES AND ADDRESSES

Agency for Healthcare Research and Quality
540 Gaither Rd., Ste. 2000
Rockville, MD 20850
(301) 427-1364
URL: http://www.ahrq.gov

American Bankruptcy Institute
44 Canal Center Plaza, Ste. 404
Alexandria, VA 22314
(703) 739-0800
FAX: (703) 739-1060
URL: http://www.abiworld.org/

Bureau of Economic Analysis
1441 L. St. NW
Washington, DC 20230
(202) 606-9900
URL: http://www.bea.gov/

Bureau of Labor Statistics
Postal Square Bldg.
2 Massachusetts Ave. NE
Washington, DC 20212
(202) 691-5200
FAX: (202) 691-6325
E-mail: hq@arrl.org
URL: http://www.bls.gov

Commodities Futures Trading Commission
Three Lafayette Centre
1155 21st St. NW
Washington, DC 20581
(202) 418-5000
FAX: (202) 418-5521
URL: http://www.cftc.gov

Congressional Budget Office
Ford House Office Bldg., 4th Floor
Washington, DC 20515
(202) 226-2602
URL: http://www.cbo.gov

Consumer Federation of America
1620 I St. NW, Ste. 200
Washington, DC 20006

(202) 387-6121
URL: http://www.consumerfed.org/

Economic Policy Institute
1333 H St. NW, Ste. 300, East Tower
Washington, DC 20005
(202) 775-8810
URL: http://www.epinet.org/

Federal Communications Commission
445 12th St. SW
Washington, DC 20554
1-888-225-5322
FAX: (866) 418-0232
E-mail: fccinfo@fcc.gov
URL: http://www.fcc.gov

Federal Home Loan Mortgage Corporation (Freddie Mac)
8200 Jones Branch Dr.
McLean, VA 22102
URL: http://www.freddiemac.com

Federal National Mortgage Association (Fannie Mae)
3900 Wisconsin Ave. NW
Washington, DC 20016
(202) 752-7000
URL: http://www.fanniemae.com

Federal Reserve Bank, Board of Governors
20th St. and Constitution Ave. NW
Washington, DC 20551
(202) 452-3000
URL: http://www.federalreserve.gov/

Federal Trade Commission
600 Pennsylvania Ave. NW
Washington, DC 20580
(202) 326-2222
URL: http://www.ftc.gov

Federation of Tax Administrators
444 N. Capitol St. NW, Ste. 348
Washington, DC 20001

(202) 624-5890
URL: http://www.taxadmin.org

Government Accountability Office
441 G St. NW
Washington, DC 20548
(202) 512-4800
FAX: (202) 512-7726
E-mail: webmaster@gao.gov
URL: http://www.gao.gov

International Monetary Fund
700 19th St. NW
Washington, DC 20431
(202) 623-7000
FAX: (202) 623-4661
URL: http://www.imf.org

Investment Company Institute
1401 H St. NW
Washington, DC 20005
URL: http://www.ici.org

Office of Federal Housing Enterprise Oversight
1700 G St. NW, 4th Floor
Washington, DC 20552
(202) 414-3800
FAX: (202) 414-3823
E-mail: ofheoinquiries@ofheo.gov
URL: http://www.ofheo.gov

Office of Management and Budget
725 17th St. NW
Washington, DC 20503
(202) 395-3080
FAX: (202) 395-3888
URL: http://www.whitehouse.gov/omb

Organization for Economic Cooperation and Development
2 rue Andre Pascal, F-75775
Paris, Cedex 16 France
33-1-45-24-82-00
FAX: 33-1-45-24-85-00
URL: http://www.oecd.org/home/

Social Security Administration
Windsor Park Bldg.
6401 Security Blvd.
Baltimore, MD 21235
1-888-225-5322
URL: http://www.ssa.gov

U.S. Census Bureau
4700 Silver Hill Rd.
Washington, DC 20233
(301) 763-4636
E-mail: pio@census.gov
URL: http://www.census.gov/

U.S. Consumer Product Safety Commission
4330 East-West Hwy.
Bethesda, MD 20814
(301) 504-7923
FAX: (301) 504-0124
E-mail: info@cpsc.gov
URL: http://www.cpsc.gov

U.S. Department of Commerce
1401 Constitution Ave. NW
Washington, DC 20230
URL: http://www.commerce.gov

U.S. Department of Health and Human Services
200 Independence Ave. SW
Washington, DC 20201
(202) 619-0257
URL: http://www.hhs.gov

U.S. Department of Housing and Urban Development
451 7th St. SW
Washington, DC 20410
(202) 708-1112
URL: http://www.hud.gov

U.S. Department of Labor
Frances Perkins Bldg.
200 Constitution Ave. NW
Washington, DC 20210
1-866-4-USA-DOL
URL: http://www.dol.gov

U.S. Department of Treasury
1500 Pennsylvania Ave. NW
Washington, DC 20220
(202) 622-2000
FAX: (202) 622-6415
URL: http://www.treasury.gov

U.S. Equal Opportunity Employment Commission
1801 L St. NW
Washington, DC 20507
(202) 663-4900
1-800-669-4000
E-mail: info@ask.eeoc.gov
URL: http://www.eeoc.gov

U.S. Securities and Exchange Commission
100 F St. NW
Washington, DC 20549
(202) 551-6551

E-mail: help@sec.gov
URL: http://www.sec.gov

U.S. Small Business Administration
409 3rd St. SW
Washington, DC 20416
1-888-225-5322
URL: http://www.sba.gov

The World Bank Group
1818 H St. SW
Washington, DC 20433
(202) 473-1000
FAX: (202) 477-6391
URL: http://www.worldbank.org

World Intellectual Property Organization
34 chemin des Colombettes
PO Box 18
Geneva, Switzerland
41-22-338-91-11
FAX: 41-22-733-54-28
E-mail: wipo.mail@wipo.int
URL: http://www.wipo.int/

World Trade Organization
Centre William Rappard
Rue de Lausanne 154, CH-1211
Geneva 21, Switzerland
41-22-739-51-11
FAX: 41-22 731-42-06
URL: http://www.wto.org

RESOURCES

Several government agencies provided invaluable economic data and information for this book: the U.S. Department of Commerce's Bureau of Economic Affairs (BEA) and U.S. Census Bureau, the U.S. Department of Labor's Bureau of Labor Statistics (BLS), and the Federal Reserve Bank.

The BEA compiles the *National Income and Product Accounts*, which include detailed financial information on gross domestic product, personal income and outlays, saving, corporate profits, and international trade and balance of payments.

The BLS publishes statistical data on wages, benefits, and income; inflation and economic indexes; employment and unemployment; industries and occupations; employment demographics; and worker health and safety standards. In addition, BLS posts many of its publications online, including *Employment Situation*, *Occupational Outlook Handbook*, *Monthly Labor Review*, and *Occupational Outlook Quarterly*.

The U.S. Census Bureau provides comprehensive economic and demographic data. Particularly useful for the study of the American economy are the Census publications *Historical Statistics of the United States, Colonial Times to 1970*, Bicentennial edition; *Income, Poverty, and Health Insurance in the United States: 2003*; the *Economic Census of 2002*; and *Statistical Abstract of the United States: 2006*, 125th edition.

The Federal Reserve Bank publishes economic data and papers on a variety of economic subjects, including housing, consumer spending, interest rates, consumer credit, net worth, wealth distribution, and debt. Especially useful is the series titled *Federal Reserve Statistical Release*.

Other government agencies and offices consulted during the compilation of this book include: the Government Accountability Office (*Federal Debt: Answers to Frequently Asked Questions, An Update [GAO-04-485SP]*), the Social Security Administration (*A Summary of the 2006 Annual Social Security and Medicare Trust Fund Reports*), and the White House (*Economic Report of the President* and *Budget of the United States Government: Fiscal Year 2007*).

Important information was also obtained from the U.S. Federal Trade Commission, U.S. Department of Energy, Commodities Futures Trading Commission, U.S. Department of Health and Human Services, U.S. Department of Agriculture, U.S. Department of the Treasury, U.S. International Trade Commission, International Trade Administration, Office of Management and Budget, Office of Federal Housing Enterprise Oversight, and U.S. Small Business Administration.

A number of independent, nonpartisan think tanks and private organizations were consulted to obtain various points of view on socioeconomic issues. These organizations include United for a Fair Economy, the Economic Policy Institute, the Center for Corporate Policy, the Center for a New American Dream, and the Center for Responsive Politics.

Finally, the Gallup Organization was the source for numerous public opinion polls conducted to gauge American attitudes on economic topics.

INDEX